STEP BY STEP

A
Journey of
CONQUERING
PTSD, Depression,
Anxieties, Problems
THROUGH
God's Presence and Power

PSALM 142

Christopher Paul

Step By Step: A Journey of Conquering PTSD, Depression, Anxieties, Problems Through God's Presence and Power

ISBN: 979-8-218-58845-8

Printed in the United States of America

This book was in the editing process when Chris suddenly passed away from a heart attack. His family and friends decided to go ahead and publish his book "as is" in hopes it will help others who suffered like he did.

Christopher James "Chris" Paul, 67, of Fairfield, IA, went home to be with his Lord and Savior, Jesus Christ, Wednesday, March 27, 2024, at University of Iowa Hospital in Iowa City, IA.

Chris was born in Chicago, IL on May 2, 1956, to Vernon G. and Ardath C. (Breitenbach) Paul, who married in 1949. Soon after his birth, the family moved to Morrison, IL, where they would reside most of their lives. Chris graduated from Morrison Community High School in 1974, and later went to Morningside College in Sioux City, IA. He worked for the American Cemetery Association, Greene Building Supplies, and was in the ministry for many years. He was in youth ministry at Grace Church of DuPage, IL (1990's), youth staff at First Baptist Church of Sycamore, IL (2000-2006), and youth pastor at First Baptist Church of Fairfield, IA (2006-2017). Chris' love for Jesus and his passion for the Chicago Cubs, Bears, and Bulls will forever be remembered by his family and friends, who dearly loved him down to his last moments.

Surviving are brothers, Timothy (Bobbi) Paul of Crystal Lake, IL and Dr. Theodore (Dawn) Paul of DeKalb, IL.; sister-in-law, Erma Paul of Spring Hill, TN; nieces and nephews, Carolyn (James) Jett of Spring Hill, TN, Jason (Shelly) Paul of Green Bay WI, Jennifer (Nick) Orifici of Long Island, NY, Mackenzie Paul of DeKalb, IL, and Matthew Paul of DeKalb, IL; grandniece and nephews, Addison Paul, of Green Bay, WI, Benjamin Jett of Spring Hill, TN, and Joseph Jett of Spring Hill, TN; and dear friends who he considered his family, Jason, Lisa, Chance, Sage, Addison, and Emma Crandall.

He is preceded in death by his parents and half-siblings, DorothyMae (Tony) Dazey and Terry (Erma) Paul.

Services for Chris will be held on Monday, April 1, 2024, at First Baptist Church of Fairfield, IA at 10:00 AM with Pastor John Kermott officiating. A graveside service and burial will be held at Grove Hill Cemetery in Morrison, IL at 3:00 PM on the same day. Pallbearers for the funeral service will be Benny Jett, James Jett, Jason Crandall, Chance Crandall, Sage Crandall, Saban Simons, and Zane Richmond. Pallbearers for the graveside service will be Timothy Paul, Jason Paul, James Jett, Jason Crandall, Chance Crandall, and Sage Crandall.

Cranston Family Funeral Home in Fairfield, IA is assisting with the arrangements.

Selah.

CONTENTS

INTRODUCTION AND OVERVIEW
of what was happening to David
1 SAMUEL 17-23

Have you ever felt depressed, lonely, oppressed, abandoned, not understood, and perhaps even suffering from PTSD and the subsequent episodes that come from being triggered? Then I hope that these Cave Psalms of David will speak to your heart and the Holy Spirit will use this to help you recover and rebuild. Many people suffer from Spirit Depression. Yes, even Christians suffer from this. As we can see here through these Cave Psalms of David that David for sure suffered with this. He also, I firmly believe, suffered from PTSD and as I said depression and feelings of abandonment and even from times of abandonment from the Lord Himself.

If you have these Spirit Depression times, then I pray that this book can be used by the Lord to help you in Spirit Revival. You are not alone. David "a man after God's own heart" as mentioned suffered from this. As you read through this book try and see how David fought through these times. See David's strong view of the Lord and how he saw his personal close relationship with the Lord. Yes, David had his ups and downs in this battle of PTSD and Soul Depression, but he did not give up fighting. We must not also.

This book while it is about how to fight Biblically against our depressions, PTSD episodes, anxieties and other troubles that invade our lives that wage war against our souls it is more I would say about "Beholding Our God." Beholding God in all His glory in who He is, what He does and is like and His amazing never-ending love for us and who then we are in Christ. Behold Our God! There is nothing that can compare to our God! He reigns forever! He has ultimate power and authority! Hs is sovereign over the whole universe and what it contains and is! At the same time, He is sovereign in and over our lives through the valleys and the mountain top times! Behold our God! Behold Your God!

As we do this more and more revealing to us in a deeper and deeper way who God is and who we are to Him we can be more than conquerors in this spiritual battle for our spirit. We can have soul revival from our soul depression. More than conquerors even in our valleys. This was the example that David gives to us in Psalm 142. He also does so in his other cave/valley Psalms that we will also touch on as we go on. David, through the Holy Spirit, wrote a lot of cave/valley Psalms as he was in a lot of cave/valley times. How the Holy Spirit maintained

David through those times and propelled him forward during those cave/valley times is what we see in Psalm 142. David gave us a Biblical pattern to follow as we walk through our own valleys of life.

I will be right up front and open and say that I have been diagnosed with PTSD with its subsequent battles with episodes as I'm triggered with bouts of depression and sense at times of hopelessness and abandonment. Apparently, I had this PTSD from my earlier teen years that was never diagnosed or dealt with and then when I was hit with a horrific life changing situation my PTSD got worse and deeper. Depression has followed along with it. It is a daily if not at times a moment-by-moment struggle to fight through it.

While in my latest struggle from my situation I felt driven by the Holy Spirit to park myself in the Psalms. I have always loved the Psalms but six years ago (from this writing) I felt such an urge to absorb the Psalms. Eventually I came to again park myself in the Psalms of David whereas I discovered through those Psalms and through the background of them from 1 Samuel how David was constantly going through dire circumstances and attacks that ultimately drove him to what I believe was PTSD and episodes from that along with depression and thus soul depression.

At times David did bring on some of his own troubles but these cave/valley Psalms arising out of what was happening as we will see in 1 Samuel were not of his making but rather flowed from his calling of God to be king. God's great calling on our lives does not mean our lives then become worry free and we sail along with the wind always at our backs. Usually, it means just the opposite as we also see from the earthly life of Jesus. Conflict, confrontation, and subsequent pains often accompany a deep calling of the Lord.

David experienced this firsthand. Jesus experienced this firsthand. I am not alone in this. You are not alone in this. David experienced deep valleys of pain and soul depression as we will see. But David did not desire to stay in the valleys. How did David, through the Holy Spirit, come out of the valleys? This was my quest as I began to do a deeper study into this. Since David experienced these deep dark valley times of his soul due to these difficult circumstances and he came out of them how can I learn from what he did in order to fight out of mine?

As I moved from David's various Psalms and studying them a pattern emerged that I saw. I saw four distinct areas of truths that were I think in most of if not all his cave/valley Psalms. Let me briefly reveal them here and then as you see this book is sectioned off into each of these areas for further study.

1) SITUATION

David was very open and clear about the circumstances that surrounded him. David did not paint over these trying times and just say whatever. He declared what was at the core of his problems. In the Psalms he was somewhat general in nature so as I sought to seek out what exactly was going on I discovered that the book of 1 Samuel gave us a very detailed picture of what David's circumstances were during the writing of these Psalms.

Let's begin by looking at the context of these Psalms as a whole. This will help us to get a clearer vision of what David was going through as the Holy Spirit moved him to write these Psalms. To narrow that down 1 Samuel 17-23 gives us our background for our cave/valley Psalm studies and here in Psalm 142. David throughout doesn't sugar coat anything and lays it out what he is going through.

2) SOUL IMPACT ON DAVID

Then David writes about how all these troubling times and circumstances affected his spirit. His soul was being attacked as a result. What exactly is meant by our soul and David's soul depression as we will be talking of this all through this book. The Hebrew has several words for "soul" – Ruwach and Nephesh. They both mean virtually the same thing. Our soul is the seat of our emotions, passions, desires and character. It is the breath of our lives and strength of our lives. It is the eternal aspect of everyone living and while living it is who we are in those areas just mentioned of emotions, desires and passions.

Obviously, our circumstances good and or bad do affect our soul – our spirit. It affects our emotions, desires and passions for things and people. All areas of our lives. As I was studying out these cave/valley Psalms of David I saw how David also did not hold back how his dire circumstances also affected him inside in his soul. David was very open about how deep into sadness and depressions he fell into as a result of what was going on around him and to him. David felt abandoned by friends and family (sometimes true and sometimes a misconception made of David due to his depression and PTSD.) David also felt at times abandoned by God as well. That was obviously not true, and David knew that, but he still feels so low at times that knowing the truth that God would never abandon him was overwhelmed by his troubled spirit so much that he declared several times to "where are You God?" Dark periods of the soul even for a strong believer can flow from deep valleys of life.

3) SOLUTION FOUND IN GOD

David did not just accept these valleys as the course of his life. I saw two specific areas that David constantly did in order to fight back in this battle for his soul. Not a battle for his salvation but a battle for his daily living. The first line of offense and defense for David as seen in his pattern of Holy Spirit writing was in God Himself. David had and developed this upward pursuit of God. Yes, as mentioned, there were times that even David lost and couldn't find this upward focus but overall, this was his main focal point in his battle for soul revival during soul depression.

David remembered who God was. David remembered things that God had one in the past for him and others. David remembered the love, compassion and power of God. David remembered also who he was to God and who he was in God. David "beheld his God."

David showed that our main line of defense and offense in this battle is getting to know who God is and then also remembering who he was in Jesus Christ. I saw as David did this so many names and epithets of who God is came shining through. An epithet of God is a word or phrase that is used to describe one of His qualities. It is a description or characterization or portrayal of who God is and/or what He is like or does. While an epithet per say might not be an actual Biblical direct name for God, they virtually do the same thing in helping us to see God more clearly. In our study, I will be using the phrase "name/epithet" of God. This will be a key point of our study as it is a key ingredient in our soul revival. Knowing God. Behold Our God! This was David's pattern and this we must pursue to do ourselves as we fight our own personal battles with soul revival.

As we like David have and develop (yes it takes development too) this upward focus on God this is the fuel the Holy Spirit can use to restore, revive and encourage us through our valleys. Our valley times can become times of a greater awareness of God and experiencing of God as He invades our lives – our souls with who He is and what He does for us and others. God is the ultimate source and power and love to pull us up out of the valley and to not just pull us out as we will see but to get us on our journey up the mountain. God does not just desire to pull us out but more so to then get us going again on our journey. Then if we fall back into another valley God will pick us up again and get us going again – and again – and again as many times as required.

This is the key as we will see repeated throughout this book as it is repeatedly seen in Psalm 142 and other Psalms and for that part all throughout God's Word. This is our call to develop, maintain and relentlessly pursue knowing God. Not just theology words to impress others but flowing from that knowledge a deeper relationship with Him. To "Behold Our God!"

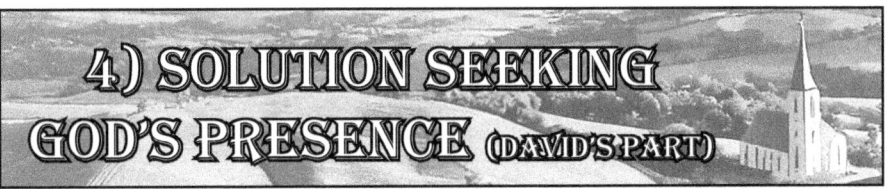

4) SOLUTION SEEKING GOD'S PRESENCE (DAVID'S PART)

I also saw as a pattern of David as he fought his own soul depression was that he had an active part in this battle. I call these at various time Participation Points or Action Steps. David did them and so is our call to do them as well. Yes, it is all of God in this soul revival. God is sovereign. Yet within God's sovereignty He is calling us to participate in this battle for soul revival. We are not to just sit back and do nothing. We will look deeper into this as we get into this section but briefly here, we are called to rest and wait upon the Lord. This we must do. We are also called of God to be active in this process of His journey for us.

There may be times when all we can do is simply raise up our heads to look at God and God even enables us to do this too. There are times in our valleys when we can seek God with a strong pursuit. There are then the middle ground times. We flow it seems like David did from being in the valley to climbing out to mountain top times to then falling right back into another valley and the process starts all over again – or so it seems. But I discovered that even when we fall back again into another valley that we thought we had already climbed out of that the falling back was not to the beginning but to another area of the valley. Our journey upward is a journey of stages from one point to another as we are healed and driven by the Holy Spirit. It is important to know this ebb and flow of this spiritual battle that we are in to know this can help us to fight off discouragement when it seems when we are not progressing when we should. Keep on fighting!

As we participate with the Lord in doing these action steps, we will have times of slipping back. You know why? Because we are human! Don't jump on yourself too quickly when you sense and even know that you are not seeking God and participating like you should – simply start from where you are at and get going again. In this section we will look at how David participated in this soul revival, and we will see some very specific ways in which we can participate as well. Always knowing that this is fully of God, yet He also calls us to participate in the process.

Those are the main four points of our study. I have also put in the back an addendum which contains some areas of review plus I hope some helpful additional action steps you can participate in.

To start out as I have mentioned before we get into our main body of our study of Psalm 142 is to see in an overview the specific circumstances that David was living in as he wrote through the Holy Spirit Psalm 142. As I mentioned we will be looking at other Psalms that I will reference to from time to time. What I am giving here now is an overview which I have done for an easier reading style of going chapter by chapter through 1 Samuel 17-23 and numbered them out. Again, I have done it this way just for I hope to simplify in an orderly way all that David was going through. I would encourage you to on your own read through 1 Samuel 17-23 directly from scripture as this will help as we go into Psalm 142 more directly. Let's begin our study of Psalm 142 by looking at the situations David was facing which is found in Isaiah 17-23.

OVERVIEW OF DAVID'S SITUATIONS

David was going through a multitude of trials and situations at this point in his life. David struggled with anxiety, depression, fear, abandonment. David knew terrors. David knew and experienced betrayal. David knew and experienced grief. David was hunted by armies that were out to not only capture him but to kill him. David had periods of extreme loneliness and even crying out to God, "Where are you God?"

All these events led to what I feel David developing PTSD. This seems so clear to me as you begin reading through David's earlier Psalms during this time period to the final ones. You can see a pattern of being up and full of energy and vigor for the Lord to times of great depression and anxiety. In one verse of these Psalms David can seem very strong in the Lord and in just a few verses later he is in the pit of despair. We don't know exactly how long it took David to write these Psalms. Perhaps some were written in one sitting and perhaps some or all were written over a period which could account for these great ups and downs that we will see. But it all points to David's ongoing battle with PTSD and depression – Spirit Depression.

I would like to add a personal note that I don't like the term PTSD (Post Traumatic Stress Disorder.) I think it should be called PTSI (Post Traumatic Stress Injury.) Whatever it is that has brought a person to this condition I feel that it is an injury to the mind, emotions and spiritual realm of a person. I agree that psychologically it is probably determined to be a "Disorder" but again I feel that saying it is rather an injury could take some of the stigma away from this.

Some of you reading this also suffer from PTSI or depression or anxiety or such. Whatever has caused this in you as you read through these Psalms and see that even David suffered from this. I hope that you can see that you are not alone in this battle. God is there for you. Open your heart to the Lord like we will see how David did. Fight back the way David did as he focused on the Lord and how great He is and how much God loved him – and you!

How do we get through these times of great Soul Depression. I am not a counselor and I do not attempt to replace someone that you might be talking with as it is important to have someone that will listen to you and help you in the battle. David had Jonathan who risked so much to travel and be with David to "encourage him in the Lord." What I am trying to do here is to open God's word in a deeper way that we can sense the depth of David's pain which can then I pray help us to overcome in and through the Lord.

What brought David to this sense of depression and PTSD? Let's look at those chapters in 1 Samuel. David was called by the Lord to be king over Israel. God sent Samuel to David's family to call the king whom God would pick from them. As Samuel went to David's father, he brought out all the kids and Samuel said no not them, and do you have any more? His father said, "well yes I guess David who is out tending the sheep." Even back then we can see a glimpse of David virtually not getting any recognition from his dad at all –even forgotten by him to not even mentioning him until Samuel directly asks.

Maybe this was an ongoing thing for David to handle as being looked down on and not valued. This is even seen more through the story of David and Goliath too. David was not just sitting on the grass watching the sheep and playing the harp all day. Tending sheep was a vital job and a stressful one and could be a dangerous one as well. David had to be constantly on guard for predators who would attempt to come and kill the sheep (good training from the Lord for future endeavors that David would have.) When some sheep would wander away and not stay with the fold David would go and search for them to bring them back (again more training for when David had to deal with some of his own soldiers who would not follow him.) When some sheep got taken by lions and bears David went out single handed to get the sheep back. I don't know about you but as of yet I have not had personal one on encounters with lions and bears – although came close once in Colorado! So even though David had proved himself time and time again with his care and protection of the sheep he would not get any recognition or even thanks from his father or brothers.

Even when David brought bread to his brothers at the time of the Goliath stand off and David said he would fight for Israel and God's honor he was ridiculed by his brothers. It seems that David was under slight pressure already to be an outcast even in his own family. David then fought Goliath in this battle. God gave David a strength and accuracy to bring down Goliath and save Israel. But instead of being honored by Saul as we will see this eventually brought Saul to great envy of David which started out all of David's troubles.

David fought many battles for Saul and Israel and even when Saul was suffering from some kind of depression would call on David to ease it through David playing the harp for him. While David was helping Saul this event turned Saul away from David. David for his service had spears thrown at him not just once but several times trying to kill him. Maybe you have been serving the Lord with all you have yet some even in the church are coming at you. This I have experienced many times and it is very heartbreaking to see and experience and can lead to a building up of anxiety and depression and abandonment feelings. This is what David was experiencing.

Perhaps at your workplace you have also experienced this similar type of rejection and or ridicule. Perhaps you have attempted in the Lord to raise godly children and it has not yet proved very fruitful. Maybe you have had a serious illness or a loved one. Was perhaps you have suffered through a horrible accident or witnessed one. We all probably have had times like these of rejection or unjust criticism or severe circumstances like these.

David experienced many tough trials and hardships. David had personal encounters with bears and lions and then had spears thrown at him to kill him. I'm sure many readings of this have experienced difficult life-threatening situations. Situations that can stir up and play havoc with our minds, bodies, emotions, and spiritually. They did for sure with David.

This background setting of when David wrote Psalm 142 is again vital to help us in our own personal battles. I feel so strongly that we have such a good grasp of this Psalm 142 background that I would like for us to dig into a bit further into it.

Let's explore more thoroughly what is transpiring in 1 Samuel 17-23. To do this I have broken down Isaiah 17-23 chapter by chapter to hopefully make this more readable and I have broken it down further by numbering situations. Keeping in mind that as we travel through Isaiah 17-23 it is all for a deeper understanding of Psalm 142. Let's explore together to prepare us for Psalm 142. You will also note in the next section that under each chapter in 1 Samuel there are Psalm listed underneath. The Psalms listed there are ones that scholars see as being written by David during that time period. This might be a good time to read through those Psalms as it were to give a solid base leading up to Psalm 142. I have also included these in chronological list form in the addendum.

1 SAMUEL 17
(Psalm 9)

Before I summarize 1 Samuel 17 let me also highlight some areas leading up to this chapter.

1) David was a shepherd and the youngest son with several brothers. While being a shepherd David had the duty of taking care of the sheep. Google at some point and see all that a shepherd had to do with this. At some point lions and bears would come and take some sheep. David pursued the lions and bears and would fight them to get the sheep back. I don't know about you, but I have yet to wrestle and fight a lion or bear, but I would assume it is a potential life-threatening event. David did so with courage.

2) God had appointed Samuel to pick a new king for Israel out of the sons of Jesse. None of the sons that Jesse brought forth to Samuel were the ones. Yet Jesse had one other son – David – whom he had not brought up for Samuel to see. David being overlooked due to his youth? Not sure of the reason but he was being overlooked by his own father. Being a shepherd then was considered one of the lowest jobs to have so is this how David's father saw him?

3) King Saul was tormented by evil spirits and found out that David could play the harp and so Saul summoned David and David's playing soothed his soul and David found favor in Saul's court and life.

4) Enter Goliath in 1 Samuel 17. The challenge was on. Goliath calls any person in Saul's vast army to come out and fight him and the winner takes all. No soldier had the courage to do so. David was sent by his father to bring food to his brothers at the front lines – obviously his brothers also were not stepping forward to fight Goliath. David comes on the scene and sees what is happening.

When he started asking some questions about what was going on his brothers became angry with him and ridiculed him. They would not step up to fight yet they ridiculed David for doing so. David said that he would go up against Goliath. He knew that God had been with him when he went up against lions and bears and so he knew that God would be with him in taking on Goliath. God used those earlier tough situations with the lions and bears to strengthen David for this calling. (We need to see that some of our trials and troubles are sent by God to prepare us for something even bigger that God would be calling us to do.)

David went up against Goliath despite all the criticism and potential fall out if he lost and surged out in the strength and power of the Lord. How David trusted God is so encouraging. Scripture tells how David prevailed over Goliath and then how his reputation grew among the Israelites.

1 SAMUEL 18
(Psalms 23, 5, and 12)

5) Because of David's growing popularity this became a pride issue with Saul and while David was serving Saul by playing his harp Saul threw a spear at David with the intention of killing him. David escaped Saul's presence "twice" we are told in 1 Samuel 18:11. David continued to prosper in the Lord as a commander in Saul's army and this angered Saul even more.

6) Then Saul even attempts to use his own daughter as bait to get at David. Saul learned that his daughter Michal loved David. Saul approached David to offer him his daughter. Saul felt that Michal would become a snare to David and be killed in battles with the Philistines. David continued to go to battle for Saul and with the Lord's enabling kept on defeating the Philistines every time they fought, and David's popularity grew even more.

1 SAMUEL 19
(Psalms 59, 11, 22, 7, and 25)

7) By this time when Saul saw how great David's victories were and his growing popularity; on top of that David was now married to his daughter Saul felt a change in heart towards David and wanted now a deep and great father-in-law to son-in-law relationship with David. Wrong – just the opposite as we see in 1 Samuel 19:1. Saul was so enraged against David that he commissioned his son Jonathan and his servants to put David to death. Another death threat for David from Saul. If this were me, I would begin to come a bit unhinged at this point. Lions, bears, Giant's in the land, spears thrown at me, going to battle time after time would he be enough for me. Now another death threat with a conspiracy as Saul was now entreating others to join in with him to kill David.

8) Thank goodness for great close friends. Jonathan, instead of becoming David's assassin, became his greatest friend of all time. Jonathan tried to smooth things over with his dad and David and brought David before Saul. David once again began playing the harp for Saul as another evil spirit was harassing Saul.

Instead of gratitude Saul picks up yet another spear and tries to kill David. In my counting so far, this is the third chucking of a spear at David from Saul. Thank goodness his aim was not that good! David had to flee in order to escape from Saul. Saul then tried to chase after David.

Pause for a moment and take in all that is happening to David. Just these situations and issues would be more than enough to bring in a counselor to help David deal with any potential PTSD, depression or anxiety issues. But even more is to come upon David. Let's continue.

1 SAMUEL 20
(Psalm 26)

9) In 1 Samuel 20, we see how Saul now also threatened his own son Jonathan and in his fierce anger showed Jonathan the door, Jonathan saw how his father Saul still wanted to kill David. Jonathan went to warn David of his fathers continued desire to kill him and as a result this forced David to flee. The song of Willie Nelson came to my mind "On the Road Again." This was David's life now.

1 SAMUEL 21
(Psalms 34 and 56)

10) 1 Samuel chapter 21 shows us a very sad situation developing that pained David's soul greatly. As David fled, he went to the town of Nob where he received some bread from the priest Ahimelech. We will soon see the dire consequences of this simple act of getting food was.

The sword that Goliath had was being kept by Ahimelech and David retrieved that sword at this point to keep. Now at first glance this might not be such a bad thing. But go back to the story of Goliath in chapter 17 and verse 4. Where was Goliath from? He was from Gath! And now David was going there for protection and on top of that carrying the sword of Goliath, the one he had slain. What was going on with David. Mind collapse or brain freeze? David was going to go into the land of Goliath whom he had just recently defeated and killed!

He probably felt that since Saul was an enemy of Achish and Achish was Saul's enemy that he would be safe there. But soon David's identity became more evident that he was the one who had led the army of Israel, and this probably led David to fear for himself there too. What a growing list of troubles and fears that were continuing to build up in David's life. But David dealt with this in a great way – he pretended to be insane. Really? Come on not in brave or good I don't see in my eyes a big trust in God from David at this point. Maybe I'm wrong this was David's life now, but David seemed to be going in the wrong direction here and perhaps he was starting to experience some PTSD effects with all that was going on around him. This could very well be a possibility. Despite of all the mistakes of David God protected him and he was able to escape there.

1 SAMUEL 22
(Psalms 142, 141, 64, 35, 52 and 57)

11) David continues his run from Saul as we get into 1 Samuel 22. Here David escapes to the cave of Adullam. Psalm 57 was written by David from this time period. We can see from some verses there how David was feeling. He felt his soul was among lions and he was hiding from those breathing forth fire. He said that they had prepared a net for him and had dug a pit for him. His soul was bowed down and he was very discouraged.

12) At this point other men started to gather with David. We see that they were not the cream of the crop. They were men of distress, debt and discontented. Not a good list of three D's. There came to him about 400 of such men. And David became their captain. David was once again at war with Saul having his vast trained army and David with his 400 "D" men that he would have to train and deal with. This would not be an easy task as we will soon see. But this can also be seen as a great picture of how God uses the weak instruments that we feel are weak all to his glory. We will also see how God used these weak unprepared and untrained men to defeat the Philistines at the city of Keilah. God uses what appears to be the weak to show forth His strength. Do you think that you are weak and unusable by God? Think again as you are in the perfect place to be used of God for great and mighty things for His kingdom – through Him using you!

13) David warned by the prophet Gad now goes to the forest of Hereth. David once again on the move. While this is going on Saul continues his pursuit of David and he finds out how David had gone to the city of Nob. Through it all

Saul had Doeg, who was one of her men, turn on the priests and city of Nob and he killed eighty-five priests plus all the men, women, children, infants and animals of the town. Only one escaped, Abiathar, and he ran and fled to David and told him all that had happened.

David said in 1 Samuel 22:22 that he was the one responsible for all their deaths. Can you imagine the weight and burden this must have been to David. David was a man after God's own heart. God is one who has great compassion and love for others. David must have been crushed in his spirit for feeling such a heavy burden of a whole town being wiped out – priests, the other men and the women plus all the children and infants and babies. What a load to carry. On top of being pursued time after time and now continually on the run for his life and being the leader of a rag tag group of men who David knew would also be killed if Saul caught up with them and now – all in the city of Nob except this one man had been killed by Saul. All because he had just basically stopped by there. Burden upon burden heaping up on David outwardly and inwardly within his spirit and soul.

1 SAMUEL 23
(Psalms 140, 31, 13, 54, 17, 16 and 35)

14) Now comes the situation at Keilah in chapter 23. Keep in mind that these events that we have been looking at have been happening in rapid sequence, so David is not getting much of a break to just chill out and try to regroup physically, emotionally and spiritually. As the town of Nob was being slaughtered and David was feeling the tremendous guilt of all that, on top of it all he gets word that the Philistines are attacking the town of Keilah and plundering it. Keilah was a town in Israel, so David's heart was with them.

David does right and went immediately to the Lord God for direction on what to do. His heart I'm sure was to go and save Keilah but David wanted to make sure that this was the Lord's will for him to do. God gives David the go ahead. So now a battle is in the mix. David goes to his men and explains the situation to them and immediately say they will follow him to the ends of the earth. No, they don't. They tell David that they are afraid to go and protect Keilah.

Now David has an additional problem in that he has received his marching orders from the Lord but his "fighting men" are too afraid to go and do it. Perhaps David is now wondering what he will do since his own men won't follow his lead and direction. David again does what is right and goes to the Lord with it.

David has an upward focus rather than the downward. He doesn't give up during the problem but goes to the Lord.

The Lord once again tells him to move forward and that He would give the Philistines into the hands of David. David must have gone to his men again because immediately Scripture tells us that David AND his men went to Keilah and fought with the Philistines and defeated them. They even took all the Philistines' livestock. David and his men through the Lord were victorious – just as the Lord promised David. I'm sure that this inspired David's heart even though it must have been a physical drain on him and his men.

15) But hold on, before David even gets to catch his breath and enjoy victory things start to go a bit south for him again. Just after he had rescued the town one or many of the inhabitants decided to betray David's great loyalty to them and went to Saul to report to him where David was and that he could capture David there. David must have been a bit thrown back by this. He was human too. Imagine doing something great for someone and they immediately turn their back on you and worse betray you. Think how this would impact on you. David again goes to the Lord to seek His direction. During great turmoil David continues to seek the Lord.

The Lord reveals to David that Saul and his men would be coming to get him, and that the town of Keilah would surrender him to Saul. Now David is experiencing an even more massive betrayal as the whole town would turn him in. David had just saved their lives and their town and now boom they turn away from David and would have turned him over to Saul to be killed. Back to the wilderness David and his men go. Rugged country it was too. The wilderness of Ziph was now their home or place of escape. Plus, on top of that we are told in verse 14 that Saul was continuing with his pursuit and hunt for David in order to kill him. No rest for the weary David and his men.

16) As David is hearing of this continual search by Saul for him, he gets a reprieve and a visit from his good friend Jonathan. What a relief and sense of blessing David must have felt when he either saw Jonathan coming or being told of it. At this point David must have just been totally exhausted on all levels. The Lord knew this as we see how God Himself, we are told in verse 14 was protecting David and was not allowing Saul to get him. Then the Lord also adds to this blessing and sends his good friend Jonathan to encourage him in the Lord. God knows our needs even before we do, and the Lord reveals again how much He cares for David. God knew that David at this point needed someone to come up and walk along beside him to strengthen him in the Lord. We don't know how long Jonathan stayed with David, but David received some spiritual fuel to keep on fighting both physically, emotionally and spiritually.

17) God knew he would need this as now the Ziphites also turned against David and went to Saul to gather up with Saul to go and find David to kill him. Since David was in the wilderness of Ziph the Ziphites knew the land and places where David might be hiding so now David had some new enemies coming

against him. When it rains, it sure does seem to pour at times. More pressures falling upon David more people pursuing him to kill him.

18) As we see in verse 25 Saul had heard where David was and began an assault along with the Ziphites to capture and kill him. They were getting now very close to David and his men. Saul and his army along with the Ziphites were fast approaching David as David was on one side of a mountain and they were just on the other side. Image watching this as a movie with an aerial view with David running away with his men as they were being pursed. Scripture tells us that David was very disturbed and making haste to get away. He was alarmed and fled as fast as he could along with his men. Fear was surrounding them just like Saul and his army was. David was literally running for his life. We don't know but maybe David was even wondering what was happening and why. God had appointed him to be king of Israel and now he was the one being sought to be killed and it looked like it just might happen. Confusion must have been adding to David's dilemma that day.

19) "But God," – again we see how God miraculously intervened in David's life here. We must let this sink in as I'm sure David saw it as well. It was almost over for David. The edge of night was almost gone being followed up with complete darkness and defeat. But God – Look at verse 27 and we will see how God came to David's rescue once again. Off in another area of Israel the Philistines were at it again and were making a raid on the land of Israel. A messenger came running up to Saul to tell him what was happening. Saul being king of Israel had to protect the land and as much as he wanted to kill David, he knew he had to go and protect Israel from the Philistines. Saul and the Ziphites therefore broke off their pursuit of David. David must have seen this happening and wondered what was going on? They are leaving and no longer pursuing us. What a relief that must have been.

Let's look at bit deeper at this sequence of events to see how awesome God is. God used the evil Philistines at the right moment and right circumstances to once again attack Israel and invade. They had just been defeated at Keilah, but they kept on coming in their attacks on Israel. God using the evil intentions of the Philistines to accomplish His purpose and plan for David. Then God had a messenger come to Saul to tell him what was happening. We are not told the name of this person and whether he was a believer in God or not. Perhaps he was and perhaps he was not as we simply do not know but what we do know is that God used this unnamed messenger to find Saul and relay the message of the attack. Without even knowing this man this messenger was being used of God to get this message to Saul. See how the Lord can weave together so many events for our good. God created the universe with a single breath so He can certainly move what He needs and desires to move for our good and His eternal plans for us. Don't lose sight of this major event. "But God" – do a study some time even in just the Psalms of that two-word phrase.

When you feel that you are under attack and being pursued and the enemy is just over the ridge ready to pounce on you and end it all – remember – "But God!" David must have seen God's hand in this all which must have again encouraged him to keep on going. That place got named for what it was – the "Rock of Escape."

20) Now David had it all easy and life was a breeze. Not so much. Look at the end of chapter 23 in verse 29. Once again David and his men ended up in the wilderness lands. This time at Engedi. Does the phrase "out of the frying pan and into the fire" mean anything to you? It sure did to David.

This is where we will stop in our background setting for our study in Psalm 142. Somewhere in this timeframe and sequence of events David through the Holy Spirit wrote Psalm 142 plus several other Psalms which we will reference from time to time. It was obviously a very difficult and trying time for David. These events had a huge emotional and spiritual impact on David which we will see as we progress with our study. Let me encourage you as you study Psalm 142 to go and read and even study a bit more this section in 1 Samuel 17-23 as it gives a great look into what David was going through.

Let's proceed then into our next section where we will dive deeper into Psalm 142 by seeing it in four sections:

I) Situation
II) Soul Impact on David
III) Solution - Found in God & Who He Is
IV) Solution - Seeking God's Presence (David's Part)

What is exactly the EHGV? This is a brand-new expanded version that will hopefully help us to see a more in-depth and at the same time a clearer view of what is being said by the Holy Spirit. We will do this by looking at the original Hebrew and Greek words and tenses along with the Strong's Concordance, and use of English synonyms to expand on the verses. It is not adding to the meaning but giving more depth. Our English words can simply not come close to properly convey what the hearers would hear when this was originally said and written.

The layers of the depth in the Hebrew and Greek words are so heavy with meaning that if the whole Bible were expanded like this it would simply be too heavy to even carry. In this book unless noted it will be in the EHGV. With that in mind the following pages will give us a good glimpse into what I stated here. Our book is mainly focused on Psalm 142 which has just seven verses. In the coming few pages you will see that I have written out Psalm 142 in the NIV and then right below each verse you will see the EHGV which again does not add or subtract from the Hebrew but simply gives the fuller sense and truth of what is being said. Along with examining the tenses of each word we can also gather a deeper sense of the meaning. Plus, this also gives us an enhanced view of what David was experiencing in his emotions and mindset. Here we go!

"PRAYER FOR HELP IN TROUBLE"

MASKIL OF DAVID, WHEN HE WAS IN A CAVE

PSALM 142

Lord, I'm in a cave – this time literally as I am fleeing from Saul who is trying to kill me. I know he is serious as he has already thrown spears at me attempting to kill me. Now he has gathered his army in search of me. I am hiding out in this cave which is in a desolate barren place. Along with the ones who have now gathered with me here it is even hard to find any water or food to survive on. If we venture out will Saul, then be alerted to where we are? Will there be enough food and drink for us all? Did You not appoint me King of Israel and now I am hiding out in a cave.

So here is my prayer that I lift to You, O Lord. I ask for You to intercede on my behalf and on behalf of all of those who have now gathered with me in this cave. Please step into my situation Lord. Here are my requests through this Psalm and prayer that I am lifting-up to You. I am seeking You in this time of severe troubles.

Lord, I also ask that this prayer and Psalm be used of You as a teaching for those who are also going through troubles of their own – whatever they might be. Let this help them in You and through You to be able to navigate their troubles as You lead and guide them.

"I cry aloud to the Lord; I lift up my voice to the Lord for mercy."

~ Psalm 142:1 ~

Lord, You are Jehovah. You are the Sovereign One. You are God Almighty. I am looking to You as I am in this cave. I am crying out to You. I am pleading with You through this prayer as I am in desperate need. I am asking You to come to my aid. I am asking You that we be joined together as these troubles surround me. Let them draw me closer to You. I am shrieking out to You in my anguish and the dangers I am in. I am crying out to you in my time of distress. These troubles have even caused my heart to become rattled and disturbed within me. I direct this prayer to You for help. It is Your help I request and need O Lord.

I am troubled by anxiety with all the commotion that is raging on all around me. As I am shouting out to you loudly, I am doing so with reverence for You. My voice thunders emphatically in my requests in my desperation for You and Your help. I don't care who hears me as I am in deep need and despair. Lord, let the depths of these troubles release the depths of Your love and power to me and for me.

Lord, I am asking – rather I am begging for Your mercy in these situations. I am imploring You to move in on my behalf. You are the Lord of lords and King of kings. You sit enthroned in heaven and Sovereign over all Your creation. I realize I am but a man and dependent upon You. I ask – I beg that You reach down from on high from Your heavenly thrown to give me relief and bless me with Your mercy. I ask for Your aid and help as I am overwhelmed and have not the resources or energy or wisdom to come through this. Therefore, I know that I need You. You brought me to this cave for protection. Perhaps You have allowed all of this to happen so that I would stop and look up to You more and see my complete dependency is upon You and not me or anything I have or anyone with me. Let us be joined together in a deeper relationship than ever before because of all of this. There is nothing that You can't do. Help me to live in that truth.

"I pour out before Him my complaint,
before Him I tell my trouble."

~ Psalm 142:2 ~

Lord, I am bringing to You the full weight of my grief, sadness, fear, discouragement – I am dying inside. I have nowhere else to go but to You as I pour out my heart - my emotions to You. I am here completely pouring out my soul - the seat of my emotions and all that I am. You are the only one who can help me. All my anxieties and distress and troubles I am coming to You with. I ask that as I am pouring out my soul to You that you will change me –change me to trust You more. I need Your heart guarding peace. Let me sense Your presence as we meet in this prayer. While others may hear I am praying specifically here to an audience of one – You! I come into Your presence to be lifted by Your presence.

As You know I'm surrounded by trouble. These dangers and adversities make me feel like I am in a strait which is being pressed in with nowhere for me to go. The storms are raging all around causing great turmoil around me and inside me. There is such distress and anguish in my soul. I am therefore pouring myself out to You. I am empty inside and so I empty myself into Your hands.

"When my spirit was overwhelmed within me, it is You who watch over my way, in the path where I walk people have hidden a snare for me."

~ Psalm 142:3 ~

Lord, as all these troubles are happening all around me and to me, they have caused my spirit to be overwhelmed. My strength and desires have dried up and have led me to become greatly discouraged even to the point of spirit depression. My thoughts, emotions and energy of life have become so troubled as my life feels like it is uncontrollable. This darkness has enveloped my spirit. I am fainting away with exhaustion and my life is ebbing away.

However, when all this is happening, I also know that You, Lord are paying attention to me. You fully understand all these trials, troubles and dangers that have led my spirit to this depression. Through this all You will reveal Yourself to me in a deeper way that I have never understood before. I hang onto this truth. My very footsteps I know are ordained by You the Sovereign One. My path is under Your care, compassion, guidance and control. Yet I feel even now – even knowing these truths about You and my relationship with You – that my spirit is still slipping away. How can this be? My focus is slipping back again to my enemies and my situations. My enemies have intensely and intentionally with repeated actions hidden traps for me to fall into. They are planning adversity and hardships for me. They desire to bring multiple distresses into my life and bring me down. They are a source and the agents of calamity to me. They want to simply wreck my life as I know it.

"Look and see, there is no one at my right hand;
no one is concerned for me. I have no refuge,
no one cares for my life."

~ Psalm 142:4 ~

Lord, I know as I've just proclaimed that You are there – yet it still hits me hard that I have looked intently for help to come, but none has. If just one person who would be close with me through this all. No one cares about me or my situation enough to hang in there with me. No one is looking intently at me to reach out to me with help. Instead, they all pretend to be strangers to me. They ignore my cries for help and reject my calls to please reach out to me.

There is no one I can run to for safety. No escape for me. No place for shelter. Nowhere to flee to. No place to escape from all these dangers, depression and sense of hopeless despair. No refuge for me.

No one has thoroughly studied out why I am in such a place of despair as they don't care enough about me to do so. No one reaches out to help me. I feel like my soul is in a state of disarray. My seat of emotions, passions and thoughts are drying up inside of me. I am in the pit of deep despair and no one even cares.

"I cry to You, Lord; I say, You are my refuge,
my portion in the land of the living."

~ Psalm 142:5 ~

In my desperate need Lord, I am again calling unto You for help. Since no one who is coming to my aid or even seems to care enough to try, I am reaching out to You. I am desperately crying out to You. I look to others and there is no one who cared enough to help me in my deepest time of need. They are always around yet run away when I try to share my hurts and my pains. Friends and even blood family keep me at a distance. They say that they are there for me yet hide when they see me coming or try to share. I asked for help, and they disappeared. This has brought me to look to You, my Lord. You should have been my first look to person anyway. You are my God who cares and cares for me. You are my God of refuge. You are my shelter in these storms that I am in that don't seem to go away and I see that You will not go away even in the darkest of storms, You will stand with me and by me.

Let me be joined together with You – You who are Jehovah the Sovereign Almighty One. You are my portion – my stability. My flesh and my heart may fail me. My flesh which represents my blood relatives who have forsaken me and failed me. My own heart represents the seat of my desires, emotions and courage that fails me. I fail myself time after time as I try and work through this depression of mine. Yet I know that You are my strength and my portion and my stability for ever and You will not fail me. Join with me now Lord. Help me to join-together more with you. I need You Lord now more than ever.

"Listen to my cry, for I am in desperate need,
rescue me from those who pursue me,
for they are too strong for me."

~ Psalm 142:6 ~

Lord, I ask that You take notice of my shouts of grief and cries for help to You. I am growing tired and feel very weakened through this all. I am hanging limp as though I am dangling over a deep cliff. I sense and feel this deep state of depression with these extreme dangers that have led me to be greatly diminished in all that I do and am. This is my constant sense of living now. I am completely engulfed in it, and it is intensive, abundant and a persistent danger. The subsequent depression then gets louder and louder and deeper and deeper. I am being pursued and I am being attacked with this unbroken continuity. They come after me with great eagerness to destroy me. They are too strong for me, and I simply cannot handle it anymore.

Deliver me Lord. Rescue me, Lord. Defend me, Lord. Help me, Lord. You are my great God who is the great Cause and Effect of all things. Help me to stand strong as You step in to deliver me. Deliver me from these dangers and troubles that the enemy has brought upon me. Deliver my spirit from these depressions. Don't let these anxieties rule over me. Let Your spirit of peace rule in me.

"Set me free from my prison, that I may praise Your name. Then the righteous will gather about me because of Your goodness to me."

~ Psalm 142:7 ~

Lord, bring me out of this deep dungeon of depression and dangers that I am in. My emotions, my passions, my will and mind need rescue. Energize me once again Lord. Not only rescue me out but take me forward to green pastures. Take me out of this to go forth with purpose and for results for and with You. Take me from this to proceed to something great. Just like You took the Israelites from slavery in Egypt You didn't just take them out of there, but You also took them to the Promised Land. Make this a great "coming away" to a great "going to" event for me. Let this be another source of praise and worship that I can freshly raise up to You as You do this. Let this also be seen by others so that then we can gather as one to praise You. Lord, take me out of this and take me to something great.

PSALM

142

I) SITUATION

In the title of our Psalm 142 we are told by David that he was in trouble and was hiding in a cave. I'd like to give a brief overview and I would ask you to refer more to the previous section on 1 Samuel that gives a more detailed look into the circumstances that were surrounding David.

More than likely scholars place this Psalm 142 along with Psalm 23 and Psalm 54 flowing from 1 Samuel 22 where David was in trouble hiding in a cave – hiding for his life. David was fleeing from Saul who was on the march seeking to kill him (1 Samuel 20:33; 21:10). This came right after David had feigned insanity with Achish and then escaped to the Cave of Adullam. David was on the run from King Saul and his vast army. Saul had his army and David also had his – but there was a huge difference. David's army as we see in 1 Samuel 22:2 consisted of a total of 400 me who fell into three categories: 1) Everyone who was in distress, feeling hardship, in trouble, in anguish, feeling oppressed and in desperate situations. 2) Everyone who was in debt fleeing their debtors. 3) Everyone who was discontented, in anguish, ruthless, very upset, bitter in heart and angry in heart. Wow! Such a great group of men to call your army. David did not do well as it would seem on the draft day. His picks appeared to be in the late 70-80th round at best. King Saul's army vs. David's army – take your pick for who would be victorious!

The men, who became David's army, had heard about David being on the run and they gathered themselves to David to be their leader. Soon after this gathering David was told by the prophet Gad to leave the cave and head into the Forest of Hereth (1 Samuel 22:5). The Forest of Hereth was not so much a forest full of lush vegetation but more of a desert – dry and arid – where no vegetation could grow. Jeremiah 17:6 describes such a situation, "dwell in the parched place of the desert where no one lives." Not a pleasant place to be sent to. Cave times to Desert times. Seems it was growing from bad to worse for David and his men. David found himself in the desert of limitations and fleeing for his life. With a rag tag army at best with him. David was anointed to be King by God. David was supposed to be on the throne yet now he was in a desperate time of fleeing from King Saul while in a cave then transferred to a place of desert conditions. David himself expresses what was going on in several verses in Psalm 142. Let's look at verses 2,3 and 6 to see how David, through the Holy Spirit describes his situation here.

Verse 2 – "I pour out my complaint before God; I declare my trouble before Him." David says that he is in trouble. The Hebrew word for that here is Tsarah (Tsaw-raw). David had problems and he was in narrow straits that were full of calamities, dangers, storms, suffering, distresses, anguish, and adversities. He had enemies, adversaries and oppressors who were actively pursuing him. Not a pleasant time.

Verse 3 – "In the way where I walk, they have hidden a trap for me." Besides the obvious meaning for trap, it also means that it comes from a source or agent of calamity. King Saul and his army were the source and agent of these troubled times for David. David was experiencing hardship, adversity, and a possible catastrophic collapse of his life. There was danger around every corner for him.

Verse 6 – "Deliver me from my persecutors, for they are too strong for me." David had persecutors, He was being pursued and chased by Saul and his army whose aim was to secure David in order to kill him. David was being harassed being run after by those who had obvious hostile intent. These pursuers-persecutors were simply too strong for David. They were determined. They were resolute. They were persistent. They were relentless. They were tenacious. They were strong and powerful. They were after David.

Take a moment and ponder all that David was facing and going through. This was real for David. This was not just a Bible story but his life. Now bring this home to your life. Perhaps some of you right now are going through your own great troubles. Obviously different from David's but you have your own time even right now perhaps where you feel surrounded by troubles. You have struggles (whatever they may be) swirling all around you. Storms and adversity so strong you sense that there is no way out for you. You feel that you are in a cave or desert and in an adequate time of your life.

Your cave or desert time could be revolving around family troubles, financial troubles, relationship troubles, work troubles, emotional troubles, physical troubles – fill in the blank of what you may be going through. All of them or even just one could bring about a desperate sense in your mind and heart. All of that could open the door to depression. Depression can be brought on by so many varied circumstances. Spiritual depression then can creep into your heart and mind and soul. Difficult to describe and difficult for those around you to understand. David experienced these times of great trouble and distress, and they had a significant impact on his mind, emotions and in his spiritual life impacting his soul.

Perhaps you will see how your times of caves and desert situations you are facing have also impacted you. Some might say that it does no good to rehash and to voice your feelings as it is only complaining. That is simply not true according to what we will see right from the Bible. David was very clearly stating how all his circumstances were affecting him spiritually. I also feel from my own experience that if one keeps it all inside it does nothing to help move forward. This is where God through our David example here tells us to spill out our hearts to Him and let Him know how you feel and how it is all impacting you. To sit down and being able to talk with someone on a regular basis I see is a vital step to moving forward. Don't keep it all inside. David did not keep all inside but just the opposite. David was honest by God on what was happening to him. He didn't sugar coat it with "awe shucks it isn't all that bad." It was bad and David shared that with God. All these rough situations had an impact on how David was feeling. It impacted his thinking. It impacted his emotions. It impacted his very soul. In our next section, we will see how David was impacted and how honest he was to God with them too.

II) SOUL IMPACT ON DAVID

As we will see and just mentioned, all that was happening to David and around him had a great effect on his mental, physical, emotional, and spiritual life. Throughout this Psalm David lays out how he felt. Perhaps you can relate to some of these. I don't want this section to be discouraging to anyone going through some of the same emotions and despair that we will see David had as a result of his situation. But it is very important for us to see the depths of David's despair and then have God and David dealt with it. This can also help us to feel like we are not alone. Keep in mind as we work through this section that there is another section following – Solutions to our deep despair. For now, let's go verse by verse and try to see. The soul impact his situation had on him.

Verse 3 – "When my spirit was overwhelmed within me..." Spirit there is the Hebrew word ruwach (roo-akh) and it means one's feelings, disposition as troubled, bitter, discontented, uncontrollable impulses, the seat of one's emotions and energy of life. One's life breath per se. David's situation had a standing impact on him. He said his spirit (ruwach) was overwhelmed. Overwhelmed is the Hebrew word ataph (awtaf). It means to feel feeble, faint from exhaustion, faintness, despair. It carries with it the idea of darkness and feeling that darkness has enveloped you or surrounded you. That is a deep reaction to what was happening to David. This was not a simple mild setback or ho hum, but it was deep despair that engulfed his spirit. A man after God's own heart was in the throngs of deep depression.

I feel since this Psalm is one of the early cave Psalms about what we have looked at in 1 Samuel I sense this is the beginning point of David's PTSD episodes which flourished into depression in him. This is a continual battle that David experienced throughout this part of his life and even into his later days. This spiritual dependency for David was an ongoing battle. This is not to discourage you if you are facing some of these same emotions and feelings of spiritual overwhelming as it can be fought and won in Jesus Christ, but God does not always remove this spiritual battle immediately or even fully while on earth. Paul even had a thorn in his side that God would not remove for His reasons and purposes. Maybe it kept Paul dependent on God? Maybe God allowed David to experience and not get fully away from this Spiritual Depression so that he would also rely on God and to keep seeking God for his times and moments of refreshing. We don't know all the reasons why God does not automatically lift the despair from one's soul. But that does not negate the hope and trust in God that we still need to have and develop as we fight through it. For some these times of Spiritual Depression are only for a short season and for others it is like David a lifelong battle. Either way we can fight through it as we will see in the Solutions section coming up.

Verse 4 – "I look to the right and see; for there is no one who regards me; There is no escape for me; No one cares for my soul." David, in this overwhelming despair began to feel that he was all alone. There was no hope. No escape. No one cared for him. He felt he had no place to run to for help or safety. No refuge to run to. No place he could hide. Right now, David is feeling this about the people around him. David even in Psalm 31:22 and other places felt that God had abounded him too. This can be an overriding sense for many people who are experiencing PTSD, depression, anxiety, and such. You can feel like David did that no one cares for you. You can sense a deep feeling of no hope and no escape from your troubles. But there is hope. It is ok to acknowledge these feelings that you have and even beneficial to talk with someone about them. Maybe sometimes they are real as I have experienced firsthand through my own PTSD episodes that some people even former close friends and family cannot understand what I am going through and since they can't handle the episodes of doubt, depression, and hopelessness that they turn and run away. Yes, at times this abandonment can be real. And there are also times when it is not true, yet it still feels like it.

Once you have been abandoned by someone close and adding in what PTSD can do to a person no wonder one develops a mindset that everyone will eventually abandon me. Keep in mind that even if that is true (hope it is not) but if it is we still have Jesus who said He will never leave us or abandon us. Keep asking the Lord to send you someone or several people who can help you walk through these struggles. People who will, even though they might not understand all the feelings you are going through, won't abandon you. For David right now this is how he felt - that all have abandoned him.

Verse 6 – "Give heed to my cry, For I am brought very low..." The word "brought" can't be passed over here. It is the Hebrew word dalal (daw-lae). It means to be brought low, greatly diminished, grow tired, emptied, to be low, of distress, look weary, to be oppressed and feeble. It is the same word for "low" that is used here. Then David adds the word "very." It means exceedingly, greatly, huge amount. David was entangled in these feelings of spiritual and emotional depression. It was continual and something that was wiping him out mentally, physically, emotionally, and spiritually. This was excessive distress that tired David out. It weakened him. It emptied him. Have you ever felt this way or are you living in this right now. It can be devasting to try and get up each day. Even the smallest thing that you need to do can seem like a mountain when you are under such stress and oppression.

I have three fish tanks in my small little home that I live in now. Each one has its own setting and types of fish. My bed is right next to the biggest tank and when I wake up and the fish in that tank see me getting out of bed, they all swim to that corner of the tank and start getting excited as they see me awake and know that they are about to be fed. Fish do recognize the ones who are their caregivers and obviously have memories. One morning when I was going through a very difficult time and feeling some of these things that David was feeling when I woke up, I thought how in the world am I going to manage and feed all three tanks. I also had to make lunch for myself as work was very busy and I would not have time to come home. So now add having to make lunch in the morning along with my normal taking a shower, making coffee and breakfast. Let's be real here. None of those things in a normal thinking process for a person are difficult things to do and can even be enjoyable. But on this morning, I was so overwhelmed that even the thought of having to feed three different fish tanks and make lunch was almost too much for me to overcome. I honestly felt that. How in the world could I possibly do that this morning. Well, thank goodness I was able to make it through that morning. Obviously looking back those thoughts I had were not rational but right then and there they were as real as can be. This is what spiritual depression can do. It can take what are the normal everyday simple things and turn it into a mountain.

One who has experienced trauma or other reasons and has developed PTSD, depression and anxiety even having to feed the fish in the morning can seem overwhelming. Don't condemn yourself for these moments (even though some around you may).

Verse 6 – "Deliver me from my persecutors, for they are too strong for me." David felt overwhelmed at the opposition that he was facing. Here is a man who didn't flinch when he took on Goliath. In the whole army of Israel not one person walked forward to take on Goliath. But David did. David was so strong in the Lord that he knew that even the great strength of Goliath was no match for God. David stepped out in confidence and in God's strength took down the mammoth Goliath. Yet here we see David feeling that he was no match for Saul's army. Things that we used to be able to do when one experiences great trauma, hard times, PTSD, depression, etc. now seem too much for us to handle. Remember my fish story I just wrote about? This can also be in other important areas of our lives too. Bringing up kids can become an overwhelming "I can't do this anymore" feeling in a person. A job that a person has done for a long time now is too overwhelming to take on. Depression can rob us of our strength and our reliance upon God to accomplish every day and great tasks for Him. David was experiencing this.

Verse 7 – "Bring my soul out of prison…" Again, David's soul was the seat of his emotions, passions, appetites, will – his very life breath. David felt like his very soul was in prison. The word prison means dungeon. A shutting up of oneself in this darkness of times and darkness of spirit.

David was in deep despair. He had troubles all around him. Saul along with his army was seeking to find David in order to kill him. David was hiding out in a cave and having to go into an even more desolate dry place in order to run from Saul. David was perhaps even wondering what was going on since God had appointed and anointed him as King of Israel, yet he was the one on the run for his life in the wilderness of a desert and now in the wilderness of his spirit. What was David to do? What are we to do when we are faced with our own tough times? Our own times of PTSD episodes or depression. Our times of anxiety. Our times of when our tough situations just do not seem to end and there appears to be no one who cares for us and no hope on the horizon. What do we do? Scripture here in Psalm 142 gives us a great blueprint to follow as we fight back for Soul Revival. Soul Revival can be a reality and we can through the Lord overcome Soul Depression. We don't need to stay in any Soul Depression, but the way David did. If you slip and fall back in don't give up and get back on this Holy Spirit inspired blueprint for Soul Revival that David gives us here. We need to keep on keeping on.

As we move towards the Solution for fighting for Soul Revival, I see it in two parts. The first one is the cornerstone of all revival - the utmost Solution is found in God and who He is and who we are to Him. The other part of the Solution that I see is what was David's part in participation with God for this Soul Revival. And this is also a part that God calls us to likewise participate in. But God even helps us to do that too. Let's go into our next and more encouraging section – Solutions to our Soul Depression.

III) SOLUTIONS – FOUND IN GOD

When we are found in difficult situations in our lives, we all want solutions. David did not deserve to stay in his physical and spiritual battle. David wanted solutions. David's life was unraveling, and he wanted some inner and outer peace. So do we.

Perhaps today you are struggling with some deep troubling issue in your life. You might be in distress. Distress is a sense of suffering, anxiety, dread, dejections, sorrow, unhappiness, acute physical, mental, and suffering. There is great pain, agony, grief, heartache, hardship in your life. All of these could manifest itself in depression – mental, emotional, and spiritual.

It's hard to just wake up every day and be determined to just "get over it" and move on. Yet by saying that let me encourage you that there are solutions to whatever situation you are now facing. This has been the focus of my study over the last multitude of years to find a solution! I wanted solutions! I knew I was in emotional and spiritual pain. I knew my personal struggle with PTSD and depression, I wanted solutions! I knew the episodes that came from PTSD were pushing away close friends from my life who didn't understand it and couldn't cope with it. So instead of helping me they abandoned me. I wanted solutions!

I poured myself into the Psalms that David wrote during his great times of spiritual depression. I wanted to know what he did to fight though his struggle and to keep going. How did David find solutions? As I began to do this (with my Bible and notebook in hand) the Holy Spirit kept leading me to see that David knowingly or maybe even unknowingly was following a pattern to fight for spiritual revival in his life.

I began to see after a long season of study that David found solutions to his spiritual depression through focusing on two major areas. Each of these areas have many connection subparts as we will see but the solutions to his drive for spiritual renewal centered on the two overriding truths.

The first overriding truth from scripture to find solutions to our spiritual depression is – Found in God!

The ultimate solution is always God. God can bring this about in so many of His unlimited was and means. I saw David know this and how he was good at seeing God as his first "run to" person. David struggled in doing this at times due to his own personal bouts with episodes resulting from his PTSD and depression. I saw how he continually kept fighting back and sometimes even crawling back to spiritual revival through who God is.

David did this and we will see very specifically here in Psalm 142 how he focused the truths of God is. I saw that David did this in a specific way. He saw God as He reveals Himself to us through all His various names and epithets. An epithet is a truth or character of God that reveals who He is. An epithet of God is much like a name. For our study here I will refer to God's names/epithets.

The truths about God that reveal who he is through His vast name/epithets helped David to fight through his times of deep despair and spiritual depression. These were brought on by all his various troubles and situations that he was facing and going through. These names/epithets of God can be our steppingstone solution to our spiritual depression as well.

Walk through to finding solutions as we focus in an who God is through His names/epithet. Just like David did we can also experience spiritual revival as we do so too. Take time to ponder all these truths about God that we will see. They also reveal how much he loves us. Let the truths of God soak into our hearts, minds, and spirit. Memorize them, remember them. Let them become a part of who you are. David did! Let us so likewise do! Let's begin with our first name/epithet of God from Psalm142 – Jehovah Yada.

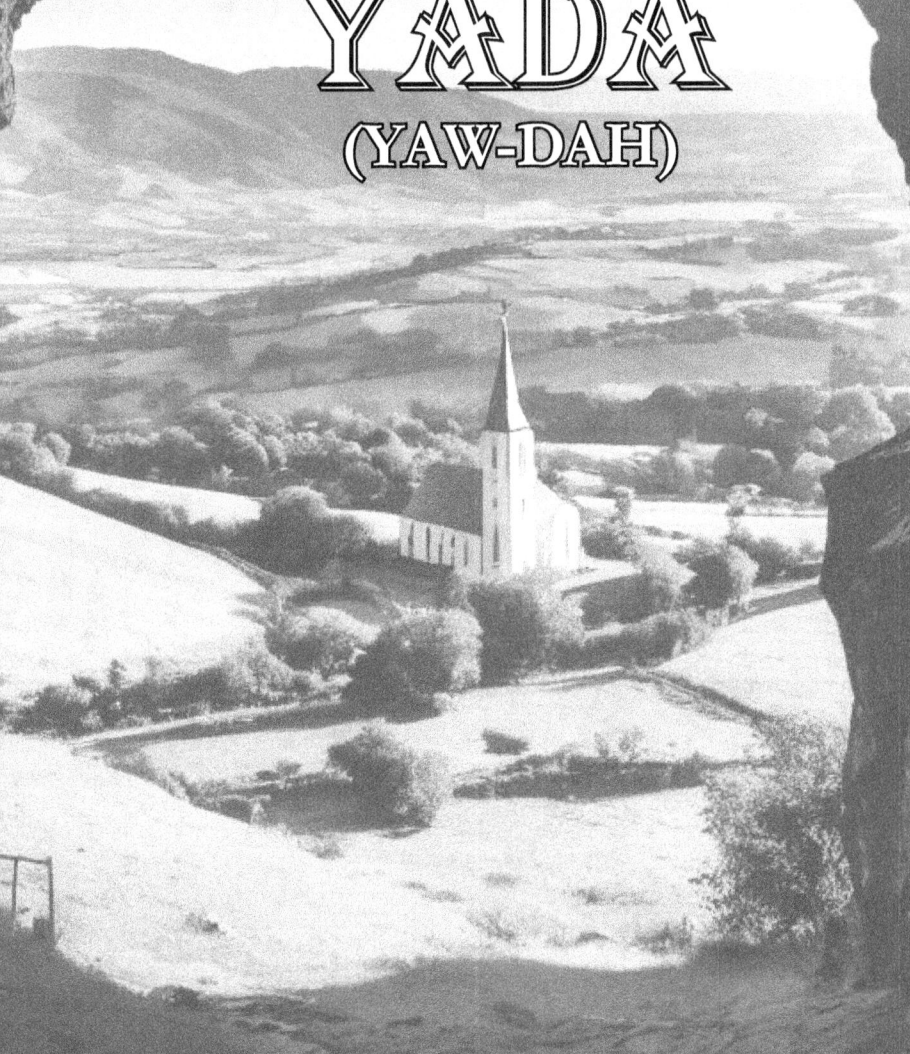

JEHOVAH

YADA

(YAW-DAH)

JEHOVAH YADA

To know by experience
Personally experience
Understand
Fully Understand
Pay attention to
Acknowledge
Determine
Leading
Gives Instruction
Be wise
Familiar Friend
To make oneself known

1) Verse 3 – Jehovah Yada (Yaw-dah) "When my spirit was overwhelmed within me, You knew (Yada) my path. In the way where I walk, they have hidden a trap for me."

David knew that his enemies were out to get him and that they had laid traps for him. His enemies were the source or better put the agent of the ultimate enemy who was attempting to bring calamities into David's life. As these attacks were coming against David, he kept this two-word phrase in his mind – "But God." But God – God was aware of what was happening to David. David also knew that God allows things to come into our lives at various times so that we would ultimately look to Him and seek Him more diligently to rely on God more deeply.

The word Yada carries with it know by experience. Jesus knew full well the experience of facing attacks from the enemy and some of His attacks were directly from Satan the truth to himself like in the wilderness in Matthew chapter 4. Then Satan used his agents of doom to harass Jesus throughout His earthly ministry and with the ultimate attack at the cross and in the Garden. Satan thought he had won but it was his doom. Jesus felt the horrors of physical pain along with the emotional pain of his disciples abandoning Him. This is for another time of deeper study but the Greek states that in the Garden Jesus even felt the pangs of depression so bad it was unto death – mainly because of the disciples not even willing to fight the call of sleep over Jesus' call to them to pray with Him. Jesus knows the depths of despair that many of us feel. He understands firsthand what it feels like to feel like David did here. He knows for sure what it is like. He knows your pains and your struggles too! Jesus knows through His own experiences.

This makes it a lot easier to know that at least one somebody understands your troubles and depression and anxieties even if no one else does. This "one" is Jesus! You can run to God with all your troubles, despair, hardships, PTSD, depression, abandonment plus anything else. You can cry aloud, pour out your heart and even complaints to the Lord. He gets it. He has been through it. He knows and understands your pain. That is comforting to me when I am in the depths of despair. I might not get it fully when I am sinking in the mud, but it can help to fight to come out of it and then looking back to see how He pulled me out. Know that Jesus understands and gets how you feel. Many people, even close friends and loved ones and family just can't get what is the trouble with us and can even expect us to just snap out of it. But God – Jesus knows and understands.

Yada also means to determine, lead, and giving instruction. As we've seen Jesus fully understands our pains and savior as He personally went through His own as He walked this earth. But Yada goes beyond just knowing about it as Yada also carries the truth that God in His sovereignty is fully involved in the whole process. God is orchestrating all our life events. Even the difficult trials I'm going through? In all things God is sovereign. God has a purpose for us and others even through our difficult troubles of life. Things here in David's life were not just random acts that God couldn't keep under control. Do I understand this? No, I don't or can't or will ever be able in this life to see all the why's of things – But God – He does. He is working all the events of our lives to our good and for His glory (Romans 8:26). We need to trust Him in His Yada – sovereignty of our lives.

Yada also has another truth to it. It means that Jesus is our familiar friend. I like that! He is there with us as we walk through our difficult times. He is your friend! The creator of the universe is your friend. Let that sink into your heart and mind.

Yada – God knows. This is an attribute of God that is also connected to God being Jehovah Yada. God is Omniscient. Omniscient means that God is in total knowledge of all things. This is also connected with his sovereignty.

1 John 3:20 tells us that God knows all things. Psalm 139 again is a great Psalm to see this truth. Matthew 10 tells us that even when one sparrow falls to the ground God knows it. God also knows the number of hairs on our head. Now multiple that times the number of people in the world and that can tell you a bit about God! When all of this was swirling around David and David's emotional and spiritual states were not strong David held on to the truth that God was Jehovah Yada and Omniscient. God was all knowing. David was being attacked by Saul and his army. Yet David also knew that God was fully aware about it and that He was there with him. David's heart and soul were being overwhelmed to the point of spiritual depression and a sense of feeling abandoned. Yet David held on to the truths of who God was and was for him.

David also wrote Psalm 139. Try to read and study through that Psalm some more as it deeply reveals the truth of Jehovah Yada and God's Omniscience running together. Verse 5 of Psalm 139 is key to David's thinking as he knew the truth of Jehovah Yada. Verse 5, "I look behind me and You are there. I look ahead of me, and You are there. I look to my left and You are there. I look to my right, and You are there. You God surround me with Your presence. Your hand is on me everywhere I go." (EHGV).

David said in verse 8 that he knew he could not flee anywhere to get out of God's presence. David knew that the darkness that surrounded him was not dark to God. Darkness here was David's misery, sorrow, and the sense of being in a deep dark dungeon due to all that was going on around him and to him. David knew though that God's light was brighter than any darkness that the world could throw at him. David knew that God's presence was with him.

Think about Shadrach, Meshach and Abidnego on how even when they were thrown into a fiery furnace that God was there walking with them. God was not taken off guard while this was happening to them. God knew all about it and the three knew that God would be with them. David knew about Joseph and how he was literally thrown into a dark prison unjustly and that God knew all about it and was not caught off guard there either. David knew that Joseph knew that God was with him and that he was under God's sovereign protection even while being falsely accused and thrown into prison. God had a purpose for it all.

Even through our difficult times we need to grab hold of these truths of who God is, He is sovereign over all even our storms that we are in. It is still difficult to be going through them but hang on to the truth that God could be using our storms for His purposes down the road for us and for others. Let this truth of God being Jehovah Yada/Omniscient sink in I give the Holy Spirit fuel to help us to stand firm against the enemy's attacks. We may get hit and wounded through our trials – "But God!" David was hit and wounded through his trials and troubles but he knows – "But God." We will ultimately prevail through Him. God knows about our trials and troubles. God cares about us and is with us. Jesus is our familiar friend as we walk through our fiery trails.

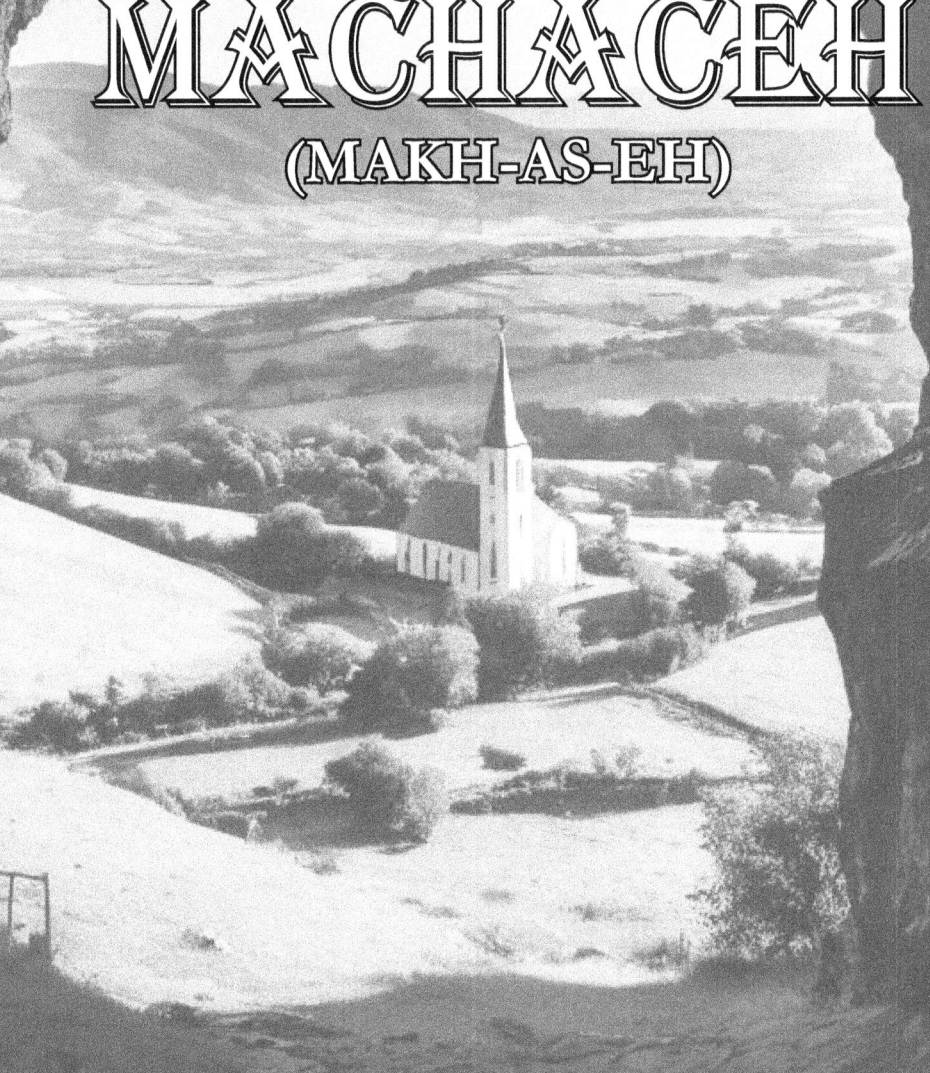

JEHOVAH

MACHACEH

(MAKH-AS-EH)

JEHOVAH MACHACEH

Shelter

Refuge

Safety

Source of Safety

Hope

Trust

Shelter and Refuge from Rain, Storm,
Dangers or Falsehood

Guardian

Security

Preserve

Sanctuary

Anchorage

Harbor

Retreat

2) Verse 5 – Jehovah Machaceh (makh-as-eh) "I cried out to You, O Lord; I said, "You are my refuge (Machaceh)..."

David saw God and knew God was his shelter, safety, source of safety, hope, trust, shelter from storms or dangers or falsehood. God was his personal harbor in the storm – no matter how violent the storm was David knew that God was stronger than the strongest storm. Psalm 93:3-4 shows this too where it says that the floods have lifted up, O Lord, the floods have lifted up their voice, The floods lift up their pounding waves. You can see a progression there of intensity with the floods. First it says they have lifted up. The Hebrew word Nasa – they are beginning to rise, and they are stacking up and even in this state they can be unforgiving in their destruction and force. But it can get worse. Just like storms our trials and troubles can get worse. Verse 3 goes on to describe the floods then as lifting their voices. The Hebrew word there is Qowl. Now you can begin to hear these flood storms. They are shouting with their thunder and commotion. Their noise is getting louder and louder as they cry out. It is almost like a battle cry coming forth from them as they attack you. David must have felt that here. They were thundering loudly – no more whispers from them.

This is what the Confederate army would do during the Civil War when they would attack. They would yell and scream as they began their assault. Imagine how this must have affected the Union forces at times. This can be what it feels to us as well when troubles seem to mount. One thing happens and then another and then another and with greater intensity. It begins to pile up on you and it is difficult to keep fighting. But here in Psalm 93 in verse 3 it says it can get even worse. The floods then lift up their pounding waves. The troubles come crashing down on you relentlessly and with great intensity. This can bring deeper misery and hurt and suffering into our lives. The anguish piles up. Sorrow grows deeper. The torment of physical pain, emotional pain, spiritual soul pain can almost seem unbearable.

BUT GOD!

I love that two-letter phrase that is seen all throughout the Psalms. That little two-word phrase would be worth a deeper study to see the depths of truths in that for us.

Verse 4 of Psalm 93 gives us the good news – "More than the sounds of many waters, more than the mighty breakers of the sea, THE LORD on high is Mighty. That's another name for the Lord – Jehovah Addiyr (Ad-deer). God is majestic is His power. God is all high and mighty in His power. God is The Great One. God is mightier than the shouting and yelling of the great waves of whatever troubles you are facing. He is Almighty God the ruler of the universe and your life!

Psalm 93 acknowledges that we will face at times difficulties and those troubles and trials can also grow up into even greater troubles that seem overwhelming like it did to David. BUT GOD – remember those two words. BUT GOD! God is more powerful than any trouble or situation you may face. God is The Wise

One who knows how to handle the situations. Yes, God may allow and even at times send these troubles to us for whatever purpose or plan He has for us or for others but remember that God is sovereign and in control.

Is this difficult to remember when going through our despairs of life? Yes, it is. This is also why we need good friends to help us navigate through our rough times as I know when we are in them it can be difficult to focus right. But we do need to train ourselves like David did to keep looking up to Jesus as our ultimate source of safety and refuge and strength. I do admit that this will require some self-training on our part. We might stumble and fall at times as we train our hearts and minds to keep trusting in God. David struggled at times with this too, but he kept on remembering – But God!

This truth that God was David's Jehovah Machaceh is also true for you as your walk through your struggles. Look at the list of words that help describe what Machaceh means. God doesn't promise that our lives will be free from storms but in those storms, He is there for us and with us!

When the storms are raging their fury down on us, we can go into God's harbor and anchor ourselves there – in Him! God is our security in the storm. Jesus is our source of safety in the storm. Jesus is our hope and one to put our trust in within the storm. Let us retreat and run to Jesus in our storms.

Let's continue in Psalm 142 is verse 5 and see another name/epithet of God that can help us in our storms.

JEHOVAH

CHELEQ

(KHAY-LEK)

JEHOVAH CHELEQ

Portion

Allotment

Inheritance

Territory

Associate

Enjoy Prosperity

Stability

Continuance Without Change

Steadfast

Constant of Character and Purpose

Sticking Together

Attachment

Security

Strength

Support

Abiding Endurance

Shield

Protector

Selah

3) Verse 5 - Jehovah Cheleq (Khay-lek). "I cried out to You, O Lord; I said, "You are my refuge, My Portion (Cheleq) in the land of the living."

David knew that he needed to concentrate on these names and truths of who God is on these names/epithets of God also reveal our relationship with Him as well. David could feel himself probably sinking into some depression or episode as we see in verse 3, "my spirit was overwhelmed within me." Verse 6, "I am brought very low." Verse 7, he felt "his soul was in prison in deep darkness." David was in a very precarious place in his spirit from all the troubles that were swirling around him and the pain of knowing of all the lives lost at the town of Nob just because he visited there. Depression was on his doorstep knocking very loudly. He needed to turn them around, to do so David had to focus on who God is. So must we in our rough times. Here David declared who God was and especially for him as he got personal as he said "my", portion in the land of the living. While here on earth God was David's personal portion – his Jehovah Cheleq.

At first, I just gave this Hebrew word Cheleq a passing glance and did not feel to go too much deeper. I felt that it was great to see this in God and know that He is my inheritance and my portion too. I didn't see at first all the depth that was in that one name/epithet of God. Being Jehovah Cheleq to David and all believers goes into great depths of God's heart, passion, and love for us. Who we are to Him should drive us to a deeper love for Him a deeper trust in Him. As I was studying this, I put on some Michael W. Smith songs and one song came up was "Deep in love with You." This word Cheleq and the depth of it as I studied it and pondered on it moved my heart to really feel this for God as I heard it. Knowing these names of God and epithets of Him is a part of our spiritual armor that the Holy Spirit uses to enable us to fight our battles (another great Michael W. Smith song – Fight Our Battles).

A whole bunch of words started floating through my mind as I studied this name of God – Jehovah Cheleq. These words can help drive home the depth of truth that is contained in this one name/epithet of God. These words had a huge impact on me and led me to a deeper worship as I was studying this. This verse 5 in Psalm 142 reads again, "You, Lord Jehovah when I'm facing great troubles, trials, heartaches, depression, anxieties – You Lord are my portion, my strength, my stability, my security, my support, my shield, my protector – my Cheleq" (EHGV)

Whatever our troubles are the Lord is our stability. The Lord is my balance, my harmony, my friend, my peace, my tranquility, my consistency, my calmness, my serenity, my stillness, my Selah, my rest, my composure, my quietness. In the midst of my storms, You Lord are all of this to and for me.

Lord, in all my troubles You are my shield, my protector, my resistance, my abiding endurance, my steadfastness, my relentless shield. You are determined and resolute to shield and protect me in these storms. You even make my storms purposeful for me as You work out Your sovereign plan for me. You did this for Job, Joseph, Elijah, Peter, Paul and all the disciples. You do this for me too. Whatever you decide to purpose for me in the storms even though I may slip at times help me to know that Your eyes are on me. The wicked have no such hope – but David did and so do all believers in You saved through Jesus Christ.

The deep care the Lord has for me as my Cheleq is unshakeable and relentless He is protecting me. It is unswayable, immoveable and it is set-in-stone that God is there for me and with me. Through this God enables me and make me to hang tough in any situation that comes my way.

Lord, You are my portion (Cheleq). I am integrated with You and connected with You, surrounded by You, unified with You. We are allies together and banded together. You're surrounding me is impenetrable, bullet proof and indestructible. You are adamant in this truth and reality for me despite all that the enemy tries to throw at me. Lord, this is what You are for me during all my storms no matter how fierce and strong they are You are stronger.

Psalm 73:25-26 are two key verses to hold on to and remember as we go through storms and to help ward off episodes, depression, and anxieties. "Whom have I in heaven but You? And besides You, I desire nothing on earth. My flesh – my blood relatives and close friends and even other Christian friends may fail me – walk away from me, disappear from my life, become exhausted and frustrated with me because of my problems and are finished with me. I can even fail my own self in my passions, my emotions, my courage, and my desires when I get too down and depressed in my troubles. But You Jehovah God – You won't fail me. You are my strength, the Mighty One. You won't leave me even in my darkest days. Even when I'm so depressed and everyone else has walked away and I have even given up on myself – You won't walk away" (EHGV). The Lord was David's and our friend forever. Our stability. Our calm. Our rest. God is steadfast and relentless in pursuit of us and holding us up in His love. He will never forsake us or walk away from us.

That truth that is seen here in Psalm 73:25-26 are two verses that we need to be preaching to ourselves repeatedly especially when the storms hit but also before so that we are getting stronger in our spiritual walk before the storms even hit. David also said in Psalm 16:5 "Lord, You give me stability as my portion (Cheleq) and You hold me together in and with You. You make me now and my future secure and, in Your hands, You hold me and keep me." (EHGV)

This is also seen in Lamentations 3:24 "My portion (Cheleq) IS the Lord. I have said to myself, so I will put my hope in the Lord." Despite all our problems we must preach this truth to ourselves so that the Holy Spirit can have this fuel to sift through our minds, hearts and souls that can bring us to trust Him more and wait upon Him more. Then I can know that whatever the Lord decides to purpose in and through my storms that I can stand fast through as He enables me. We might slip and fall at times, but He will never let us go. Memorize these two verses in Psalm 73 and His various names will also help us to fight off the enemies attacks.

The enemy is relentless in his attacks on us. God is relentless in defending us. We must also be relentless in our fighting in this battle as well. We must put on our armor in this battle. We must not and cannot give up. We are in a spiritual battle and thus we must battle it spiritually. Yes, get counselors and if needed medication to help but we must also see God's role in all this as well. Fight back with God's truths. God is our Jehovah Cheleq. David knew this truth about God, and it helped him to fight his battles. This truth of God sifted into our hearts and minds. Can be used by the Holy Spirit to help us fight our battles – with the Lord and through the Lord.

JEHOVAH

CHAY

(KHAH-EE)

JEHOVAH CHAY

Fresh
Flowing Fresh Water
Revive
Full Life
Renewed
Reviving as in the Springtime after a Long Winter
Surviving
Sustenance
Supports Life through Nourishment
Sustains
Life
Living
Alive
Prosperity
Inspire - Ignite - Rekindle
Spur on - Energize
Keep from Sinking
Keeping Afloat
Encourage
Revive
Buoy
Overcome
Strengthen

"My portion in the land of the living (Chay)." We just examined how God is our Jehovah Cheleq – our portion and our security. The next phrase "in the land of the living" could carry with it several meanings and translations from that. It could mean what it says in plain English in that David could have been simply that he was alive and walking among the living. That translation can fit with the context of Psalm 142 and is faithful to what "land" (Erets) means in Hebrew as well as what the word "living" (chay) means in Hebrew.

Let me throw out another possible translation of those two words "land" and "living." Just as I was meditating and thinking about this verse and looking at those two words in the Hebrew, I saw that there could be another way that they could be translated and stay true to the context and their meanings. Since both translations are true to the context and the word meanings then it is possible that the Holy Spirit had in mind both for our benefit. This other potential translation of those two words drove home to me a deeper truth of verse 5 plus another name/epithet of God – Jehovah Chay. This I know is going to help me and strengthen me as I fight my own personal battle with my PTSD episodes and bouts with depression.

For a brief review of the first translation that we have looked at verse 5 could read, "God is my Jehovah Cheleq – my portion, my security as I walk through earth among the living." That translation again is fine and is the one mostly used. Yet as mentioned there is a second translation that is also true to the context and meanings of the words.

The word "land" in Hebrew is erets (eh-rets). It can mean exactly how the first translation has it – land. It can also mean ground, country, territory, area, earth's surface, surrounding lands, and inhabitants. Basically, the meaning – land. But like many other Hebrew words erets "land" also has other meanings and then one must decide which meaning is more accurate depending on a variety of considerations including most of all the context in which it is written.

Erets "land" can also mean dry desert, fell to the ground unfulfilled. Unfulfilled can mean discontented, disquieted, afraid, apprehensive, distressed, afflicted, anxious, distraught, confused. Now take all those words and compare it to the context of Psalm 142 and we can see that this is what David was feeling through all the problems, trials, troubles, and attacks that were happening to him. Then comparing to the overall context of 1 Samuel 17-23 then using the translation of erets to mean "living in a dry desert," "fell to the ground unfulfilled," discontented, afraid, distressed, afflicted, anxious and distraught would fit in and I feel even more in line with what David was going through and trying to get across to us.

David was seeking God and relying upon God while he was feeling so distressed, afflicted, distraught, and anxious to be his Cheleq – his source of safety. Then David adds another pursuit of God as he was feeling all this to also be his Jehovah Cheleq.

With this additional translation in mind let's look at how it comes together in verse 5 which could then be translated like this: "I cried out to you, O Lord; I said, You are my refuge and my portion and my security while I am here in this spiritual dry desert that I am in due to the attacks coming upon me. These attacks have left me feeling unfulfilled as I should be king but I'm on the run from the king. I am due to all this feeling distressed, confused, anxious, distraught, apprehensive, and afraid. In all of this Lord be my buoy. Keep me afloat and do not let me sink and drown. Sustain me. Revive me in my spirit. Help me to overcome this severe danger I'm now in. Be the fresh flowering water in my spirit that gives me renewed life that spurs me on and strengthens me. Help me to not just survive but to flourish." (EHGV)

That is what the Hebrew word "Chay" means. It is to be fresh, revives, full life, surviving, renewed, fresh flowing, flowing fresh of water, reviving as in the springtime after a long winter. It can also mean sustenance. Sustaining meaning that which supports life through nourishment and something or someone that sustains or comforts someone especially through spiritual support. That sure seems to be who God is for us. God is our nourishment during the good times as well as in times of famine.

God also has all His various ways by which He can do this for us. He can bring forth water from a rock. God can tell a raven to feed Elijah. God can turn a little bit of food into months and months' worth. This is on the physical realm and God also does this for us on the emotional and spiritual side of things too. The Holy Spirit sustains us through our darkest valleys and trials. This is what I sense that David was asking of God for himself as well as acknowledging that God IS Jehovah Chay Himself. God is our source in surviving what the world and our enemy attempts to throw at us.

Let me add another layer of depth to the word Chay. It comes from the Hebrew word Chayah (khaw-yaw). Chayah can also reflect Chay in that it can also mean revive, surely live, recover, restore, restore life, to quicken, revive, refresh, and then cause to grow. It also means to preserve and to be revived from sickness, discouragement, or faintness. This is what David was going through and experiencing emotionally and spiritually. God is the ultimate one who can and does revive us and restore what is broken in us and or around us. God as the Holy Spirit is the one who quickens us and restores us back to life during our discouragement. Psalm 142:5 could be translated. "I cried out to you, O Lord; I said, You are my refuge and my portion and my security while I am here in this spiritual dry desert that I am in due to the attacks coming upon me. These attacks have left me feeling unfulfilled as I should be king but I'm on the run from the king. I am due to all this feeling distressed, confused, anxious, distraught, apprehensive, and afraid. Through this all I realize that You are Jehovah Chay. You are the Living God who is the Great Sustainer. It is through You, O Lord, who enables me to survive all this as You choose to revive me and renew my life. Flow forth fresh spiritual water from the Holy Spirit into me to where I can feel like it's springtime after this hard cold dry winter that I'm in right now. Brace me up to survive this and even cause me to grow in it and through it. Bind me closer together with You. Encourage me. Energize me. Empower me. Through this all also prepare me for whatever next calling that You will give me." That is obviously a bit longer than the NIV version, but it goes into more depth of what David was saying.

David was fighting through so many circumstances, and he simply needed the Holy Spirit's renewal in his spirit to keep on going. David needed the Lord's fresh flowing water inside himself. We all need a springtime revival at times and especially after and during a cold hard winter of life.

In the New Testament God is also referred to as the "Living God." The Greek word for living is Zao. It means to be fresh, strong, efficient, powerful, active and alive. This is who God is and what He can infuse into us with His fresh flowing spiritual waters to revive us and renew us. You may be in a battle with depression, anxieties, PTSD, troubles, illness or whatever else you are dealing with. All of this could be draining you physically, emotionally, and spiritually to the point you are feeling overwhelmed. Remember – BUT GOD – God can break through any darkness. God can work through any difficulties, hardships, heartaches, and any troubles we may be in.

Spend time in God's presence as this is where the refreshing begins. Pour out your aches and pains to God as He wants to hear from you. He already knows them all, but God wants a relationship that is a two-way street. Open up to God and be honest with him like David was. The same God to David is also our God here and now. Spend time with Him. Get into His Word which He uses to refresh and restore us and helps us to carry on through the valleys of life. Listen to your favorite style of worship music. Soak it in. Spend time in prayer with God – speaking and listening to Him. Absorb who He is and all that you are to Him. God is our ultimate source of fresh revival which also enables us to persevere through the storms. God is our Jehovah Chay.

JEHOVAH

NATSAL

(NAW-TSAL)

JEHOVAH NATSAL

Rescue
Deliverer
Save
Escape
Defended
Vindicated
Carried Away
Snatched Out
Resist
Kept
Help
Preserve
Recover
To Deliver from Enemies, Trouble or Death
To Deliver from Sin and Guilt
Involved
Without fail

In verse 6 David keeps on the right path in his fight against spiritual depression as he continues his focus on who God is and his pursuit of Him. We also see David's dependency upon God here as he starts out by pleading with the Lord to "Listen to my cry…" David knew from past experiences that God listened to his prayers, and he here also asks for God to hear his desperate cry. His cry here was a cry of grief as a deep anguish was within his heart. David was full of distress, suffering and pain. He was in deep despair with a sense of hopelessness which had enveloped his spirit. Despondency had set in with a depression of his spirit with a loss of courage and hope. Dejection was finding root in his heart. If you have ever experienced this depth of soul depression or are now, then you know how David felt.

As we have looked at, he was "brought very low" in his spirit. What does David do to fight and try to climb out of this darkness? He once again looks up. He looks up to the Lord. David's deep dark dungeon of depression moved him to desperately seek out God. He asked God to be his personal Jehovah Natsal.

This name/epithet of God is used many times within the Psalms by David and other writers. It reveals in David a constant need and cry out to the Lord. Natsal means to rescue, deliver, save, escape, vindicate, carry away, carry out, snatch out, resist. All those words carry with it the truth that God does so without fail. God does not always immediately remove all our troubles and storms, but He does promise that He will be with us as He does call us at times to sit within the midst of our storms as we continue in our dependency upon Him. Joseph, Job and Jonah are just three examples of how God at times calls us to go through some storms and some brought on by our own disobedience or wrong choices. Sometimes we are living righteously, and the storms still come. Remember this Natsal of God is all within His sovereign timetable.

Joseph went through years of pain and suffering and false accusations before being restored and carried out of his troubles. Job went through many painful times before being restored and carried out of his troubles. Jonah as we know spent three days within a whale's belly before God restored and carried him out of his troubles. Keep this in mind as difficult as it may be. But also remember that Jesus immediately stopped the storm with just the words "be still". Let us cry out to the Lord while living in His sovereignty.

Besides Natsal meaning to carry us out of our troubles we need to see that it also means to preserve and keep someone. To help a person to resist and recover. God may have as His grand design to help us in the storm and while in it He will keep us in His sovereign hand. Nothing can come to us without it first going through God. That again is a tough truth, but it is truth. If God does not remove the storm, then cry out to God to also help you to persevere through it and to keep you in His hand. Trust in the Lord in the storm.

This was the confidence in God that Shadrach, Meshach and Abednego had as we had seen in Daniel 3. As they were to be thrown into the fiery furnace, they could say that if it be so that their God whom they serve is able to deliver them from the furnace of blazing fire and He will deliver them out of the hand of the king. But even if he does not that they were not going to serve their gods or worship the golden image that they had set up.

What faith in God they had. It was not just with words but backed up by their actions. God can deliver us immediately from our own fiery furnaces but if God decides not to and we perish physically within the fire we still know God loves us and we will be with Him eternally. This is the kind of faith we need to fight with through our troubles and storms. We must have their faith to know that God can deliver us/me from the storms and if he does not for His sovereign purpose then I hope and desire to continue to worship Him through it all. I know that even my storms are guided by God's sovereign hand. I hope I can develop a faith that can help me to stand strong in Him. Even though I may falter at times my desire is to develop this kind of growing faith in the Lord. Those three men who faced a literal fiery furnace stood with the Lord as they knew the Lord stood with them. This same God stands with us too!

David's desire was also to do this. Yes, David faltered at times like we all do but he continued in his cry out to the Lord even in his doubts. This faith development builds over time. Psalm 31, which was also written by David reveals this heart of faith in him. Psalm 31 was written by David roughly at this same time period as Psalm 142 was written and it is evident that he was in deep trouble and experiencing some soul depression. Yet David had this Shadrach, Meshach and Abednego faith when he said in verse 14-15, "But as for me, I trust in You. I depend on You. I am secure in You. You even cause me to trust in You, O Lord. I say and affirm that, "You are my God. My times and circumstances are in Your hand and under Your authority and I trust in Your ability to accomplish mighty deeds and to defend me, rescue me and deliver me from the hand of my enemies and from those who persecute me." (EHGV)

Can you see David's growth here even during his growing continuous troubles? God did not deliver David from all his troubles right then and there, but He did preserve David and kept David in His hands. God was still his Jehovah Natsal. David could say because of his growing knowledge and relationship with God that God could deliver him and yet if the storms remain to keep him. He knew that his life was under God's control and all things went through God's sovereign hand. This is the faith that I desire to pursue and to live in.

God is also calling us to be involved in this process as well. Challenge yourself to ask some of these questions. What am I believing – God's truths or the enemies lies? What am I allowing to be poured into my mind by what I watch and hear? That is a part of taking captive our thoughts. Invite the Holy Spirit to take control as we can't on our own. Ask yourself what kind of fruit am I eating and or serving to others? Look at Galatians 5:19-23 and look at the fruit of the spirit and the fruit of the flesh and compare with your life. Through my rough times and still pursuing Holy Spirit fruit in my life?

1 Co 15:2 tells us we are to hold firmly to the message – the Word of God.

This means we are to cling and hold on for dear life the truths of God. Hold on to the truths of God being Jehovah Natsal in your life. Hold on to these truths in your spirit. Keep them secure and ready to use when the attacks come - and they will come. Keep these in your memory tucked away for the Holy Spirit to use at the appropriate time for you and for others.

For myself I have found out that keeping index cards with all the various names/epithets of God handy as I walk through the day. I also write on some a brief explanation of what they mean and some corresponding words. Attacks from the enemy come at all different times and places and we need to try and be always prepared. I realize we will have slips in this, but our goal should be to keep on trying to fight. Due to my own PTSD and episodes that can arise from triggers I feel a special need to carry these cards with me. When Satan tries to pour out his lies to me in so many varied ways and sources, I can fight back with remembering the truths of God in who He is and who I am to Him. Again, I am not always successful per say in these battles, but I try to keep on fighting.

Another way that we can fight in this battle as God being our Jehovah Natsal is by being a part of a solid church where we can receive and give to the body. Eph 4:11-12 tells us that pastors and teachers are there to build us up. The word build means just that. It's an act of one who promotes another person's growth in Christian wisdom, happiness and holiness.

I worked in Washington D.C. for many years when I was in my twenties. D.C. was in a huge growth spurt building wise. Our office was at 19th and L Streets, and we were on the 8th – top floor. There were new building projects going on all around our area there. I could go and look out the window where I could see several of these projects going on. One thing that caught me is that most of them, before the new building could be constructed the old building first had to come down. That hits me that some of us in our battles must be willing to crush down the old strongholds that the enemy has in our lives. These can vary from our wrong thinking to some wrong friends that we let influence us to old sinful habits that we must let the Lord tear down in our lives. David asks the Lord in Psalm 39:8 to Natsal him – deliver him from his sins and rebellious ways and actions. We must be willing to let God "de"struck areas in our lives before He constructs newer and stronger areas for us. I also noted that to build high the building must have a strong base. Our base sites to build on must be in the Lord.

Another part of our active involvement is through prayer. For yourself but also for others and asking others to pray for you as well. Asaph in Psalm 82 gives us this truth from the Lord. "Rescue them the weak and the needy; deliver (Natsal) them out of the hand of the wicked." Asaph is asking others here to pray for those who are weak and needy that they need a special rescue and to be brought into God's security. As you are going through your storms part of our armor is prayer. That is, you pray directly to God and also hopefully you also have people you can call upon to pray for you. Then ask God to let you also be a prayer warrior for others as well. You will be amazed that as your heart turns to others to pray for them how the Holy Spirit can also begin to bring a lift to your spirit through that. A double blessing from the Lord.

Psalm 31 is also one of my favorites to dig truths from in times of our storms. Verse 15 reveals another avenue by which we can participate with the Spirit as we fight on. Verse 15 reads, "My times are in Your hands; Deliver (Natsal) me from those who are my enemies and adversaries." The phrase "My times are in Your hands" we see that through all of his storms and troubles of his soul that He knew and believed in God's sovereignty in his life. Here we see him like he is placing his life at the altar of God and saying here it is Lord – I trust in You.

David also does this in verse 5, "Into Your hand I commit my spirit...". The heart of Jesus as well when He was on the cross dying for our sins. Even though David was in great distress and felt alone and abandoned he still relied upon God and His sovereign plan and purposes for his life. As we do this through our storms it can fuel the Holy Spirit to enable us to keep on going. God is our anchor in the storm. The anchor does not keep the ship from moving around or take it from the storm but rather keeps the ship stable within the storm. As we trust in our ANCHOR – Jesus Christ and how even in the storms that He is sovereign overall then we are more equipped to keep on battling. This we need to keep on doing. Never give up. Never give in. Charge ahead in and with the Lord. Remember that God is your personal Jehovah Natsal.

I realize that some even right now could be in the midst of a great storm. Perhaps the storm has been going on for some time and your strength and endurance is beginning to waver a bit. There could even be some sneaking into to your heart and mind. "Where is God? Has God left me? Does God even still care for me?" Don't condemn yourself for those thoughts but also don't let your heart and soul camp out there. Walk away from things that are not true and pursue to live in the truths of who God is and how much He does love you. Take the garbage out. Let the truths come in to replace the garbage.

Psalm 69 which was also written by David during a time of great distress and soul depression is another great Psalm to learn how he fought back. Verse 14 of Psalm 69 reads "Natsal me – deliver me, resend me, defend me, save me without fail from this reality of my instability, my loneliness, my sense of helplessness – the mood that I'm in that is about to sweep me away don't let me drown Lord. Don't let me sink down in the depth of despair and settle down there as I go through these troubles' preserve me Lord. Keep me going through it all. Be involved in the situation I'm in and in my spirit to spare me on and keep me going." (EHGV)

Let our spirit be in this frame of mind as well. Ask for God to deliver you and as the storm or if the storm continues around you that He will preserve you through it. God was David's Jehovah Natsal in the storms. God is my Jehovah Natsal in my storm. God is your Jehovah Natsal in your storms.

JEHOVAH

YATSA

(YAW-TSAW)

JEHOVAH YATSA

A	B	C
Remove	Burst Forth	With Purpose
Escape	Traveled	and For Results
Come Out	Go Forth	Proceed from
Draw Out	Set Out	something to
Departed	March Out	something
Carried Out	Lead Out	(Exodus)
	Flows	Intends for
	Proceed Active	Desired Result
	Participation	Impact

MAIN PURPOSE:

To see who God is and to draw closer to Him.

It is a taking 'From' (A) and then to going in a 'Process' (B) with a distinct 'Reason' for Purpose and Result with one of those Purposes to see more clearly who God is and to draw closer to Him.

Jehovah Yatsa – As David begins to wrap up this Psalm it appears that he is bringing all of Psalm 142 together in this verse 7, "Bring my soul out of prison, that I may give praise to Your name; Your people will form a circle around me because of Your goodness to me."

* David states how he feels = his soul is in prison
* David realizes only one can bring him out = God
* David takes steps himself to fight = Prays to God
* David states his dependency upon God to do this = above two points
* David looks to the future and does not hold on to the current situational problems as if that is all there will be
* David ends with a praise and acknowledgement of God

In this verse we can see many truths, names/epithets of God that can be used of the Lord to draw us closer to Him in our times of troubles and to catch a deeper glimpse of who God is.

Jehovah Yatsa. Such a deep deep name/epithet of God that I would venture to say that most Israelites knew this name of God well and very much so the leaders and now David. Let us grab hold of this truth of God as well.

This truth of God as being Yatsa and all that it contains and revealing who God is and His love and care for us is vital to hang on to. From this truth, name/epithet of God there are many other ones that flow from it and connected with it. Anyone who is desiring to draw closer to God while struggling and dealing with PTSA, depression, anxiety, fears, troubles, despair (and the list could go on and on) this name of God can be used of the Spirit to lift our spirits and enable us through Him to endure, persevere and come through our own particular struggles.

There is so much depth of truth here that I can only prayerfully attempt to convey what I have studied. I am sure knowing that we are only barely touching the depth of this here, but we will go forth with that. The word Yatsa is used 992 times in the Old Testament. Here as we go, we will endeavor to look at it within its context here and then try and give a bigger overview of the meaning it had for them and can for us.

As I am writing this, I am looking at my study notes that I had as I was studying Yatsa out more. In my journal for that day, I wrote down, "feeling the I don't care and despondent and hopeless today." I also wrote down that I felt like David must have felt like in Psalm 142:3 when he said he declared his trouble to the Lord. As a review the word trouble means to be spirit overwhelmed, weaker, energy ebbing, despair, fainting, to grow weak, be faint, from idea of darkness to languish within you, be overwhelmed. Despair is the loss of hope and to give up, which is in essence depression. To be in anguish, which is to be in agony, misery, sorrow, torment, affliction, discouragement, sadness. I wasn't having a good day, and neither was David when he wrote Psalm 142 and many other of His Psalms.

As I'm looking at my study notes of that day, I was for sure struggling. David as he wrote Psalms 142 was struggling to say the least. On that particular day when I was really struggling, I can look back and see that at first I wasn't giving up. I was pursuing God in His word, and the Holy Spirit was using this time to help me to preserver though the troubled spirit that I was in. One of the major ways the Holy Spirit was accomplishing this was by sending some more names/epithets of God.

I know by personal experience that I can share with you all who are struggling that seeking out God by knowing and studying His names/epithets can help us to fight on during our days and moments of intense emotional and spiritual battles. This brings me here now to where I was at on my day of struggling – seems God's name/epithet of Jehovah Yatsa then from that it was like the Holy Spirit flew open the gates for me to see so many more names/epithets of God that flow directly from Him being Jehovah Yatsa.

As I studied this truth of God out, I began to see three distant areas or phases of what Yatsa means for us. In the following pases I have broken down each section. I have also put in at beginning of each of the three area/phases a review of what each one specifically is. I hope this helps.

I see three areas or phases of truths from the Hebrew word Yatsa as describing who God is. This helped me to see the depth of what God did for Israel and then for David and can for us as well. Since God does not change and God was Jehovah Yatsa to Israel and David, so He still is for us. Let's begin looking at Jehovah Yats with the first area/phase of it.

JEHOVAH YATSA

AREA/PHASE #1 OF YATSA

Remove
Escape
Come Out
Draw Out
Deported
Carried Out

WITH THE MAIN PURPOSE:

- *to see who God is*
- *to draw closer to God*

In this first area/phase we go back to the time that Israel had while they were in bondage in Egypt. Here we see how God reveals Himself as Jehovah Yatsa. The deep truth of what Yatsa means is seen very clearly in how God dealt with the Israelites in the book of Exodus. We will spend some time digging through this truth of God that David leaned on by looking at the Exodus of Israel from Egypt.

"Therefore, so now go, and I will send you (Moses) to Pharaoh to bring (Yatsa) my people the Israelites out of Egypt." – Exodus 3:10

"Say, 'Therefore, to the sons of Israel,I am the Lord, and I will bring (Yatsa) you out from under the burdens of the Egyptians, and I will deliver you from their bondage…" – Exodus 6:6

God pulled the Israelites OUT OF bondage. That is the first area or part of what Yatsa is. Bring out, remove, come out, draw out, bring out. This is what God said He would do for Israel and what He did do for them. That is one example of God being Jehovah Yatsa. It is also one of the greatest example of God being Jehovah Yatsa on display for us.

Another is found in Genesis 19:15-17 when God was revealing Himself to Lot when He was about to destroy Sodom for their great sinfulness. "When morning dawned, the angels urged Lot, saying, 'take your wife and your two daughters who are here, or you will be swept away in the punishment of the city. But he (Lot) hesitated. The men (angels) seized his hand and the hand of his wife, for the compassion of the Lord was upon him; and they (angels) brought (Yatsa) him out and put him outside the city."

With Lot notice how he hesitated. In the Hebrew it says that Lot delayed and didn't get going right away and stayed where he was. He questioned God's leading and hesitated. Did Lot's hesitations and doubt thwart God's plans and desires for Lot? No, of course not as man cannot stop God's sovereign plans. But like Lot at times, we will need to be dragged out if we don't follow God's leading. And at times God may let us stay where we are at in order to discipline us as well. With Lot God had the angels seize Lot by his hand. They held him tightly so he would not resist, and they pulled Lot and his family to safety.

God was not stopped by Lot's hesitations. God was not stopped by Pharaoh's desires to not let the Israelites depart – Yatsa out. Moses as well as you read that story also had his doubts and reservations with God about doing it. God is more powerful than Lot's doubts. God is more powerful that Moses' doubts. God is more powerful that Pharaoh and his vast army and resources. God is more powerful than your PTSD symptoms and episodes. God is more powerful than your depression. God is more powerful than your anxieties. God is more powerful than any troubles or disasters that you are facing and going through. When it is in God's plans and timing, He will Yatsa you out or give you the strength to endure.

Did Israel immediately listen and follow Moses out of Egypt? No, they did not. There are times when we don't follow God like we should because of all the troubles and despair that we are in. This is how I believe the Israelites were like during their living conditions when Moses told them how God was going to Yatsa them out of their bondage to Pharaoh. Their response in Exodus 6:9 "So Moses spoke and gave encouragement and promises to the Israelites. Moses told them of God's predetermined plan of escape for them out of their bondage, but they did not pay attention to what Moses was telling them and even ignoring what he said with regards to this. They acted this way due to their great anguish and discouragement that had taken root in their spirits with a result of being discontented and agitation arising from the harsh, difficult, burdensome, unrelenting, severe and rigorous labor and assigned tasks and responsibilities and oppression through their bondage to Pharaoh." (EHGV).

So yes, the Israelites were not at this time willing to follow God through Moses because they were so destroyed in spirit. That does not give them the right or blessing to be disobedient, but it does give us a glimpse into how harsh conditions and repeated difficult events including depression and such can have on one's soul, heart and mind. It can happen to us too!

Moses was telling them that God was going to set them free! But they did not even have the power or energy to hear, listen and trust that this would happen. All those years of their cruel bondage had so discouraged them physically, mentally, emotionally and spiritually that they were simply so wiped out they could not even follow the one who said would free them. Dejection and discouragement had weaved their spirit through their spirits so that they were so disheartened, scared and even suspicious of any good news happening to them. They were broken.

Ever been there yourself? Perhaps this is where you are right now or have been for some time or know someone who is so overwhelmed like this by all their troubles that they can't even hear or believe that they can or will or could be delivered from all of their situations. Battling PTSD, depression, anxieties and troubles of life can bring one to such an exhaustion that even if they desire to be delivered and set free that they can't believe it will ever happen and as a result that person can shut down. I have been there, and it is a very difficult dark hole to climb out of. It can be for some a daily or even moment by moment battle of discouragement.

Those who are reading this, if you are there right now, I plead with you not to give up. God is working in you and around you even when we fail to see it or even feel it or even believe it. When I travel out to Estes Park, Colorado and as soon as you round that last turn from the winding highway that leads there you will see the majestic mountains. How beautiful they are. At times one of the hotel rooms that I would get had an incredible view of those mountains. On a clear day it would almost feel like you could reach out and touch them. However, there were days when it was so cloudy that those clouds engulfed those same mountains, and I could not see them and sometimes for days. I never thought to myself and wondered if the mountains had moved or disappeared. I knew they were there but due to the clouds and me not having x-ray vision to see through the clouds I could not see them but that again did not stop me from knowing and believing that they were still there. We need to fight the battle on those cloudy days and periods of time to know that God is still there – even through our times of great discouragement and even depression. God has not left you. He is still there!

David also had these times of great soul depression episodes. One such time occurred around the writing of 1 Sa 23:16. David was so discouraged and weighed down with all that was going on around him. God was moving in the situation directly Himself as He was not allowing Saul to find David and kill him, and God was also working through Jonathan to seek out David to encourage him in the Lord. Jonathan had to travel a great distance through the wilderness and desert, plus hoping his father Saul would not find out he was going to help David. The clouds were so great that God sent Jonathan to encourage David to keep on going. The clouds of despair were so great for David that perhaps he was even doubting where God was (Ps. 13:1). God intervened by sending Jonathon who was David's loyal friend to encourage him in the Lord.

Moses was in sort a Jonathan to the Israelites while they were in bondage. At first, they did not listen, but Moses and God did not give up on them. For David - he obviously listened to Jonathan and went to the Lord and got revived in Him to carry on some more. I hope each of you reading this has a Jonathan in your life who can come along beside you to encourage you and help you to see that God is still there. Perhaps God is desiring to use you through all your experiences of tough days to be a Jonathan to someone who could use your encouragement in the Lord.

God wanted to save Lot and his family from disaster. As we saw with the Israelites how God Yatsa Israel from a horrendous life and here God was Jehovah Yatsa to Lot and his family. He was calling them and bringing them out to escape from being destroyed with Sodom.

All of us at times like this could be like the Israelites and Lot and not even believe that this first step of Yatsa in bringing them out could happen to you. This is when we need to do what a great friend of mine has told me when I enter an episode – "Pump the brakes!" Slow down and look up to God. If God is sending someone to encourage you and start the process of bringing you out of your situation or helping you to endure it – listen. Fight back as best you can and cry out to God. Believe that He can Yatsa you out.

Philippians 2:13 says, "...for it is God who is at work in you, empowering you, energizing you, accomplishing in you to even desire and become resolved to the point of taking pleasure in and delighting in doing His will and then to even long to do it." (EHGV) Ask God to give you this desire to first believe that He will rescue you out and deliver you in His sovereign timing and purpose. Gods purpose could also be to strengthen you to endure as well. Whatever His purpose is. God does have a purpose for you while you are in the storm and if He takes you out of it or if He holds you in that storm, He will enable you to endure it.

I say all of that because I want to emphasize that when the Israelites could not bring themselves to believe what Moses was telling them would happen in that God would not desert them because they were momentarily "disconnected" and could not believe. God isn't like that to His children. Yes, God will at time chastise His children in order to get them back on the right path, but God will never abandon His children. The Israelites were not alone in their struggles to believe what God would do for them. In that same chapter 6 in Exodus, we see towards the end there that even Moses complained to God that how could he be the one to do all of this. That didn't cause God to abandon Moses either, but God worked through his doubts and fears.

This verse in Philippians and here in Exodus is speaking to me even today as I am writing this section of this book. Today I feel like I am really struggling and feeling little worth and even a sense of hopelessness. Even as I am writing this book on how to fight and overcome this through God, I am going through it. As I see this verse in Philippians and in Exodus that even through my own struggles with doubt and fears that I am reminded that God will not abandon me in my struggles of disbelief and discouragement.

My depression today as I am writing this has not and will not cause Jesus Christ to walk away from me. Friends, family and even church members and some of them Christians might abandon me because I can't at times seem to get a handle on these episodes, but God will not! I can rest in that truth. I'm also thankful for my friends who have not abandoned me, and some have been my Jonathans.

The truth that God won't abandon us is found throughout the pages of Scripture when God dealt with others who struggle with depression and at times disbelief. That truth is also seen in who God is. That truth is also seen in the promise of Jesus in that He will never leave me nor abandon me – even when I am struggling and not thinking right.

The Holy Spirit is still fighting for me today during these struggles that I am having right now. Right now, as I am writing this. God is working in me to do His good will and pleasure. I feel this book is one of those good wills and pleasures of God that He has for me, and I know strongly then that this book will get done despite my momentary times of doubt, fear, episodes, or depression. I know that I cannot produce the sense of this truth in myself, but I can rely on Scripture which tells me that God is at work in me to do so. How much I need Him for everything. How much you need Him for everything.

Keep this truth in mind as to why God Yatsa's us out – this truth can help you stay in the fight when like the Israelites you feel you have no fight left. Psalm 18:19, "God Yatsa me out into liberty and a wide-open place in my life and God delivered me and pulled me out and removed me from my distress because He delights in me and takes pleasure in me and has me as His treasure as God is enamored and devoted to me." (EHGV)

God the Creator of the universe delights in me. Delight is to have a high degree of pleasure or enjoyment in someone or something. God has joy and pleasure in us and yes doing things for us. The opposite of delight is disappointment, discontentment, dissatisfaction, dislike, hatred, displeasure, regret, anger, annoyance, irritation, exasperation, or extreme annoyance. Which one do you feel God is in general towards His children especially when they are suffering? Surely it is not the bad opposite side just mentioned. That is not who God is. God loves us – His children. God cherishes us – His children. If you are God's child saved through Jesus Christ, then God cherishes you!

When you feel you have failed like the Israelites did and how David often did remember this truth as David did. God's Checed love for us. This exact name of God – Jehovah Checed is not specifically mentioned in Psalm 142 but it is inherently there in and between all the lines.

God was Jehovah Yatsa to the Israelites. As we have God brought them out and rescued them. God cause them to escape and depart their bondage in Egypt that was their first phase of Yatsa for them.

I'll mention this here and keep making notes of this as the main underlying purpose for God to Yatsa then out is twofold. One main purpose for God during this is that they would see who God is more clearly and more powerfully.

The other main purpose is that they could draw closer to God through it all as God drew them out. As God enabled then to prevail though it all. Israel wasn't in bondage for a short time. The gathered straw and made bricks for a long time before God began to Yatsa the out. As they were Yatsa'd out God had then wander for another 40 years. Yet God persevered then through it all. Through it all they began to draw closer and closer to Him.

This is what God wants for us too as we journey through and struggle through our own troubles as well. Through it all God wants us to see Him more clearly and in a deeper way. Plus, He also desires us to draw closer to Him as a result of that. Don't let your situation pull you away from God but rather let them draw you closer to Him.

And through all of God working in us and enabling us to even start the process of being Yatsa out He also calls us to be in the battle with Him. Is it easy? Of course not. It is a battle. Battles are not easy and need effort to win and be victorious. God is doing it for us, yet God also says that He wants us to be involved. This is what the second phase entails a lot of – God moving us out and us moving with Him. God was calling the Israelites to action with Him. They were no longer to sit under cruel bondage under the hands of the Egyptians. God was now calling them to what I see as the second area/phases of Yatsa. This calls for our active participation. Let's get going and explore area/phase #2 of God being our Jehovah Yatsa.

JEHOVAH YATSA

AREA/PHASE #2 OF YATSA

Burst Forth
Traveled
Go Forth
Set Out
March Out
Lead Out
Flows
Proceed
Active Participation

WITH THE MAIN PURPOSE:

- to see who God is
- to draw closer to God

We have seen how God brought out the Israelites from Egypt. He called them to escape through His powerful plagues that He sent Egypt and through His selective protection from those plagues for His chosen Israelites. The next step or phase that I see included in God being Jehovah Yatsa is seen in Genesis 12:40-41. Here we see how the Israelites burst forth out of Egypt. God rescues us and then leads us out and we go forth and we are no longer stuck in where we were held captive whatever that might be for each of us. God was shooting them forth out of Egypt. The middle part of Yatza says that after God removes and causes them to escape to come out that they then burst forth, travel, go forth, set out, marched out, grew out.

Exodus 13:3-4 God brought them out of Egypt (phase 1) and then bursts them forth to travel which is phase 2 of Yatsa. As you read through the rest of The exodus this phase 2 of Yatsa in God in them bursting them forth to travel wasn't an easy time either. It was filled with many rough situations and through them if they were looking could see God's hand with them as He provided for them as He traveled them along. Exodus ends in chapter 40 with verse 38, "For throughout all their journeys, the cloud of the Lord was on the tabernacle in their presence with His presence by day, and there was fire in it by night revealing His presence in sight of all the house of Israel." (EHGV) The cloud and fire represent God's presence with them. The word journey is very enlightening for us too as we journey to our healing in our trials. The word journey means to march out – but not necessarily in a single day's traveling. Wow! That's hitting me right now. I struggle at times when I wonder as to why God won't heal me right here and now. And He could yet at times like God did with the Israelites He takes them and me on a journey of healing so that through it as we go, He keeps revealing to me deeper and deeper truths of who He is and who I am to Him!

The journey like the Israelites had to come out of slavery and David's to come out of his circumstances and depressions and then our own depressions, troubles and such can be a process and at times a long process (to us it seems long). Are there times when God heals and takes a person out of the storm immediately? Yes, of course He does but persevere if God so chooses to take you there in stages.

There are still battles as one goes out and struggles as Israel sure had them on their way to the Promised Land, but we don't have to live in what was holding us back. If it is depression, we don't have to live in it. God can rescue us out or He can wire us to be able to deal with it depending on His perfect plan and desires for each of us. This phase 2 of how God can Yatsa us out can be difficult and at times seemingly very time heavy too, but the journey is still with God's presence. As God is Yatsaing us out and moving us along He is also revealing more and more of Himself to us as we walk with Him.

God has His plans for us in and through the journey. Sometimes it could be for refining us more into the image of Jesus. Refining can be a difficult process. When God drew the Israelites out of their bondage in Egypt it was not easy road as they burst faith. Immediately after their bursting faith the Egyptian had second thoughts and they pursued Israel to bring them back.

The Israelites became trapped between the heavily armed Egyptian army and the Red Sea on the other side. But God was with them. God even purposely lead them along this long difficult path to the promised land because he knew they still needed to learn some things along the way (Ex. 13:17-18).

God led them and was personally with them. This was expressed by His presence in a pillar of cloud by day and a pillar of fire at night (Ex. 13:21). Verse 22 in Exodus is very revealing as it says God did not take away either the pillar of cloud or fire. In other words – God war always with them as they burst forth out of Egypt on their journey to the promised land.

Their first point of growth along this journey of bursting came quickly though this dilemma of seemingly being trapped in by the Egyptian army and the mighty Red Sea. What were they to do? Unfortunately, their first revelation was to panic, and they even told Moses it would have been better for them to die here in the wilderness (Ex. 14:10-12). But just as God was with them, He was also sent more to them. Moses was used by God in the release from their bondage and also as their encourager along the journey to keep on fighting. To keep on moving on when the journey got rough (Ex. 14:13-14) Moses pumped encouragement into them and truths of how God is with them and would fight for then.

As we remember the Red Sea story it reveals so much about wo God is and how much He cared for His own. The Egyptian army as no match for the protective power of God for His people. God in His amazing unlimited power parted the Red Sea and the Israelites crossed over on dry ground. Dry ground! God even took care of this detail as it wasn't muddy as it should have been but was dry.

Then when the Egyptian army tried to follow, and God just swallowed them up as the Red Sea reverted. God protects us. God shines forth His abundant power for us. God is so amazing to see in action. If God had had burst their faith out of Egypt to go directly into the promised land, then they would have missed out on seeing their awesome display of God's power In parting the Red Sea and how He did it for them!

As you burst out on your own journey of healing be on the lookout for God's hand moving with you and for you. Go on a God hunt and take the time to see God moving in your life though this journey. Replace any grumbling or complaining with having a heart of looking for God in and through all your stages on the journey of healing and revival. This sometimes-rough process of time can both mold us by od and the Holy Spirit into more of Christ's image as he grows us.

There in a song by John St. Cyr called "Weary Traveler." It's a great message song for us on this journey of reckoning and subsequent growth. This song conveys the truth of encouragement for us to carry on even when we have a tired heart and on the edge of breaking – Carry on. That we are not walking alone and to presence in God's strength and in God's power knowing that He is there for us. And with us along each and every step. Let out faith arise as there is nothing that our God can't do! ("Do it again" by Elevation Music.)

Part of our journey in bursting forth is also in the waiting. Those two ideas at first seem in opposition to each other – "Bursting forth" and "waiting." Our bursting forth does call us at times in our moving on to recovery is to also pitch our tents and wait and listen and observe God. Israel did this many a time in their exodus from Egypt to the promised land. Be sensitive to God's leading as you burst forth to honor the times of action and time of stillness (Selah.)

Let me give one more brief example of their bursting forth and waiting mold together by looking at Elijah in 1 King Chapter 17. Here in 1 Kings 17, Elijah is coming on the seen as Israel was beginning to wonder from seeking God and to even seek false gods. Here comes Elijah and he prayed to God for a drought and then he became a dangerous person to the Northern kingdom and his life was in danger. Elijah was in a tough spot to be sure.

In verse 3 God calls Elijah to depart – to burst forth to the brook Cherith. Here Elijah is on a journey from a different situation to more ministry for the Lord. During this part of the journey Elijah is waiting upon the Lord and the Lord is taking care of his needs and might we say in a way only God could do through ravens bringing him food.

Then this period of the journey was done God dried up the river (no more water to drink) and God moved Elijah to another point on his journey. This time to a widow who would provide for him (1KI 17:9)

In this station of Elijah's journey God used him to encourage the wisdom to keep on going and fighting as he was in great despair. Then he can become so sick that he died and God used Elijah to save him from the dead.

Then 1 Kings chapter 18, God calls Elijah to another station of his journey to go to Ahab. Which starts another version of Elijah's live events and station along the journey. My main point in this is that as God does burst us forth to march out there are also our times of Cherith like Elijah had – a wanting upon od to refresh us, refuel us, revive us to get us prepared to march on to the next station on our journey of spiritual revival. God moves in so many annoying ways so let us be in tune and alert to the Holy Spirit leading as we go.

Let's continue with our study of YATSA by looking at the third area/phase which contains the main overriding purpose of what the Lord is doing in all of this.

JEHOVAH YATSA

AREA/PHASE #3 OF YATSA

With Purpose and For Results
Impact
Proceed from something
to something (Exodus)
Intended for Desired Result

WITH THE MAIN PURPOSE:

- to see who God is
- to draw closer to God

When God desired to Yatsa Israel He brought them out of their bondage and then God burst them forth to march out (and here for an extended period for 40 years). All of this was done for the third phase of what Yatsa means. God was doing all of this for a purpose and for results. God was not just taking them out and bursting them forth for no reason. God has a purpose and a plan for the Israelites just as He does for us too. I just told someone today that I felt l lacked a purpose in life. How wrong thinking that was for me. It even goes against God and who He is in Jehovah Yatsa. Since I believe God is Jehovha Yatsa then I cannot believe that I have no purpose in life. I might feel it, but it is not a reality God has a plan and purpose for me. I might have to wait and do some discovery to be led more of God towards His plan and purpose for me, but He does have that for me – and He has it for you too even as you struggle through whatever problems you are struggling with now even God has a purpose in it all.

I need to pump the brakes when I "feel" I don't have a purpose in life. I need to check that wrong thinking and toss it out and replace it with right Biblical thinking which includes applying the truths of who God is to me too. God being Jehovha Yatsa to Israel and David is also true for me and you and any child of God.

God IS Yatsaing me out of my PTSA and depression as He is taking me on a journey in this all He is marching me through and leading me through some times that are there for me to grow and learn more about Him and my relationship with Him. That is a for sure a great piece of His plan and purpose in it all.

Israel had much to learn about God as they wandered in their march out of Egypt. Moses was God's chosen leader to lead Israel out and to the Promised Land. Yet Moses would not always be with them as at some point Moses would leave this earth too. God would not leave Israel leaderless and so one of the reasons I believe that God took time in leading Israel out in that second phase was to prepare Joshua for that role of leadership. Joshua who would replace Moses had things to learn and through this time of the second phase of Yatsaing them out of Egypt God used this train up Joshua for that job of leadership. Joshua had to learn some more things in order to be fully used for the Lord. Part of the purpose and plan of God's taking Israel on this 40-year journey was to prepare Joshua for leadership. Leadership that Israel would need as the entered the Promised Land.

We need to take this to heart when it seems that our journey through recovery is not moving along the time frame that we had in mind. Perhaps God is training us up for another mission in our lives. Or perhaps through what we are going through God is training up someone else through the process or journey we are on. We don't know for sure, but God does give us this example here that as we travel through our Yatsa journey with the Lord that He does not waist time on our journey, His timing is perfect, here timing is filled with so many other purposes and plans that He is weaving together. Are we patient and trusting enough in God as we travel through our own journey of life – even in the rough times?

Nothing can stop God from Him getting us to our own purpose and plans. Even the process of our journey and travels can open our eyes to see more of God and deepen our relationship with Him.

Nothing can stop God. Your troubles can't stop God as He moves you through your journey. Your depression can't stop God. Your anxieties can't stop God. Cry out to the Lord and ask Him to Yatsa you out and as He travels you along the journey be involved in the process as He calls us to do that.

See your journey as a mean by which God reveal Himself even deeper to you. Realize if your journey seems long and difficult at times remember that God loves you and is journeying through it all with you. God has purpose for you to reach your Promised Land and purposes as you journey through to it. There are obviously many reasons, and it would be too staggering to list them all out here as they are different for each of us. But there are some reasons and purposes that are universal reasons for all of us. God desires for us in our journey to:

* See God in a deeper way. God reveals Himself it seems in a deeper way
    as we walk through our "dark" hours. His light will shine though it all.
* As we see God more than this will draw us into a deeper worship and
    reverence for Him (Ex 3:12).
* See that nothing can thwart God's plan and purpose for you.
* To draw us to our knees and into a deeper dependency upon God.
* We start to pray more – and listen more intently to Him.
* We start to cry out more to the Lord like David did.
* We learn to trust God more.
* We learn to wait upon the Lord more.
* We become more aware of God's presence in our lives, and we experience
    His presence more in our lives.

God has His reasons to Yatsa us out. It is for His purpose, and He does this for results. This results in our emotions, our circumstances and our spirituality. For our lives and for the lives of others. God was Yatsa to Israel with a purpose of getting them to the Promised Land. God was Yatsa to Israel through the process of revealing more and more of who He was to them along the journey.

God is Yatsing you as well. Where you are at in this journey is difficult obviously for me to say but you are in one of the phases with the great phase 3 in mind to get you to the Promised Land God has for you and along the way to see Him deeper and to get closer to Him as a result. That alone is a great purpose of life with getting to know God deeper and to have a closer personal relationship with Him. Our valley of life has a way of bringing our eyes up to the Lord.

Before we move on to verse 7 of Psalm 142 in this section, I feel very compelled to elaborate more on God being Jehovah Yatsa as it is so key for us to have this drilled into our minds, hearts, and souls. As I was studying God being Jehovah Yatsa there were so many more names/epithets of God that are tied in with that truth of God. Let me share some of those names/epithets of God that are related to and tie in with God being Jehovah Yatsa. I will number them out as we go through them just for the sake of reference as I write and for you as you look back over them. Again, these next ten listed out and studied names/epithets of God are all connected to God being our Jehovah Yatsa.

Since the Truth of God being Jehovah Yatsa is such a vial truth, we need to spend some more time digging through it all. What better way to do this by exploring more names/epithets of God that are directly connected with His being. Our Jehovah Yatsa.

Here is a list pf 10 other names/epithets of God. Lets take some time to explore each of these in our coming pages.

Names/Epithets of God of God enter woven with
Him Being Jehovah Yatsa

1) Jehovah Checed
2) Jehovah Nahal
3) Jehovah Taeshuwah
4) Jehovah Nachah
5) Jehovah Ruwm
6) Jehovah Alah
7) Jehovah Camak
8) Jehovah Zaqaph
9) Jehovah Paqach
10) Jehovah Dalal

Let's begin then to look at these various other names/epithets of God. Again, these all flow from and are connected to God being Jehovah Yatsa. There 10 names/epithets of God here are so ones that David knew to be true of God. Lets begin by seeing how God being our Jehovah Yatsa is linked with and inter woven with His being Jehovah Checed.

JEHOVAH

CHECED

(KHEH-SED)

1) JEHOVAH CHECED

Loyal Love	Loyal
Unfailing Love	Faithful
Steadfast Love	Kindness
Faithful Love	Devoted
Fervent Love	Devotion
Intense Love	Allegiance
Passionate Love	Brotherhood
Absolute Love	Trustworthy
Persistent Love	Mercy
Boundless Love	Committed
Reliable	Faithful Acts
Dependable	Faithful Deeds
Tried-and-True	Favor of God
Rock Solid	God's Promises
Dedicated	Abiding

Everything that God does and is wraps itself and flows from this truth of God. It's main meaning is that God IS love! God does love things towards us and for us because He IS love. John says this very clearly. It's who God is. As we know the general word of love has different meanings to us and we can even say things like, "I love coffee." So what truly is love? Let's dig a little deeper into what Checed love (God's love) really means. We won't do a complete in-depth study as that could be a book on its own. For our purpose here we will look at an overview of Checed love of God. We will also look as an example in Psalm 63. Here we can see how David knew of God's Checed love for him and then how it deeply affected his being able to fight through his trouble. This is also true for us as well I our battles with PTSD, depression, anxieties, and trouble of life. Knowing about God's Checed love is a major piece of our armor to fight back in our battles of life!

God's Checed love for us is a loyal love, an unfailing love, a steadfast love and a faithful love. Loyal could mean to be intense, extraordinary, deep, extreme, energetic and enthusiastic. That's God's love for us. The opposite of that would be to be undependable, unreliable, fickle, false and temperamental. Out of those groups which one is God?

God's Checed unfailing love reveals that it is completely dependable, inexhaustible and endless. It is immense and limitless. God is all powerful so there is nothing that He can't or won't do for us in His divine plan. God's love is so unfathomable for us as human's to completely understand it and it can't be measured as His love for us is bottomless and endless and boundless while being unending. That is God's Checed unfailing love for us. The opposite of that would be limited, uncertain, unsure, finite and bounded. God is not any of those so which of these groups best describe God's unfailing love for us?

God's Checed steadfast love could also be described as firm in purpose, unwavering, firmly established. It's abiding, enduring, everlasting and persistent, constant, nonstop, steady and unbroken. That is God's love for us. God is dedicated to us. God is committed to us. God gives us His assurance that He is always there for us.

God's love for us in faithful. It is persistant. God's love for us is Him being true to His Word and promises He has made to us. God is rock solid and steady in His allegiance and affection for us. He is reliable,trustworthy and can be fully believed. God is the standard. It is who God is. God is dependable. That's God's Checed love for us.

God does not just say He loves us, but He acts on it. God's Checed love for us carries with it that He performs faithful actions and deeds for us. God backs up His words with actions. "God so loved the world that He GAVE! He gave His one and only Son, that whoever believes in Him shall not perish but have eternal life." That is God's love bursting forth with His actions for us.

The Greek word for "gave" is very revealing. In the Greek it is didomi (did-o-mee). It has a wealth of meaning to help describe God's checed love for us.

Didomi is to supply and furnish what is necessary to someone. To reach out, extend and commit to someone what they need. To give also from oneself. God gave of Himself for us. God showed His love for us at the cross – this was action in the greatest degree for us. God's love on display for us. God also has this for us not only for our eternal lives but for our everyday living here as well. That is why David felt he could cry out to God for his deliverance in the here and now because He knew God's checed love was for eternity and for while we are on this earth too. God has this same checed love for you as well. Grab hold of this truth of God's checed love and the depth of it's meaning for us. The more you see and experience God's checed love for you the more your love for God will grow and grow and affect your daily living.

One of my pastors I have had used to say, "This is where the rubber meets the road." It is to mean how do I take this knowledge and put it into practice in my own life. Specially here with regards to God's Checed love how can knowing their truths affect my life. Especially when I'm going through difficulties and even extreme troubles? This is where looking at David in Psalm 63 can help in as Psalm63 reveals how it affected David.

Psalm 63 clearly shows that David was experiencing a very difficult time. The truths of Psalm states that he was in the wilderness. It's possible this time period is close to our own Psalm 142 time.

David is in extreme danger in multiple ways. Verse 9 says that there were those seeking to take his life. Possibly Saul and his army. This pursuit of David was like a temper of a storm around him that carried with it great intensity. The kind of storm that has tremendous paths of destruction and play havoc all along its path. He was under attack. David's very life was on the line.

Because of this threat David had to flee for his life (a common theme for David at this point in time.) Verse 1 of Psalm 63 describes how he was in the wilderness or caves of dry and baren environment. It is never good to be on the run for your life and add to that the dilemma of doing so hiding in a cave in a dry and baren wilderness. NOT a fun time!

How did David fight back and get through this rough time? Verse 1 says that as his enemy was seeking him to destroy him that he fixed his gaze upward to God and David sought God! The Hebrew word for seek mean to do so with great diligence and with earnest. David was single minded in purpose in pursuing God even while he was living in a cave being pursued by his enemy.

David didn't give up. David didn't blame God. Instead, David pursued God vehemently and persistently as steadfast David's enemy was in pursuing him. David was more steadfast in his pursuit of God.

How did God reveal Himself to David as he pursued him? God revealed again to David who He was through His attributes. Here in Psalm 63 in verse 2 and 3 David revealed four specific attributes of God that the Holy Spirit used to help David to keep on keeping on in his battle. Here are those four attributes of God that He revealed to David. I'll give the Hebrew word and then its meaning.

1) Qodesh (Ko'desh) = holiness, separateness, set apart, extraordinary, special, apartness.

This reveals how God is so set apart from anything ordinary. He's set apart from us in the way that we are human, and he is God! That is a big difference. David has as His Heavenly Father on who is not hindered by our human weaknesses. God is so extraordinary that he has no equal. Nothing is too hard for him to do. When we are in our battles of life keep this truth of God alive in your heart and mind.

2) Oz (Owz) = strength, power, secure, stronghold, firmly established, thunders loudly, intensity, mightily.

All ways describe God's power. He pours down His power to us energetically and vigorously. God doesn't hold back for us. When we are in our own battle of life keep this truth of God alive in your heart and mind!

3) KaBowd (Kaw-bode) = glory, splendor, majestic, riches, grandeur, majestic glory, much wisdom, whole heart, royal authority, sovereign, awesome.

This is who God is as we walk through our trials. David knew this. When we are in our own battles of life keep this truth of God alive in your heart and mind!

4) Checed (Kheh-sed) This brings us to God's Checed love which we just looked at. David knew this truth of God and brought it home to his life and in his time of great trouble David leaned on God's Checed love for him. When we are in our own battles of life keep this truth of God alive in your heart and mind!

How did all these truths of God impact directly into David's life in his great time of struggle? Look at Psalm 63 verses 3 through 5. David was able to rise above the attacks of his enemy to even praise and worship God. David remembered who God is and realized that God is his God and his help in times of trouble. David clung to God and joined together more tightly with Him. Don't allow your troubles to push you away from Him and rather let them draw you closer to Him!

Let this truth of who God is in His Checed love for you bring you to look up to Him when you are in a valley.

Let's continue in our journey of connecting God being our Jehovah Yatsa with our next name/epithet of God – Jehovah Nahal.

JEHOVAH

NAHAL

(NAW-HAL)

2) JEHOVAH NAHAL

Guide
Led
Got Through
Carried
To Lead
Lead Gently On
Refresh
Give Rest
Place of Rest
Guide to a watering place or station
Bring to a station cause to rest there
To Journey by Stations or Stages
Lead to or Bring to a station or goal

Nahal as we see on the previous pages is to guide, lead, get through, secure, travel, carried, give rest, lead with care, guide to a watering place or station, cause to rest, bring to a station or place of rest, refresh, to refresh with food, to lead or bring to a station or goal, to run with a sparkle, to flow, to conduct, lead gently on. It also means and this is vitally important for us who struggle with depression and anxieties that God takes us on this journey of refreshing and leading by stations or stages. The Lord has been trying to drive home this truth to me over the last several weeks especially. It comes up in other names/epithets of God as well as we will explore. God does at times changes things and impacts our situations and problems in a direct "right now" version just like Jesus did when He calmed the storm in Mark chapter 4. But it seems to me the more norm is for God to transport us along by stages or stations in our healing process. By doing so he reveals Himself more and more to us through the process of stages. The Israelites were freed from Egyptian bondage, but they traveled for 40 years before reaching the Promised Land. This is not to discourage us but to help give us resolve that even when we think God is not moving as fast or the way we want but it is in His Sovereign timing and manner. But He is still moving us and with us.

One way for me to grab hold of this truth is recalling how I use to hike in Colorado. I usually had a particular destination in my mind and along the way I would pause and stop to look around and enjoy the scenery from that viewpoint and at times to rest. At other times I would pause as I was writing a new song and I had to record it with my pocket recorder or write it down. I still had my "Promised Land" in my sights of where I was hiking to but this journey to it was filled with stations that I stopped at and done in stages. At times it was hard work hiking up the steeper trails and sometimes "trailblazing" as I called it going off the trail into unchartered territory. At times there were obstacles that blocked the well-worn trail, so I had to climb over or go around. I could always go back but that was usually not the option I chose as I had my Promised Land in my mind, and I did not want this to stop me. So I traveled along to my ultimate goal of place I wanted to get to by going station to station.

Likewise, this is what our spiritual journey of healing can be like with the Lord. As God is leading and guiding us He is restoring and refreshing us in so many ways along the pathway in our healing process. Each of those stations that the Lord travels us through is for His purpose for us and or for others as we pause. Our pausing along the way could be that the Holy Spirit is desiring to use us as another weary traveler is passing through and God is calling us to be used of Him to reach out to them. So don't see the pauses and difficult hikes and even obstacles along the way are there to harm us. Maybe God has sent them and allowed them to grow us up quicker and for helping others. They could also be there to get us to pause and ponder God in a deeper way.

I know this takes extra effort as we all want to be healed up. We need to train ourselves to know and see that our journey of refreshing and rebuilding in the Lord is this journey of stations and stages. Again, along the journey that the Israelites had to the Promised Land seemed like a long way and with many obstacles, but they were there for them to further see God's incredible power and love for them in providing for their physical and spiritual needs.

Just as they were starting out and Pharaoh decided that he wanted to recapture them to bring them back to bondage in Egypt he set out for them. It seemed that Israel and Moses were trapped between them with the Red Sea preventing them to move forward. But God – we kept Pharaoh and his army from getting at them with the flaming fire and God through Moses parted the Red Sea and they crossed over on dry ground to the other side. When Pharaoh and his army followed God swallowed them up. All in God's timing and manner.

When they were running out of food and even grumbling God provided Manna from heaven. Just one time – no for as long as it was needed. They ate from the miracle that God had sent to them. Providing for them. As we travel along our specific personal path, we must know that God is in the midst. He is with us, leading us, providing for us.

I might suggest getting yourself a journal if you don't already have one and begin writing down how you see God providing for you along the journey. Be on the alert for God sightings in the "small" things as well as the big areas. I call them Holy Spirit moments when I know the Spirit is moving and being directly involved in any situation I am in. Anticipate that God will move in your day. Ask the Spirit to open your spiritual eyes to see how active He is in your life. Then write it down so you can remind yourself when you feel that God has left you. As God is Jehovah Yatsa to us, He is also within that Jehovah Nahal for us. Our journey is usually in stages as He brings us from station to station.

One of the most known and treasured Psalm in Psalm 23. This Psalm written by David could possibly have been written around the same time period as our Psalm 142. As can be seen in verse 4 and 5 David is going through some different times and be presured by his enemies.

The most vital and important was that David fights back is by bringing his focus and thoughts on the Lord. David reinforces some truths in his heart and mind that the Lord is his shepherd. A shepherd leader, guides and takes care of his sheep. The word shepherd also means that Jesus is a companion to David and us in our journey. Jesus is our close friend! A special friend through any troubles we are passing though.

In verse 2 we are told that David knew the Lord as his Jehovah Nahal. That the Lord was there even in rough times to lead him gently on. The particular place that one might be in on the journey could be one of difficulty but God is there too! He's with us and for us with His divine presence! Jesus is our personal resting place. One of the songs that I have written helps me to giht difficult times. One of the lines in the song says. "You are my resting place." We can be in the midst of a great storm but we still have and can experience Jesus there as our resting place – A shelter in the storm.

I believe that as we journey our healing proves that God still allows some storms to come our way. There storms can be there so that the Holy Spirit is teaching us to see that our ultimate "Nahal – resting place" is the presence of God Himself. Our biggest station of rest is found and experienced in God.

Our moments of being paused along the journey can be times designed by God for our healing and His rebuilding us. They can be times to make us stronger for the next stage or station in our journey of healing. Keep holding on to God at times that might seem like we are just surviving at best but keep on keeping on.

Those truths flow into our next name/epithet of God – Jehovah Quwn. As God is Yatsing us out from and to our plan of healing and renewing He is also our Jehovah Quwn is the process. Let's explore the truths together...

JEHOVAH

QUWM

(KOOM)

3) JEHOVAH QUWM

STAGE 1	STAGE 2	STAGE 3	STAGE 4
Sustained	Help lift up	Rebuild	Charge ahead
Survive	Stood up	Get ready	Accomplish
Preserve	Help up	Prepare to go	Succeed
Endure	Woke up	Heal	Action
Maintain	Grow up	Grow into	Went forth
Hold on	Build up	Strengthen	Fulfilled
Be fixed	Stir up	Established	Attacked
Not moved	Recover	To be fixed	Carried out
Supported	Ascended	Set out intact	Perform

The truth of experiencing God is seen in depth in God's name/epithet of Him being Jehovah Quwm. This name/epithet of God flows from Jesus being Jehovah Checed. As we keep seeing how all of God's names/epithets/attributes flow together within each other. This name/epithet (Jehovah Quwm) reveals who God is and what our response should be in the process as well. Remembering that God calls us to participate in this process or journey that we are into our healing, rebuilding, refreshing and revival.

Jehovah Quwm is like what we discovered about Jehovah Yatsa in that there are stages or points of progress within each meaning of this name/epithet of God. God is so deep that no one word can fully reveal who He is and even as I have seen even one name/epithet of God is so layered with the depths and riches of who God is. As the Holy Spirit was leading me in my study of Jehovah Quwm this truth and reality realy blew me away as I pondered the ocean full of God revealed here.

I saw as the Spirit was breaking this name/epithet of God down that it contained 4 various but linked stages or stations to it. Each one on its own but tied into the fullness of the word Quwm. It appeared to me that each stage then built up to the next all finding their foundation based on the previous stage. I also through my own experience realized that once out of stage 1 and moving my way along the revival of my spirit to the other stages that I would at times fall back into the previous stage. This used to discourage me but now I see that this is simply a part of the journey that even David traveled upon. This will make more sense as we look through this so let's begin now our look at Jehovah Quwm in its 4 stages.

QUWM - STAGE 1

Stage 1 of Quwm is for sure the most painful stage or station in our journey. Through studying out so many of David's Psalms that he wrote I see how David himself was parked in this painful stage unfortunately many times over. Even at times or a lot of the times within each Psalm David would be ok and seem to be strong and within just a few verses he would be back into his depression and then he would fight back. As I mentioned this can be a reality for us as well. It does not mean that we are weak, and we are failing but simply it is a part of being human and can be also God's way of strengthening and equipping us even further.

As we have looked at the background of these Cave Psalms of David in 1 Samuel, he most certainly had his ups and downs moving from stage 1 to the other stages as we will see but also falling back at times. If you sense that you are bouncing around at times this can be the norm in the process of healing and rebuilding. There is an ebb and flow to our being refreshed in the spirit. Don't let discouragement flood over you when if one day you sense you've flowed into a higher stage of your healing only to fall back. This was a major problem for me as many a time I would feel so defeated when I had a good day or even several and did some conquering and charging forward only to find myself way back down the stage process due to some trigger or something that happened.

Through seeing these stages and other names/epithets of God I see this is not to defeat me but to simply see this ebb and flow of spiritual revival. David experienced this ebb and flow so now I can fight back a bit better and not to get so self-discouraged in my low times.

I would love to live on the mountain top all the time, but I also know and have seen that the valley is also where deeper growth and a deeper knowledge and sense of God can also be found. At times the valleys can be where we experience God even deeper. When we reach our ultimate Promised Land of heaven there we will no longer have our valley times but while on this earth in this flesh our lives will be filled with valleys and mountain top times. Embrace as best you can the valleys as they can lead to the mountain tops. By saying embrace the valley times I am not saying to enjoy them but to realize that they still are from the Lord's hand for one reason or another and let them mold us more into the image of Christ. Difficult to do, especially while in the valley I agree but this can be our goal and desire to let the valley times spring us to experience the Lord's presence even deeper.

It is also in the valley times where we can be used of God in serving Him in a deeper way too. As we learn more about the stages of Quwm we can see the valley times not as defeat times in our lives but points of potential spiritual growth with a deeper experiencing of God in our lives. As we can learn to do this then our mountain top times can be more refreshing and more enjoyable. Even knowing that we might be back in the valley we can know that we will return to the mountain top.

Stage 1 is being in the valley of our emotions and troubles. It can seem like we are in a deep dark hole with no way out. David experienced this and wrote about it right here in Psalm 142 that we are looking at. Verses 3, 4, 6 and 7 all give a very good look at the deep dark hole that David felt he was in trouble wise which led him to also experience spiritual depression. There are only 7 verses to Psalm 142 and David talks about his stage 1of Quwm in 4 of them. That itself says a lot about where he was at. Let's look at each of those verses to see the deep dark hole of stage 1 of Quwm that David was in.

Verse 3 – "my spirit, my seat of emotions, desires, appetites and my heart are overwhelmed with despair which has surrounded me. I am ebbing and fainting away. I am feeble and my spirit is fainting from exhaustion". (EHGV)

Verse 4 – "I look everywhere and there is no one who understands me or even acknowledges me or has any regard for me and my problems. I have no place to shelter where I can run to for safety. I have no place to escape. No one cares about me." (EHGV)

Verse 6 – "I am greatly diminished and feel dried up as I am hanging limp with distress and troubles, I am emptied inside." (EHGV)

Verse 7 – "My soul and my spirit are in the dungeon of darkness as I cry out for help." (EHGV)

David was in a dark hole of spiritual depression. We can clearly see here that David's situations in Psalm 142 which stemmed from the story in 1 Samuel that he was left in a deep dark hole of depression and a sense of hopelessness. As we will see that stage 4 of Quwm that God calls us to "charge ahead" with actions to accomplish tasks but when we are stage 1it can be such a dark hole that we don't even have the desire to charge ahead and if we did, we don't have the strength or energy to even attempt to.

This is where God is our Jehovah Quwm who is there to simply help us or enable us to hold on and endure. Look at the page again which lists some of the meanings connected with Quwm in stage 1. It is here where we just ask God to help us to endure, to preserve us through it and at times to just simply survive. HOLD ON! Hold on to God's support!

This is what David was looking to God to be his Jehovah Quwm. In Psalm 3:5 David says, "the Lord sustain me." Sustain in the Hebrew is the work Camak. This word means to bear the weight, to support and hold, to keep alive. God being our Jehovah Quwm does so through being our Jehovah Camak. See how God's names/epithets being separate are also working together with each other. Just like God's love and God's power and God's sovereignty all work together so do His names also reveal and work together as He reveals Himself to us.

Another layer of meaning to Camak is what we are called to do in these times of deep dark holes. We are to lean on God to support us. To brace ourselves upon the Rock who is Jesus Christ. There are hours, days and periods of time where this is simply all we can do and what we are then called to do. Don't let this stage 1 be a time of walking away but rather a time to run to God. Let these rough difficult days be used by Him to twist your spirit even deeper with His. God can move you on through to the next stage that I saw in His name/epither of Jehovah Quwm.

QUWM - STAGE 2

Part of this journey is where God steps in and lifts us up out of our darkness just like He did with the Israelites lifting them up out of their darkness of slavery in Egypt. David says this truth back in Psalm 3:3, "The One who lifts me up." As God is moving in us and through our circumstances, He will begin to lift us up out of our stage 1 of where we are simply just surviving. Yes, there are times when someone goes to be with the Lord for eternity right when they were serving in this stage 1 but God desires for us within His sovereign times to come out and be lifted in our lives here. God can stir our hearts, emotions and spirits to begin and maybe to just like we do in the morning – get out of bed. God will grow us up emotionally and spiritually. He will awaken our spirit to desire to get up.

Psalm 57 gives us a good glimpse of this stage 2 in verse 4 where David says that his soul is among lions. He is ready to be attacked and eaten up. But in verse 1 at the very beginning David proclaims that his soul refuge is in God. See the ebb and flow of David going from one stage to another? Then in verse 8 David participates in this process of healing when he calls out to awaken his heart. He was preaching to himself to stir up his own heart. Wake up my heart and soul! Rouse yourself Lord to help me and I will also try to do so as well. I will act and first get up out of bed emotionally and spiritually speaking and fight on.

This work is also all the Holy Spirit working in us to even be able to desire it and then do this. Yet God is also calling upon us to participate and call out to ourselves to stir up and get out of bed. The alarm clock is going off. Don't hit the snooze button or worse turn it off and go back to sleep but rather get up. Be involved in this process of going from the various stages. We need to develop this "I will" attitude that David had. Do a study on that phrase sometime and see the meaning there more deeply. "I WILL get up and get going." As we participate the Holy Spirit nudges us even more out of our slumber. Through this the Lord can bring us into what I see as stage 3 of the depth of meaning in Jehovah Quwm.

This is where God does so much for us as He is rebuilding us. God is healing us, strengthening us, establishing us more and more. God is also getting us ready and preparing us to once again get back in the ballgame so to speak. God is growing us to be more used of Him. I feel this is where I have been for quite some time yet also falling back into previous stages where despondency lives. I don't want to live there so I must continue to fight along with the Holy Spirit in this battle.

This is an ongoing journey and process for all believers as God does not want any of His children to stay where they are at spiritually but to keep growing and maturing in the Lord. Those with deep struggles that can end up with PTSD and depression and anxieties need even more so I say to keep pulling into God's service station for regular oil changes and checking the tire pressure and other situations that need even more dealing with.

As God has caused me to endure and survive and then lifted me up out of the dark hole I want more! And that is great. I want to keep moving forward and I hope my falling back becomes less frequent. Give the Lord the time to rebuild, refresh and restore you emotionally, spiritually and even physically.

God does this and desires to do this for us because He loves us so much and wants the best for us. Living in the dark holes of despair is not the best for us. Look to Him to be lifted out and restored and rebuilt. We may need a major overhaul at times, but God is capable of that. He created the universe with a single breath – I think He can restore us and create a new spirit within us too!

God desires to do this for us because He also desires for us to be used of Him for His Kingdom work here on earth. We are all God's ambassadors as being His children. Therefore, He is reaching out to the lost world through using us in the process. He is doing the work of salvation but has chosen to use us in this process. We need to get up and get out of bed and get refreshed and rebuilt so we can be used of God in His reaching out to others with the saving message of Jesus Christ. Plus with this Truth of He can restore us and revive us.

God also desires and will use us to reach out to other believers as well in many such areas and circumstances. Perhaps the problems you are facing others are too and God desires to use you to encourage them and be used of Him to lift them up. This is one reason I am writing this book as I desire to be used of the Lord to help others through what I have been through and struggle with by letting them know that God is there and that He can revive our spirits out of these depressions. God can use you too. Look around and see where He could use you. Get out of bed and back to serving the Lord. Let these Truths drive you on too.

I hope that this encourages you. God does have a purpose and a plan to use you or else He would simply take you into eternity to your heavenly home with Him. If you are reading this, you are still here on earth. Which means that God still has a purpose and a plan for you. This flows us right into stage 4 of Jehovah Quwm.

As you look back at the page of the 4 stages of Jehovah Quwm you will see that our stage 4 is our "Charge Ahead" stage or station to accomplish God's given tasks for us. To continue to fulfill His calling on our lives. To get out and succeed with God with our actions to "Charge Ahead".

As I am sitting here and going through this right now, I am thinking about the movie "Gettysburg". I can't even say how many times I have watched it. I have visited Gettysburg several times as well Being a Civil War buff this battle has drawn my attention for many reasons. It was a key battle that turned the war for the North when the South was on the verge of great momentum and perhaps winning the war if they had succeeded at Gettysburg.

There were so many smaller battles within the overall battle at Gettysburg. One such battle occurred on Little Round Top under the leadership of the North of Joshua Chamberlain. The Union held the high ground and they had to keep holding it because if the Confederates were to gain victory there, they could easily attack the center of the Union army and win the entire battle.

The Confederates had a lot of motivation and determination to charge up that hill and take that high ground away from the Union. On they went charging up that hill several times and each time the Union was able to thwart them and send them back. Both sides received many casualties in the process. The Confederates were regrouping and getting ready to come at the Union soldiers up that hill once again.

In this eye of the hurricane moment the Union was able to report to General Chamberlain that they were virtually out of bullets and when the Confederates would charge again that they were sure to be able to take the hill. Then they would be enroute to overtake the whole Union army.

It was not a good setting for Chamberlain or the Union army to be in. Chamberlain knew they could not lose this battle and this hill. He knew how high the stakes were in this battle, but what could he do? The whole war could ride on this one battle on this one small hill – Little Round Top. Although Joshua Chamberlain did not know this then that even the whole direction of the world as we know it was also at stake. It would have been difficult at best to defeat Germany in WW1 and WW2 if the United States was not a combined country willing and finally desiring to step in and fight. A lot was on the line here on that summer day at Gettysburg.

Although the situation looked bleak at that moment for the Union soldiers we can look back now and see that God was still in control of the situation no matter how bleak it seemed. God was in still in charge and that is exactly what

General Chamberlain eventually did – he led the Union army on a charge down the hill directly into the oncoming Confederates.

Chamberlain knew they were almost out of bullets. He knew that they could not retreat. He knew that they could not give in, but how could they hold that ground without bullets. Chamberlain did what was a most unconventional and such an inspiring idea – charge at the Confederates down the hill with bayonets in their guns even if they had no bullets, they still had their bayonets. Charge ahead. Charge ahead right down the enemies' throats and hit them hard. Don't give up. Don't give in. Charge ahead. And charge ahead they did. This was such a surprise to the Confederates, and they were overwhelmed by the Union army and Chamberlain and the North were able to keep that hill and so much more. This charge ahead mentality and thinking and bravery I would say saved the day and the rest of the Union army and the war.

I hope you can see how this relates to what we are covering right now in the fourth stage of God being Jehovah Quwm and how he moves in our own particular situations. I feel this is such a strong name/epithet of God which reveals who He is and what He can do for us and calls us to do when we face our own times of difficulties that seem insurmountable. Just like what the Israelites faced. What Moses faced when God called him to be the one in whom He would work through. What David faced time after time in all his conflicts and depressions. What Joshua Chamberlain faced when he was amid a fierce battle.

What great battle are you facing right now? God knows and God is with you. God is Jehovah Quwm. God is your Jehovah Quwm. Take time to let these 4 stages siftl into your heart and mind. God being our Jehovah Yatsa means that is He is also our Jehovah Quwm and all that goes with that. Be encouraged.

God was to keep on using you for His Kingdom purposes. God wants to refresh and revive your spirit in order for you to charge ahead with Him and for Him. Lean on the Lord and don't let your enemy of depression, anxieties, or PTSD episodes keep you from living for Him! Charge ahead!

JEHOVAH

TSHUWAH

(TESH-OO-AW)

4) JEHOVAH TSHUWAH

Help
Safety
Victory
Salvation
Deliverance – usually by God through a person

Rescue
Recovery – regain something lost or taken away
Repair/Restore – to a good or sound condition after decay or damage
Restoration – to bring back to any former state or condition and even better

God is our Jehovah Yatsa Tshuwah. I hope that this encourages us in how He does this for us. At times God does step in very directly as He did with the Israelites when He was leading them by a pillar of cloud by day and a fire by night. A direct way that God intervened in guiding them and Yatsa delivering them along the journey from captivity in Egypt to the Promised Land. Through this name/epithet of God it is very clear that God also uses people – you, me and others – to bring about His Yatsa plan for us.

When God parted the Red Sea, He obviously was the One protecting them from an attack from behind by the Egyptians chasing them. Then God parting the Red Sea and they passed on dry ground before He swallowed up the Egyptians. But God also used Moses to be a part of His doings. Moses stuck his staff into the water but Moses or the staff didn't part the sea, but God did. God chose the process of using Moses. It's important point that we see this that God is doing the work and at the same time using people in the process or even things like a staff. God can even use a storm to do His bidding as we saw with Jesus calming the storm in Mark chapter 4. The main point though with this name/epithet of God is that He very distinctly uses people to bring about His divine plan.

David was in deep despair in 1 Sa 23 right after freeing Keilah as they immediately stabbed him in the back as they turned him into Saul. This caused David to once again go on the run for his life along with his army. God knew David was in need for some deep encouragement. How did God do this? He sent Jonathan as His messenger of hope to David. God using Jonathan to do His work of encouragement in David's heart and soul.

This wasn't' the first time God had done that either as in fact Scripture is full of such God intervening moments in people's lives as He used others to do it. David was strengthened in the Lord and was able to keep on going – as God used Jonathan to do this. God's work through a human agency – Jehovah Tshuwah.

In the same 1 Sa 23 we can see how the Ziphites also turned against David and allied with Saul. Both the Ziphites and Saul's army had caught up to David and were just on the verge of capturing him to kill him. God then stepped in and used a messenger, and we don't even know his name to tell Saul that Israel was being attacked by the Philistines. Saul being the king of Israel broke off his pursuit of David to go and defend Israel.

In one sense God also used the Philistines who were an evil enemy of Israel to be used for His purposes. Just at the right time far away from where David was the Philistines were moved to attack Israel. That set-in motion for this messenger to come and tell Saul – just at the right time. Again, showing that God's timing is sovereign.

On a slight detour if I could make another point within this. Sometimes in our own circumstances we may feel that God should move quicker and at our determination. But God gets things done as He moves in His timing. Remember how when Jesus was approached by Mary and Martha about Lazarus dying. Jesus did not go immediately to save Lazarus but stayed two days where He was. Was this because Jesus did not care? Absolutely not! But Jesus had a better plan that after Lazarus had died Jesus would raise him from the dead. How much a greater display of power from Jesus. If Jesus had moved at the time frame that Mary and Martha had desired, they and us now would have missed out on how Jesus had power over death.

Yes, at times what appears to us to be God delaying or not caring is actuality God moving in His sovereign plan as He is working all things for all people for His good. Suffering at times can be a part of God's plan for us or allowing us to walk through. He never forgets and is always caring and is always in control. Keep that truth rooted in your mind and heart.

Let's move back now to our point here of God being Jehovah Tshuwah. Jesus chose to use His disciples to carry on the torch of His message of salvation and how to live. Jesus used John the Baptist to pave the way for His arrival. Jesus could have used a multitude of ways for us to now have His message and He chose to Tshuwah – use people to carry it out. This word Tshuwah directly carries with it this meaning of God using us for His Kingdom work.

Know that God as He Yatsa's us goes to all extremes and ways to do this for us. Be attentive to those who come into your life and pathway as you journey through to being restored, revived and rebuilt. Plus, the truth that God can use you too.

Maybe you have heard of the story of the man caught surprised by a sudden flood and had to escape to the roof of his house? The flood waters kept on rising and the man had faith and believed in the Lord. He cried out to the Lord in prayer that He would save him.

Soon after a helicopter flew overhead and tossed out a ladder to him, but the man sent the helicopter away saying, "Go away as it's ok as he had prayed to God and God would save him." The helicopter could do nothing else but fly away.

Then a boat pulled up and they told the man to get in and the man said, "No, it's ok as I prayed to God to save me." The people on the boat had no choice but to keep on going - without the man. Soon after that with the flood waters still rising that the man's roof was covered up and the man ended up drowning.

When he reached heaven, he asked God to why He didn't save him? God looked at him and said, "I sent you a helicopter and a boat to rescue you and you sent them away." Yes, this is a made-up story but can ring quite true for us at times. There are some who simply don't like taking help or even asking for help. Yet as we have been saying since God does within His sovereignty use others to help us why should be we silent in our times of need? Don't let your silence keep you from receiving help. We were not called on to do it all on our own. I firmly believe that at times we should and need and must reach out to tell others that we simply need some help.

There could be rejection at times as I have been rejected multiple times when I reached out to others for some specific help, and I was told "no." That hurts I realize. So be conscience that when you reach out there could be rejections and disappointments from that but don't let that stop you as you feel the Spirit leading. We are there for the body of believers and the body of believers are there for us too. God using us all for His kingdom work – Jehovah Tshuwah.

I have also several times by close friendships been told that they could not help me due to reasons like they are not psychologists or a doctor. Some reason of course can be legitimate and true but some of those times it was simply them not knowing that God can use them even in their so thought of short comings.

So many of the reasons people have used for not helping me are far from the truth. Remember how Jonathan reached out to David and encouraged him in the Lord. Jonathan had no psychology training to rely upon to encourage David. What he had was a desire and the Lord moving in him to use him. Jonathan was God's Tshuwah so to speak in David's life at that time. God can send the right person at the right time just for you too. Keep on asking for God to be Jehovah Tshuwah to you and for you to be God's Jehovah Tshuwah for someone else as well.

Let me also put this forth that God could also be desiring to use you even in your time of dejection or depression. Don't feel that your time of troubles that God can't or won't use you as He can and will. Be open to the Holy Spirit's leading to helping another person who needs your help. God can use you in so many ways.

Like going to baseball card shows. One of my reasons is to sell and buy cards. But another reason for doing them is for my healing. These shows help me to get back into life. I have also prayed to the Lord that He would use me to reach out to others who come by my booth or as I am at the show and or in traveling.

I did a show one weekend in Quincy, Illinois. I broke even money wise, but I felt tremendously good going into the show. I felt good while there during the show, after the show and even driving home that night. At the show there were several times some people came up to the booth who saw something I had on the table that someone they knew would really like. But they did not have much money. They both said they would contact the person and when they came back the first one asked if I could take $20 for three items that I had for sale at $15 each. I felt that was about all they could afford so I happily said yes that would be great. That person was so excited and smiling and said their friend would really like the items. I honestly feel that God was using me to be a Tshuwah to them.

The other person had a friend who would really like this Chicago Cubs vintage scorecard I had for sale. They were going to come back the next day with the $10. While he was standing there, I was told that the card show got cancelled for the next day. That person heard it and looked disappointed since he did not have the money to buy the scorecard for his friend. I told him to simply have the item for free for his friend. Again, I felt that God was using me to encourage each of those two people and their friends who would receive the items.

Was this a huge life changing thing for them? I don't feel it would be but who knows. Maybe God was going to use such a simple act of kindness when they received those items to keep them going. I don't know obviously but I do know God was using me. God can use you too! Be on the lookout for how God could use you to be His Tshuwah to someone!

Even in your brokenness and difficult times God can step in and use you to reach out to others. Pray and ask God to use you more. Be on the lookout for God sent opportunities. Perhaps you are even having trouble with getting up in the morning. This thought and truth of God using you to help others can at times be the reason to get up in the morning – even when you don't want to get up – get up and be used of the Lord.

Get up and see how God can use you in the lives of others. Being on such a daily mission to be Tshuwah – used of God to help others. God could also be using this in our lives as well as a God-given and God-driven means by which He is restoring you too! Be a part of God's Yatsa plans for others. Be used by the Lord. He is using others to help you too! We are all in this together as His children.

Before we move on to our next name/epithet of God linked to Jahovah Yatsa I wanted to mention a few other Truths of God being our Jehovah Tshuwah. There is tremendous significance to this word meaning for anyone suffering with PTSD episodes, depression, anxieties or deep troubles. If I were to give a sermon on this I would use an outline of four R's – Rescue, Recovery, Repair and Restoration. They all tie together and are also like a staircase of upward movement for us.

1) Rescue – Jehovah Tshuwah. Just like God took out and rescued the Israelites from Egyptian bondage He can do for us as well.

2) Recovery – Jehovah Tshuwah. As God rescues us He begins a process of recovery. We have looked at some of His various means and ways by which He accomplishes this.

3) Repair/Restore –Jehovah Tshuwah. Commited to our recovery is we need some repair work done as we move forward. This is a part of the process.

4) Restoration – Jehovah Tshuwah. As the Lord journeys us onward keep in mind that He can bring us back to something even better for us. God loves us and cares for us. Let us continue looking upward to Him in thie journey of healing.

JEHOVAH

RUWM

(ROOM)

5) JEHOVAH RUWM

Snatched	**P**icked up	**R**econstruct	**R**eady to act
Away	**R**aised up	**C**onstruct	**V**ictorious
Removed	**L**ifted up	**B**uilds	**C**onfident
Brought up	**G**row up		
	Restores		

God, who is exalted and lifted up for Who He is and sits on the throne is ready to act. He can remove us from our problems as He then lifts us up to restore us and causes us to grow and be re-constructed and then ready to act in confidence in the victories that He brings us to.

God is our Jehovah Ruwm. A great insightful name/epithet of God which reveals who He is and what He does for us as we journey through our trials and troubles and depressions to His revival of our soul. Let me repeat the last paragraph which is on the previous page: God, who is exalted and lifted for Who He is and sits on the throne is ready to act. He can remove us from our problems as He then lifts us up to restore us and causes us to grow and be re-constructed and then ready to act in confidence in the victories that He brings us to.

Tremendous view and truth of God as He works in our lives. With God as our Jehovah Yatsa, He is also our Jehovah Ruwm. I need to give an example as I am writing this an incident in my younger life comes to my mind. Perhaps I have already written this in this book already and if so, then give an "old" man the privilege of telling the story again. Perhaps the Spirit wants you to hear it again or even myself as a reminder. So here it is:

When, as best as I can remember, I was in late grade school my family was on a vacation at a resort in Wisconsin. My cousin Maureen went with us on this trip, and she was maybe in high school or just out of high school as I remember. I was swimming off the dock and for some reason I started to go under. I had probably just crossed over to a deeper end and I no longer could touch bottom, and I was drifting further out. I knew that I was in danger, and I needed help. Not just a little help whenever someone could come but right then and there.

I kept yelling out and going under and popping back up and I distinctly remember and can see it all in my mind as if in a movie I was raising my hand up and yelling for help and looking at my cousin Maureen who was sitting on the dock (by the bay). Sorry, I had to write that in! She didn't sit there and tell me she would be there in a few minutes, but she immediately jumped into the water and came over to me as I can still see this so vividly in my mind as if it was still happening now. I have no doubt she literally saved my life. I still remember Maureen grabbing me and holding on to me so I would not go under. She had lifted me up out of the death grip that the water held on me. That event will always be etched into my mind.

This relates to me how God is our Jehovah Ruwm who can swoop in and grab us out of our depths of despair and depression and troubles. There are times when we are so in desperate need that we also cry out to God with our hand out of the water yelling out just hoping for someone including God to come and save us. David was doing this as well in Psalm 142 in several places as he cried out to God for help.

In our desperation he cried out to God to please come down, reach down from His throne and pull him from his troubled drowning waters that he was in.

What is awesome about this name/epithet of God is that it also gives us the truth that God will not only snatch us up but then He is also in the rebuilding process and healing process and restoring process with us and in us to bring us to victory. Maureen when she saved me did not just keep treading water with me in her arms but rather took me to shore where it was safe. This is encouraging news to those who are now feeling like they are in the pit. The pit of despair. The pit of bondage to some sin. The pit of pain physically. The pit of troubles and trials surrounding then God is there as our Jehovah Ruwm to save us and to keep us going and to bring us safely to His shores. Keep calling out to Him.

Psalm 113:7 God tells us that He does this specifically for the depressed, the needy, the weak, the ones who are low, the ones who are subject to oppression of feeling overwhelmed emotionally or physically and to the ones who are in the sense of want and need. I hope this is encouraging to those who feel in that state of mind and situation. God is our Jehovah Ruwm.

Psalm 3:3 God tells us that when we are in need that He is our shield and protector and the One who will lift us up. Like a little child who is in need and puts their heads down in despair and the loving parent comes over and puts their hand out and cups their child's chin in their hand and gently raises their child's head up to look them in the eye to reassure them and to encourage them and to say it's ok I'm here. So likewise, our loving Heavenly Father does to us. He causes us to take our gaze off the floor and to be lifted up to Him. What a difference this can make and does make in our fight against spiritual depression.

Psalm 18:48 God tells us through David that He will bring us into His security and raise us up and lift us up to victory from those who revolt against us. God is for us. God acts on our behalf. God is our Jehovah Ruwm.

Psalm 27:5 God tells us through David that in our day of troubles, depression, anxieties, misery and even unhappiness that He will step in and raise us up. He will lift us up to victory on the Rock. Jesus is our ultimate Protector. Jesus is our Rock. God is for us. God is our Jehovah Ruwm.

This name/epithet of God reminds us that He doesn't again just stop at that point but then after and during raising us up will rebuild us. He will stir us up to actions to be involved in this process. He will bring us to victory in Christ. This doesn't mean that all of our troubles will suddenly disappear but that He is there with us. David's life was full of attacks and counter attacks and subsequent depressions. Then as David turned his attention more to the Lord he would bounce back up and at times only to fall again. But then David would come back again. Our lives can ebb and flow from calm seas to great storm in such a short time. We need to train ourselves to keep looking up – up to God!

David's life was a constant battle ground fighting not only the physical enemies but also the emotional disturbances within his spirit. Some who are reading this feel like their lives are one constant battle ground and yes at times it can be. If you feel and are in a daily battle to keep your head above the water know that the Lord does not take any days or moments off in His connection with you. Keep on fighting. Keep on looking up to the Lord who is the One who lifts you up.

This truth is so vital for us to know and keep in our minds that God is our Jehovah Ruwm. Keep this name/epithet of God in your heart in your daily battles. With God being our Jehovah Ruwm in so many ways throughout scripture, we should also look at a few more names/epithets of God which wrap itself around this truth that God lifts us up. The next two names/epithets of God relate to this truth. They are God being our Jehovah Alah and our Jehovah Zaqaph. Let's look now at God as being our Jehovah Yatsa is also our Jehovah Alah.

JEHOVAH

ALAH

(AW - LAW)

6) JEHOVAH ALAH

Delivered out	Brought up	Advance	Charge ahead
	Taken up	Marched up	ahead
	Led up	Continued up	Shoot forth
	Going up		
	Restore	Stir up	
	Recover	Increase	
	To rouse	Mount up	

Accompanied
To Accompany
To join in action
To be and exist in association with
Cause to ascend or climb

God is our Jehovah Alah. As God Yatsa's us out He does so in also being Jehovah Alah to us. We can see this same pattern that has been emerging as we have dug into the depth of meaning in these various names/epithets of God. God being our Jehovah Yatsa carries with it so many more names/epithets that are connected to that God delivers us out and then restore us to enable us he stirred up and mount up to charge ahead with his callings in our lives. God didn't want David to stay in his dungeon of despair and neither does He want us to!

Charge ahead! Our situations might not automatically change but our hearts and minds and spirits can. Thus, through the Holy Spirit enabling us to keep on going through the storms. Through this process of leading us up God is also restoring us and moving us to recovery in Him in our emotions, mind and spirit. Then as we keep walking with the Lord, He then keeps moving us forward in advancing and marching onward to where we then can even charge ahead against the enemy. Through Christ we can be victorious. Again, I need to emphasize that the situation might not change and may continue but we are becoming more and more in the sense and experiencing God's presence to get us through and to keep us going.

When Jesus was praying in the Garden before His mock trial and crucifixion, He prayed with such fervency that He even sweat drops of blood. Did the Father remove the bad situation and Jesus no longer must endure the horrific trial and beatings before enduring the physical and spiritual agony at the cross? No, He still had to go through all of that for us! But Jesus was prepared in His mind, heart, emotions and spirit to endure and continue with the fight and His calling. We are also called to do this. When you fervently pray to the Father for deliverance, we cannot always expect the situations to disappear as they might continue. If this is so, then let us continue to march up to the throne of the Lord and ask for endurance and to be used in the process within the situation. Is this difficult to do? Yes, of course it is, and I have struggled with this off and on as well. Pray, pray and continue to pray for deliverance and then let us leave the avenue of His deliverance with the Sovereignty of the Lord as He always – always has our best interests in mind.

This truth of our part we will explore more in the next section, but I need to briefly fill in here is the "charge ahead" truth that is contained within the Lord being our Jehovah Alah. We do play a part in this or better said that God calls us to our participation in this process. I have already talked about the 20th Maine and how they charged forth down the hill against the enemy when they had no ammunition left and only had at their disposal their sabers. In essence that was not the only thing that they had left. They also had courage, they also had determination. They also had each other as they charged down that hill right into the face of the enemy who still had bullets in their guns. They charged ahead with such ferocity that the Confederates were so stunned that they first retreated and then gave up in a mass surrender. What a victory right in the face of for sure apparent defeat.

Let me give my personal testimony here of how the Lord has been healing me and restoring me. In what we feel are the smallest of things God can take them and use them in His process of restoring us. With my come back the Lord used baseball cards. What? Yes, baseball cards and other sport cards and memorabilia. I have collected cards since I was a kid and over the last several years, I began again with the goal of being a card flipper in order to bring in more money and to hopefully do so full-time. That has not happened yet but just within the last few months I felt the Holy Spirit prompting me to start doing card shows again. I truly felt the urging and tugging that He was giving me, and it wasn't so much to make the money but to be a missionary at the card shows. I "charged ahead" with yes, I would say with great ferocity and purchased some more items and got what I felt was a good set up for the table. I then began contacting some people and started to do some shows.

I even had a box of free items including Bibles and Christian books – but no one took anything at first. I was discouraged and even felt that I had misread what the Spirit was telling me to do in doing these shows. I also regrettably even got a bit "upset" with God and questioning Him in that here I thought that You had given me a ministry to do with this Lord and no one took even a single Bible or book. I stopped doing shows for probably three or four months and felt a bit dejected and defeated with it all.

Then the promptings started coming again to do shows. It was like a wave of the Spirit speaking with me. I started organizing and getting myself together and started contacting people to do some shows and with the main purpose of still being a missionary in this and not to make money. At first, I couldn't get into any shows, and I kept praying and then suddenly a show that did not have any openings had tables available. Within a couple of days, I had four shows lined up where I could go and set up a table. I just did a show one weekend in Quincy, Illinois where I saw the Lord move in me and possibly connecting with some people there.

For me I felt alive in a sense again. I felt like a breath of fresh air had been sent my way and was enjoying the travel and meeting with some new people and making some contacts. I felt a connection with the Lord that He was in this with me and using it to restore me back to life. I also prayed and hoped God could use me in ministering to others there. One thing that I have seen in this is that God can use what we see as small and neutral things like card collecting to use for His kingdom. I also dicovered that a few Bibles had been taken by someone, so who knows where that would lead.

Take an inventory of things that you like to do with regards to hobbies and such. Some talents that you may have. Begin praying about how the Lord might use those things in your life to be used by Him in your personal healing and restoration and perhaps so in being used by the Lord in reaching out to others for His kingdom. Start charging ahead for the Lord!

I realize that my personal example here is not in the same realm of what the

20th of Maine did at Little Round Top, but it can relate. We take what the Lord has given us even if it might seem to us as being so small and inadequate to do the job and then with His blessing and guidance we can also move forward.

This is all a part of God being Jehovah Alah in our lives. He delivers us and raises us up and calls us to charge ahead. Plus, He can use the everyday and ordinary things in our lives to do so with. Let us become more and more aware of the potential here for the Spirit's using the so-called small things in our lives to use for His Kingdom and in the lives of others that He might have us connect with.

Notice also what is within the truth of God being Jehovah Alah. It also means "accompanied." As we go about this God leading us and marching us forward, He does so by being right by our side. He is right there with you and me and every single believer. God is joining with us in our actions that we take for Him. He is in association with me when I go and do the card shows. When I am in the process of getting shows to participate in and even as I am texting with the person who is heading up the show. Plus, then also with the other vendors as we set up and throughout the show. Then with the people who attend. He is also there with me as I travel to and from the show and when I need to stay over in a hotel. I also see those "mundane" times as a part of potential God times with people who I would not normally have had any connection with. It can be with you and the Lord. It was with David as he walked through all His troubles and depression states. God was walking with David through it all and so likewise with us.

God is escorting us through these times of recovery and then the charging out and marching out times. He is our protection and our guidance through His continual presence with us. God is our chaperon who goes with us in and through the storms as He is bringing us through them. Then as He lifts us up to enable us to endure and even at times taking us completely out and then moving us forward to something He already has plans for us to do.

Just as God was with Daniel in the Lion's Den so God is with you in your Den of Troubles and sorrows. Just as the Lord was walking through the fire with Shadrach, Meshach and Abednego so He is with us. The fire may not go out and sometimes even gets hotter, but He is always with us enabling us to endure. When Jesus again was in the Garden, He called a few of the disciples that He had personally chosen to go a bit further with Him into the Garden. He asked them to be with Him during His time of crisis as He prayed and what did they do? They fell asleep numerous times throughout this time in the Garden. In Jesus' great moment and deep sorrow and even depression there God was also still with Him even if the disciples could not even stay awake with Him. No matter what dire circumstance or depth of despair, or loneliness or depression the Lord is Jehovah Alah and is accompanying us through it all. Whatever stage of recovery we are in He is there standing with us.

Keep on fighting! Keep on moving forward! Charge forward in the Lord's leading and timing. God is our Jehovah Alah. God keeps pouring this truth of how He lifts us up with yet another of His names/epithets that we find in Scripture. The next one associated with this is God is our Jehovah Zaqaph. Let's investigate this truth of God for us.

JEHOVAH

ZAQAPH
(ZAW-KAF)

7) JEHOVAH ZAQAPH

Comfort
Lifts Up
Raise
To Raise Up to Life

God is our Jehovah Zaqaph. Flowing from the truth of God being our Jehovah Yatsa the Lord keeps on drilling home into us the truth of Him raising us up. I sense the Lord is ramping up this more in me as I am writing this book. I know He is using this process of studying and writing to move me more into restoration. It seems slow but I feel, and I am told it is happening. As I am typing in this section of the book just this morning, I had an opportunity to reach out to someone who has just gone through a incredible horrific attack in his life from the enemy. He just contacted me this morning and I hope I was able to encourage him with what he was enduring through.

Through this I also saw and felt how God was still using me. I have felt my times of being used by the Lord to help others were done. God lifted me up today to tell me He still is using me in His Kingdom. God will lift you up as well as He uses you. If we are here on this earth God can and will use us or else He would call us home to be with Him. While here know that God has these opportunities for us to be used by Him and for Him. Pray for them as well. They will come. As you are reaching out to others God is not only lifting them up through you, but He is also in this process lifting you up as well. When we are active for the Kingdom's sake then we are being lifted.

We have just looked at how God is Jehovah Tshuwah and as such brings about His desires and plans through using us in this process. What a great lift that is and should be in our spirits. The Creator of the universe is using me! He is using you!

There are so many ways that God lifts us up. One is by what we just looked at in Him using us to be His Tshuwah to others. Then there are the times when all we feel is depression and despair and it's hard to even get up in the morning. This is how David felt at times. His spirit at times was crushed within him. He felt abandoned by all and felt alone, rejected and defeated. This is also where God is our Jehovah Zaqaph. God at times lifts us up simply by encouraging us through comforting us. Again, God does this in so many different and varied ways and even when we "feel" He is not active in our lives He is. These are the times when we need to simply know Scripture and the truths of Scripture and then believe these truths even when it is hard to do so. This name/epthet of God is only mentioned in two verses in the Word in Psalm 145:14 and Psalm 146:8. Let's look at them both here.

Psalms 145 also written by David and that one as a Psalm of praise to God. Verse 14 certainly calls us to raise up our praises to Him for what He does for us in our times of discouragment. Let's read through this in the EHGV.

"The Lord upholds, sustains and refreshes all who have failed or feel they have failed or fallen short. To those who are discouraged, feel unfulfilled, downcast, disheartened, terrified, overtaken and feel like they have been thrown down and have fallen flat on the ground and now live without apparent purpose. God Zaqaph's them up all who are discouraged and bowed down. God reaches out to sooth their spirits and emotions to comfort them in their time of crisis and despair to thus lift them up out of the deep well that they are in." (EHGV)

What a powerful verse for those who suffer with those strong feelings of discouragement and hopelessness. God reaches down and into our lives to cause to bring us back up again. God is there to soothe our troubled spirits and to comfort us back into hope. God is Jehovah Zaqaph to us. God will lift us up!

In Psalm 146, with whom we don't know for sure who the author is be starts out by proclaiming that the Lord is our abundant helper. How does He do this? One way is stated in verse 8, "The Lord enables and pays close attention to and opens the eyes of those who are dry spiritually and to those who are bowed down in discouragment He Zaqaphs' them up. He raises them up. He comforts them in their time of need. God is a friend who loves and is personally engaged with those whom He raises up (Jehovah Alah) to those who have been saved to be His children." (EHGV)

We also can play a part in this as well. Psalm 145 is a Psalm of Praise. One way we can fight back is by lifting our hearts in praise to God. The Hebrew word for praise used here in Psalm 145 is Tehillah (The-hil-law). It has several meanings by which we can praise and worship God during our storms. We can praise and worship with song. Singing yourself or even just listening to songs of praise in any style that is yours. Praise and thank God for His qualities (epithets), deeds or attributes. Praise Him for all His praiseworthy acts we see all throughout Scripture and in your life.

David says in verse 1 of Psalm 145 that he will exalt the Lord. David lifted his voice high to praise God. He also says he will bless God's name which also is to kneel before Him in adoration either physically or in our hearts and minds. David says he will do so by praising God's name. This is one reason why I am writing this book and focusing so much on God's various names/epithets of Him. They reveal who He is and who we are to Him and all that He is doing for us. This should bring our hearts to naturally praise and worship Him. David says he will do this every day forever and ever. The more we are worshipping and praising God as we focus our thoughts and attentions toward Him the less we are focusing on our problems and troubles. Let us fix our eyes upon Jesus!

Get to know the Lord more and more. Go deeper and deeper in your knowledge of Him which should lead to experiencing Him deeper as well. Worship and praise the Lord for lifting you up. Do so even when it is tough to do so and don't even desire to do so. It is a battle and can be a daily battle at times. To praise and worship God is a part of our spiritual armor that we must keep putting on. The more we know and see who God is the stronger our spiritual armor becomes as we do battle with our circumstances and depression.

In Psalm 145 David calls out so many of God's attributes and what He is like. Here are a few:

Verse 2 – Great is the Lord

Verse 3 – God's works and His mighty acts

Verse 5 – God's glorious splendor, majesty and wonderful works

Verse 6 – God's power of His awesome acts and His greatness

Verse 7 – God's abundant goodness, righteousness and greatness

Verse 8 – God is gracious, merciful and great in His love.

Verse 9 – God is good and merciful to all.

Verse 11 – God's glory and power

Verse 12 – God's might acts.

Our spiritual armor to do battle flows from our correct knowledge and thinking of God. In our times of feeling discouraged and overwhelmed let us remember who our God is. How much He loves and cares for us. David knew this but had to be constantly reminded of these truths and he even preached to himself these truths. So must we. God is our Jehovah Zaqaph as He lifts us up and comforts us through our trials and hard times in life. He is there for us.

JEHOVAH
PAQACH
(PAW-KAKH)

8) JEHOVAH PAQACH

Gives sight
Open
Pay close attention
Enabled
To be observant
To open the senses

God is our Jehovah Paqach. Look at verse 7 of our Psalm 142. David asks God to, "Bring me out, lead me out, deliver my very being which is the seat of my emotions, passions, desires – the very heart of who I am. Bring me out of this dungeon that I am shut down in. You, Lord are the causative action to bring this about…" (EHGV).

What a place that David was in and how this turned his soul into a blizzard of feelings. He needed the Lord desperately. David was in such a dark place emotionally and spiritually from what was happening to him that he knew that He needed God to open his eyes. David needed God to open his senses once again. Only God could enable him to do so, and David knew this. David therefore ran to the Lord begging Him to pull him out of this dark dreary place that he was in.

Psalm 146:8 tells us that the Lord is the one who does this for us. Due to our adverse circumstances, there can be times when we get a film over our spiritual eyes. These are times when it is even hard to see the hand of the Lord in our lives. Maybe this is where you are right now. You know the truths of God and who He is and who you are to Him, yet you are still struggling. This truth of God should move us to turn to Him when we are in this dark place as David was and plead with Him to open our spiritual eyes once again to Him. Perhaps you can hardly even think your way through the day let alone focus on who God is. There could even be times when you are in this deep dark dungeon that you say and think things about God that are not true. Keep fighting. Keep seeking God and His help!

If you are not there yourself but know someone who does fight depression or PTSD episodes and they say things that seem out of character for them and even about God – give them a slight break and not pounce on them or cut them off because they might say something wrong about God. These random thoughts and words arise out of the dungeon that they are in. Rather be used of God to help guide them out of this dark place that they are in. You could be that person the Lord is sending to them to minister to them for Him. Realize that they are in a deep spiritual battle and need some helping hands to guide them through this place. Gently get them back on the road of proper thinking.

Pray for them too. This is what Paul did for the church at Ephesus as we see in Ephesians 1:16-19, "…while making mention of you in my prayers – my earnest prayers for you. I have great purpose and zeal for you in my prayers. I pray that the God of our Lord Jesus Christ, the Father of glory, may give you a spirit of wisdom to discover the meaning of His words and of revelation of the truth in the precise and correct knowledge of Him. I pray that the eyes of your heart in the way you think, and feel may be enlightened and given understanding, so that you will know what the hope of His calling and confident expectation of our salvation is and what are the riches and abundance of the glory of His power toward us who believe. These are in accordance with the working of the strength of His might…". (EHGV). Paul implored them to reach out and pray for those who were struggling in their spiritual vision. Don't condemn them but rather pray for them.

This is what we see in the truths of God being Jehovah Paqach. God is the one enabling us to see Him and give Him glory. God is the one opening our eyes when the world and our circumstances have put a gloomy glaze over our eyes. As God is Yatsaing us out of our circumstances and depressions our eyes at times will become glazed over. We need God to draw us to Him again and again and again. We are also blessed to have those around us who will be praying for us when we slip and fall into those dungeons from time to time. Take heart and know this truth of God.

JEHOVAH DALAH

(DAW-LAW)

9) JEHOVAH DALAH

Lifted up
Draws
Drawing advice
To draw up
Enough

To let down a bucket for drawing out water

God is our Jehovah Dalah. Again, the Lord reveals Himself as the One who lifts us up. Since God has given Himself so many names/epithets that reveal how He lifts us up this is a topic that we need to truly let sink into our minds and hearts. God does not desire for us to stay in our dungeons and holes of depression but rather to be lifted out of them. God being Jehovah Dalah to us reinforces this truth.

There are so many reasons as to why does this for us. One is that He cares for us and when you love someone deeply you want the best for them. It is not best for us to remain in our dungeons of despair. David gives us another reason why he specifically wanted the Lord to lift him up out of this dungeon he was in. In verse 7 of Psalm 142 we see that one of David's reasons as to why he was asking God to bring him out of his dark dungeon of emotions and of the spirit and to give Him new spiritual insight was as he said, "SO THAT" he may give thanks to God's name – who He is. So that – David did not just want to be lifted out so he could feel better but also so that he could give more and deeper thanks and worship to the Lord. Let that be one of your goals for God bringing you into restoration of your spirit. So that you can worship Him deeper.

It is interesting that Jehovah Dalah carries with it the sense of being lowered down into the well and then the fresh water is drawn up. Sometimes the Lord allows us to go down into the well knowing that the lowering down will produce in us to then be lifted with fresh new water to revive us and to be better used by Him. Joseph was lowered down into a well literally and then figuratively when he was carried off into Egypt sold there by his own brothers. Those times in Egypt were full of ups and downs. His life was not easy at times. However, Romans 8:28 teaches us that even our downs can be for our ultimate good. It eventually was for Joseph and the rest of his family in the end.

God might at times lower us into what we feel is a deep dark well for His ultimate good for us and for others. I do not fully understand God's sovereignty in these moments but through the Word we see how at times these events can happen in our lives. Remember the fiery furnace our three friends were tossed into. God was with them through it all. He allowed them to be thrown in in order to more fully reveal who He was to them and all around them.

David uses this word Dalah in Psalm 30 when he was delivered by God from his enemies. He was in essence lowered into a well of difficult trials and problems time after time and then raised up by the Lord stronger than before. Yes, as we have mentioned in other places that God does allow us to go through difficult times but also again for our Romans 8:28 good within His sovereign plans.

Sometimes we don't like to hear this but the first step at times to be lifted is to be let down. To let down a bucket into a wall of water in order to then with that bucket be lifted. To be lifted with fresh water. Water is also a symbol for the power of God to purify and to provide deliverance. It can also mean destroying evil and enemies. Our lifting down at times is God's way of destroying those who are trying to destroy us. It could also be God's way of casting out the dross that is in us to make us more refined as gold. Water is also known as a vital necessity to life. So is spiritual water. It purifies us from the filth of dirt and wrong thinking while giving us freshness to live on. Try not to despise the times when we are allowed to be lowered into a well as God is using it all for His kingdom purposes and to refine us as He brings fresh water into our spirit.

Look back at the meaning of Dahal. We see that the process of God lowering us down and then lifting us up reveals that what comes up. What comes up is the water. Let's not look over this key point here. Jesus is the source of Living Water. Jesus is the Living Water. We can only live without physical water for about a week or so before we begin the process of withering away. Water helps us to maintain the right metabolism and regulate our appetite. Water can help increase our energy levels. Water can help fight off certain kinds of cancer even. Water can help with our joints and to keep our muscles from cramping up. Water can help alleviate headaches. Water can help moisturize our skin. Now take all that and translate it into our spiritual water which is found in Jesus Christ. This is true even when we are allowed to be lowered into our storms. We need to be lifted down into Jesus to be lifted to new life. We need to at times be let down into the depths of troubles and trials in order to be lifted to be used more for the Lord and for his Kingdom. We need at times to be lowered down in order to get rid of things in our lives that are holding us down and pulling us away from the Lord.

Hebrews 10:22 tells us to draw near to God. We need to draw ear to God while in the storms – even while in the deep depths of the well. My hope is that when I am in deep well that I know that God will be lifting me up. One day He will ultimately lift me up to heaven. In the meantime, I need to develop a mindset to embrace the wells of my life knowing that the Lord is Romans 8:28ing in my life. Even the wells of my deep dungeons are being used by the Lord in my life and in the lives of others. I realize that it is not easy to develop such a mindset. Apparently, I have struggled most of my life battling PTSD and not even knowing it till I was hit with my huge troubles many years ago. Then my PTSD troubles and depression escalated.

I did not immediately embrace those severe troubles which turned my life upside down. Regretfully I did not, and I went through many years of doubt and searching as to why things happened as they did. I still don't know why. Six years later and this last month or so I feel like I am just now beginning to come out of the deep end. I feel the Lord has been lifting me up all this time and I did recognize it at various times. It is becoming more and more clear to me these last few weeks and months as I am writing this section that the Lord is and has been lifting me up.

I feel it is emerging with this new "God opening up my spiritual eyes" from the writing and studying for this book. In my desire to be used of God to help others fight through their storms He has helped me. He has helped me to see that He allowed me to be dropped down into the well as He knew the fresh waters that would come from it in my spirit and life.

Just this day the Lord enabled me to reach out to someone who is also going through a similar but different deep well that they have been lowered into. I was able to talk with them and to let them know that I knew by experience how it was and that I was there for them and understood. I could not have so fully understood where they were at without my own being lowered into the well. Yes, I still could have ministered to them as we don't have to experience firsthand all things to be used of the Lord to reach out to others but in this situation, it sure helped them to know that I also had walked in those pathways and knew the hurt and pain.

God can use our troubles and heartaches and even our depressions to be used of Him to make fresh water in us and then through us to others. God is so awesome. Let's step back and give God the glory that is due His name. Our storms can help us to see Him in a deeper way and be prepared for deeper work to do.

JEHOVAH GAMAL
(GAW-MAL)

10) JEHOVAH GAMAL

Deal bountifully
A benefit
To Good to
To deal bountifully with
Treat a person well
Aid
Relief
Care
Help
Assistance
Encouragement
Abundantly supply
Be in plenty

"Burst forth my soul which is my seat of emotions and passions and even the very activity of my mind – in essence who I am – out of the dungeon and prison of my emotions that I am in now. Lord, I know that You are the causative action to enable me to be capable of marching out of this depression and even possibly these circumstances if it is Your will. But if the circumstances don't change, please I beg help me to come out of this emotional roller coaster and to march forth and proceed toward something for You. Release me from this pit of despair so I may praise Your name and give You thanks for my delivery. Let other believers gather around me too so that they can see how bountifully You have dealt with me." – Psalm 142:7(EHGV)

What a powerful verse that is from the heart of David. So much desiring to be out of his pit of despair and the circumstances surrounding him. Yet how wonderful it is to see how David desired to also live under the sovereignty of God. If God so chose to keep him in his circumstances, then he could live with that as it was from God's hand. Yet at the same time if those circumstances were not lifted away David still cried out to be freed from his depressions arising from it all. David was revealing that with God he could withstand his circumstances. However, the spiritual depression and aching in his soul David could not stand and wanted relief from the Lord. How vital it is to be released from our spiritual depressions. They seem to hinder our walk with the Lord even more than our circumstances can. We need to fight back with the Lord to conquer these dungeons of despair. David's valley times were robbing him of sensing and experiencing God's presence like he so desired to do.

I feel like I am in such a valley right now. I am trying as I write this book to be up front with you all as to where I am at in my pursuit of restoration and healing. I am writing this book probably over a period of months and months so there will be a sense of per say jaggedness to it possibly. I'm just trying to be real so that you all can see that even though I am in the process of this upward journey with the Lord to "get better" there are still periods of time which are very difficult to navigate. Today as I am writing this is one of those valley times where I feel I have slipped from my journey up the mountain.

I won't go into detail as I'm unsure of what has triggered me into this sense of depression that I am in today. But it's here. I have reached out to some of my friends who understand or try to, but I isolated myself today and told everyone as I'm reaching out that I needed to be alone. Somehow in retrospect that doesn't even make sense. I'm reaching out to my friends for help yet telling them I need to be alone. In looking back that seems to be a contradiction but that's what happens when I get into a certain valley.

So maybe not the best move to go it alone but from past experiences when I get to this point this is apparently what I do, and I have done it again. I am alone and I don't necessarily recommend this if you are struggling but I sent out the memo I wanted to be alone and so now I am alone. When I get like this, I feel that I don't want to "contaminate" other people's lives more than I already have with my constant battles. Even though I have gone several months without a major episode today and last night the throngs of depression and despair and tired of fighting has swept over me. I am a bit shocked that I picked up my computer to write today but I wanted to somehow convey to you all that this battle that I am in and some of you may be is and could be a continual one. I pray you don't become discouraged in the fighting.

I am discouraged today so I am trying to pass on to keep on fighting – even though today I feel like I am so tired of this all. With all that in mind I am now writing verse 7 of our Psalm 142. It is here that I park myself and a place and verse that I so much need today. Today's writings are for me, and I hope it helps someone out there as well. I am trying to preach to myself and lift up my emotional pain to the Lord for some help. So here we go with verse 7.

As David is coming to the end of this Psalm as we see in verse 7 it is a mixture of pain and a prayer of looking up and forward to what could possibly happen in a great way from the Lord. I am trying today so badly to have this attitude. It is very easy to sound off right now and tell the Lord how much pain and ache I am in today and again I am not totally sure what has triggered me. It is July 4, 2022, and I did a baseball card show in Janesville, Wisconsin yesterday after I had a great visit with one of my brothers and his family. The card show was ok, and I had a good number of conversations with people that was fun. I am very tired and for me when I get physically tired it is harder for me to fight things off so maybe that is a part of it too. Without going into more details, which again I am not even sure what is going on, I am at a very low point today. This is how David felt when he was writing Psalm 142.

God's word is inspirited and breathed out by the Holy Spirit, but the Spirit did not nullify the writer's personality or circumstance when it was written. Here David is in a lot of pain, and he is open about it and pleading with God for His help.

David reveals here through the Hebrew tense of some of the words here is that he knew God was the causative action needed to bring him out of his deep pit of despair. He starts out by saying "free me." The word "free" is the Hebrew word that we have already looked at "yatsa." David not only wanted to be freed but to go forth to something. What was David desiring to be freed from? Here it was not his circumstances which are just hitting me now with regards to how I am feeling. Yes, I wish some of my circumstances were for sure different but here as David was seeking God, he was imploring God to set his spirit free from the dungeon that he was in emotionally.

David was exhausted spiritually as well. He was worn out. That is how I am feeling today as I am freshly studying this out. I need to do what David did here and just cry out to God to bring me out of this depression and despair that I am in this very day. I can't fight this on my own. As great as some of my few friends that I have who are so supportive of me they are there for me only through the caring giving of the Lord. God is the causative agent and the one who can bring me up and send me forth. He uses others but He is the causative action in it all.

I can't tell God how to do it but in essence I may have today by telling some I needed to be alone. Perhaps in doing so I cut off the person who God was going to use to help me fight today. I can't bring back those texts to say please come over and be with me to help fight this. Perhaps God wanted me to be alone so He could personally restore me today. I don't know so I just must go with the flow of where I am right now and maybe it is in studying and sharing from my heart right now with you all.

Maybe someone reading this today is also going through what I am feeling right now too. The sense of just being worn out from fighting all the time to get better and feel "normal" again. To not have depression lurking over your shoulder as I wait for it to pounce out. I understand if this is where you are right now. Don't give up. Keep fighting. It is very difficult as I know from personal experience but don't give up. Keep On Keeping On. I can't do this on my own as only God can bring me out to send me forth. So like David I am openly acknowledging that it is God who is the causative action in this battle to bring me out to march forward. Lord, if you don't change my circumstances, I am still asking to bring up my spirit. This was David's prayer as well.

One of the reasons why David wanted the Lord to rescue him from this pit of despair was so that he could freshly praise, worship and give thanks to the Lord again. I know that we are supposed to praise the Lord even in the valleys. However, when you are in the valley if we all were to truly be honest it is difficult to do so. I am not super Christian who when depression hits that I can immediately starting praising and worshiping the Lord in it. I am getting better when it hits to try and put worship songs on to listen to even if I can't sing along but I still struggle with when I get into my deeper valleys it is difficult for me to look up.

I think David realized he also had this inner difficulty and was being honest with God about it. "Hey, Lord, I am in this dark valley, and it is very difficult for me to worship You right now and sing praises of thanksgiving to You." But then David offers up this honest prayer of "OK Lord, help me to praise You again. Help my spirit to be able to lift praises and thanksgivings to You as right now I am so dry. I need Your help today to enable me to do this."

If you fall into this kind of rut, then simply be honest with God and tell Him how difficult it is to worship Him right now. Being honest with God is always the best policy as He already knows your heart. Be honest with the Lord and then ask Him to change your heart to give you a fresh heart to be able to praise Him in the storm.

David then even goes further. He asks God as He lifts his soul from the dark and dreary dungeon he was in spiritually and emotionally to then additionally deal bountifully with him. David did not stop by just asking to be taken out of the hole but to also continue and bless him as he was lifted out of the hole he was in.

Here we jump into our next name/epithet of God. This Hebrew word for "bountifully" is Gamal (Gaw-mal). God is Jehovah Gamal. This means to deal bountifully with or to treat a person well as well as to give benefits to them. To abundantly supply and be in plenty. God generously and lavishly gives to us of His benefits. They are great, large and broad. They can't be contained. Benefits are for our good and advantageous for us. They are there to help us while at the same time revealing all the boundless love God has for us. God puts Himself on display when He pours out His bountiful blessings to us.

When God does this for us these blessings are flowing from an act of kindness and care for us. So as David was crying out for God to so greatly bless Him this reveals this truth about God. David would not ask this of God if he knew God would not do this. David knew that He was Jehovah Gamal and so David offered up this prayer of help and support to the One Who could do this for him.

Isaiah 63:7 reveals why God desires and does this for us. In Isaiah we are given three reasons why. First because He is Jehovah Checed. His great love for us. Springing forth from God's love is His desire to bountifully bless us.

He is also Jehovah Tuwb which describes His great, abundant, numerous and enormous goodness. Flowing from that God desires to bountifully bless us.

Thirdly because He is Jehovah Racham. This reveals and describes God's deep compassion and how much He cherishes us. Flowing from God's deep compassion and from being cherished by Him comes His desire to bountifully bless us. The multitude of God's character all flowing together like the sunbeams breaking forth through the clouds.

I am trying right now to remind myself of these truths of God as I am desiring to come out of this hole that I am in today. I can see that even amid all of David's troubles which brought him to his spiritual depression that he fought his way back by knowing who God was and how much God loved him. This helped David to let it all go so to speak and plead with God to bring him out of his spiritual depression and to go even further in blessing him in a great and huge way. It's ok to ask God to bless you. David was doing just that in verse 7 and we can take his example as we reach out to the Lord.

David was attempting to do what Joshua Chamberlain did on Little Round Top when he was stacked with great odds. God dealing with us bountifully is not all about money being poured into our laps. It is as we see here in this circumstance all about the spiritual end of things. It's getting wisdom in time of need. It's getting direction when a decision needs to be made. It's being given strength when we feel we are so far from the finish line. Does God step in at times and bless us financially? Of course, He does but it's not always about that.

Today when I am struggling, I am not asking God for a knock on my door with someone blessing me with an envelope full of money. I am asking for God's bountiful blessings for me to be lifted out of this dark pit that I have fallen into.

That is my prayer right now as I am writing this that the Lord can give me such a spirit to fight on even when part of me is so tired of it and is tired of fighting on – but God – help me to keep fighting on like David did.

Knowing that God is your Jehovah Gamal can be a significant piece of your armor to fight off feelings of abandonment, depression, isolation, despair and anxieties. David experienced this and sought out the Lord as his Jehovah Gamal. Looking at Psalm 13 reveals this very strongly.

Psalm 13 was written by David and is also very close in the timeframe with our Psalm 142. Scholars believe Psalm 13 along with Psalm 142 were written by David through the Holy Spirit during the timing of 1 Samuel 23. That is when David was once again hiding out and running from Saul.

In 1 Samuel 23 the Ziphits also enter the picture with Soul. They were beginning to work with Saul to capture and kill David. Things were piling up against David and Psalm 13 records how David was reeling in spiritual and emotional pain from it all. He even was asking God multiple times "how long" Lord "how long."

David felt that God had forgotten him, rejected him, disregarded him, overlooked him, ignored him, ceased to care for him, had put him out of His mind, abandoned him. Get the picture on how David felt with regards to his relationship with God? Keeping in mind this is what David was also feeling in Psalm 142.

David was in pain and simply not thinking right. David felt that God's presence was no longer with him. How discouraging the depth of despair that David was in – to feel that God had pulled His very presence from him. Have you ever "felt" that way at times? Has anyone whom you have shared these deep painful thoughts and feelings with come back to you with "why are you feeling this way and stop it?" If that ever happens remind them that besides David even our Lord Jesus Christ felt this when He proclaimed to the Father, "Why have you forsaken Me."

It is not a spiritual crime to have these thoughts and feelings flood over you, but it is not a good place to park yourself in when it happens. We need to fight back and get back to the truth that Jesus said that He would never leave us nor forsake us.

Back to Psalm 13 – in verse 2 David even asks God how long he must continue to feel like this. I have been saying this to several of my "go to" people when I get into a spiritual depression time. I have said to them that I was simply tired of feeling this way all the time. I get David's pain and questioning God even with this.

David battled with deep depression, and no one can deny this and yet he was called a man after God's own heart. David was not a lesser Christian for battling this but was what he had to deal with. Although David being a warrior and one who could attack lions and bears along with giants, I feel he was still a kind and tenderhearted person deep down. Through this makeup of his personality, he felt deep emotions and so when he was down and out, he was down and out. We see so much of this pour through many of his psalms.

David was a warrior, leader and king but he was also tenderhearted as well. It's possible today he would have been made fun of for being so tender in his heart and emotional. I have been and that even hurts too. Psalm 139 so clearly tells us that everyone is wired and knit together by the Lord in the womb. David's personality was carried with it multiple characteristics like ours do too. His gentle and compassionate side carried with it some capabilities to slip into deep depression at times. This he had to do battle with when it came to emotional and spiritual depression.

In Psalm 13:3 this is clearly seen in David. During this great time of depression and feeling overwhelmed by his troubles he pleaded with God to hear him, pay attention to him and to do something about this spiritual depression that he was in. David asked if the Lord would do it quickly. David was in dire straits, and he needed the Lord to step in now to help him.

As David was lifting this prayer to the Lord, we began to see a shift in his spiritual and emotional state. A great reversal is happening. A recovery per say. Psalm 13:5 from David to the Lord, "But I will trust in You Lord and put my confidence in You. In You I feel secure and depend upon. I can be bold and confident no matter what my circumstances are as I trust in You. I can trust in You because of Your Checed love for me. Your love for me is unfailing, it is faithful, it is steadfast. You are loyal and devoted to me. So therefore, my emotions, my passions, my thinking and my heart will greatly rejoice and celebrate the victory and deliverance from You. I know you will and are intervening in my heart right now. In this I will trust and rejoice in." (EHGV)

Then David continues with this upward emotional and spiritual revival in verse 6 of Psalm 13, "I will sing my praises to You Lord because you are my Jehovah Gamal – You deal so bountifully with me to abundantly supply all my needs physically, emotionally and spiritually. You lavishly pour out your blessings to me that are so great, large and broad. Your blessings cannot be contained as they flow from You and who You are." (EHGV)

David began to remember who God is and who he is to God! David went from sighing in despair and spiritual depression (vs. 1-4) to singing praises to God (vs. 5-6). David went from the Pit of Despair to Praises to God. What happened between verses 1-4 and verses 5-6? As just mentioned, David had a mind shift which brought about a spiritual shift. How did this come about? I believe we need to return to the setting of Psalm 13 and 142.

1 Samuel 23:14-17 we see how Saul who was his enemy and oppressor sought David every day in order to kill him. We see here two words, "But God." God did not allow Saul to capture David. God was intervening in David's life as it was not David's time to come and be with Him in heaven. God had more plans for David to achieve here on earth, so God supernaturally intervened in David's life and did not allow Saul to capture and kill David. If it is not in God's will or

allowance for whatever reason. He has the enemy cannot harm us. David himself probably did not remember this truth at that point in time. This is where David was visited by Jonathan.

As we see in those verses in 1 Samuel 23 how Jonathan being David's close friend had traveled over a long and grueling distance in order to encourage David in the Lord. Jonathan told David to not be afraid that Saul would not get him and how David would rise to his appointed kingship given to him by the Lord through Samuel.

This helped David to see the "But God" truth. Even though Saul was charging against him relentlessly and even gathering more forces like the Ziphits to help him that he was safe in the Lord's hands. David's enemy was to be allowed to only go so far and so close to David. God was in control not Saul. Not even David was in charge – God was. We need to remember this truth as we walk through our valleys. God is the same God now as He was then and is just as much sovereign in our lives as He was then with David.

David was helped to see all of this or be reminded of this through his friend Jonathan. As we talk about God's abundant blessings, we need to remember what a great blessing of God to us are the friends that He sends our way to help us. Our Jonathan friends can help us to look up when we are looking down.

This all moved David in Psalm 13 to begin his upward focus towards God and away from his circumstances. How long did it take for David to stop saying "how long" to the Lord? We don't know. We are not given through the Word how much time passed in Psalm 13 between verses 4 and 5.

Scholars have said that we don't have any exact way of knowing how long it took each Psalm to be written by David. Maybe some were written all at once. Maybe some took days or months to fully write them. Perhaps David wrote several verses and then later added more. This seems to apply here in Psalm 13. Perhaps David in his throngs of depression wrote the first part of Psalm 13. Then David had his great friend Jonathan come alongside him to encourage him. David through Jonathan's help began to remember truths about God and His Checed love for him. David began to remember that God was his Jehovah Gamal and all His great and wonderful blessings that the Lord gives him. He must have been reminded or reminded himself of God's great ability to deliver him from anything. How he could from the Lord be delivered from his circumstance to his emotional and spiritual needs. Even if God did not deliver him from these enemies and it turned out this was his time to depart this earth which is only our temporary home anyway and to go and be with the Lord eternally. It is a win-win situation. David began looking upward instead of downward and it began an inward change in him.

Before Jonathan came to encourage David, he was in this deep depression with nothing but the air he was breathing to hold on to and that was not a good support system. Now David had the Lord to grab hold of. God had seized David's spirit which enabled David to hold on. Even though David felt like he was falling off the cliff he now knew that the Lord in all of His love and strength was grasping and taking hold of David's hand to get him through this.

If you have ever seen a little cartoon or something of a person dangling off the edge of a cliff with someone holding on to him this is how I picture God here with David. This is also how I need to picture God with me as I travel through difficult days. So must you as well. See the Lord Himself holding onto you. Even in the times of your great despair God is there holding on – grabbing your hand so that you will not slip. This is also another one of God's abundant blessings for us. He will never leave us nor forsake us and is always holding on to us.

Remember the story of the person who was struggling and walking on the sand? This person looked back on the sand and saw there was only one set of footprints? He might have felt that he was walking through it all by himself What in essence we are told are the footprints that he saw were the Lord's and not his. Jesus was carrying him through it all. A good story to help us to see how the Lord is with us even when we feel we are alone. Even when we like David cry up at times "how long Lord" He is still actively carrying us. Allow Him to carry you. Give in to His loving arms. David did and so can we! Even when like I was today so discouraged and down that I told my friends I want to be alone –Jesus was here with me and carrying me.

Jesus will strengthen us. Even if we don't have a close friend to do so like David had Jonathan, we can know that Jesus is our Friend and will carry us through. Jesus will hold us. Jesus will enable us to carry on. Jesus will encourage us to keep going even when we don't desire to. Jesus will overpower the enemy that is oppressing us to again enable us to keep on fighting. Jesus will help us to be bold in the face of the enemy and dire circumstances. Jesus will enable us to prevail and be victorious no matter the outcome. Jesus will hold strongly with us. I believe David was reminded of all these truths in one way or another which caused him through God to have such a mind and spiritual shift that we see in Psalm 13. This resulted in his upward viewing of God. We can also have this even in our darkest of hours. Like David we need to lift our eyes up to the Lord.

I'm reminded of the time in Mark 6 when Jesus had his disciples go over to the other side of the Lake while He went to spend some time with the Father. During that time a great storm arose on the Lake and the disciples had difficulty in rowing over. Enter in Jesus as He walked on the Lake. So many truths to be seen in this event. Jesus is God as only God has such power over the elements as to be able to walk on water. There is more…

As Jesus was approaching the boat it says that He intended to "pass them by." This phrase had been so confusing to me until further study brought to light what was meant there. Jesus would not have just simply kept on going as they struggled with the storm. That is not what is meant there by how He would pass them by. It means instead just like God passed by Moses to reveal who He was, and His glory Jesus was now going to "pass by" the disciples revealing His glory to them. The glory of who Jesus was would "pass by" them like God did with Moses. Jesus was about to sweep over them with a blazing picture of who He is.

Scripture tells us that the disciples were filled with great fear not only with the storm but also in seeing Jesus walk towards them as they first thought Him to be a ghost. Jesus calmed them by speaking with them. How incredible the ways the Lord works in us. Here Jesus calms their fear and terror by speaking with them. We can also experience God's speaking to us when we are in the Word. God speaks to us through His Word. God speaks to us through the Holy Spirit residing in us. God speaks to us through our friends and circumstances but here in point Jesus calms them with just His words.

Jesus encourages them to take courage. To rise out of their fear and trust in Him. The gospel of Mark does not speak to when Peter also walked on water. For that we need to shift to Mathew 14. Here we see how Peter was taking Jesus' words literally to have courage and he said that if Jesus told him to that he would also get out of the boat and walk on the water with Him. Jesus gave him that directive and Peter being Peter does what he did so many times and goes at it. He gets out of the boat and walked on the water towards Jesus.

However, Peter also having another side of being Peter began to falter. Peter began to take his gaze off Jesus and onto his circumstances – being in a storm and walking on water. He does good and cries out to the Lord to save him and Jesus immediately takes a hold of Peter and raises him up from his slipping into the water.

When our circumstances are like we are in a fierce storm our peace is not ultimately found in the storms or circumstances changing but rather our peace is found in Jesus Christ Himself. Peace is not found in the absence of the storms but in the person of Jesus. Jesus never promised us smooth sailing as we walked here on earth and even the opposite of that in this earth, we will have troubles. Just look at Jesus' own time here on earth and what He endured. Our first line of prayer should not always be for the Lord to take away our troubles but rather to experience His presence even while in the storm. The storm did not stop when Peter stepped out of the boat, but it continued. What changed was Peter's focus which at first was on Jesus. When he faltered the Lord did not condemn him and let him drown but reached out and took hold of him.

Without Jesus we will sink with the storms that come at us. Like David we will even question God as to how long is He going to allow this to continue. Thankfully, like Peter we see in Psalm 13 how David's focus was changed to look up and have his gaze fixed on the Lord. So must we in our dire circumstances of life. Our fears can be replaced with peace. The peace that only Jesus can give you. Fears are foundationless where there is the presence of Jesus. Our experiencing the presence of Jesus becomes more real when we fix our gaze upon Him while in the dire straits we pass through.

Jesus then takes Peter with Him, and they get into the boat and then the storm is subdued by silence that the Lord gives to it. Jesus first wants our focus to be lifted to Him. He desires for our spirit to become more entwined with

His. Storms can have a way of doing this for us and then even in the middle of a storm we can walk in His peace. The peace of His continual presence with us.

Jesus is there to give you victory amid apparent defeat. Even if in His sovereignty He does not remove the obstacles or problems when we want Him to that He is still there with us orchestrating events for our good (Romans 8:28). He can give us eye of the hurricane moments to help revive us to keep on going. Even amid your storms, fears, anxieties, PTSD episodes, depressions and dire circumstances we can know like David and Peter did that God loves us and cares for us and is sending us His blessings from above. One of the greatest blessings is the experiencing of His presence with us.

This is also what David was doing in Psalm 142 in verse 7. Just like Psalm 13 where at the beginning of Psalm 142 David was in deep despair. Yet he began to recall how much God loved him and would pour out His great Gamal's – His blessings – to him. How this helped transform and renew his mind to trust in God.

What we need to do and attempt to do in our valley times is to surrender to God and the truths of God and take hold of Him like David did. Like Jesus did to Peter. Brace ourselves on the truths of God and God Himself. Rest in the Lord and who He is and how much He loves us and cares for us. Stay in His Word. Be in prayer and talking with the Lord. Listen to the Lord. Seek out friends that you know can help you and don't isolate yourself from them. Yes, there are times when just like Jesus did, we go and pursue alone times with the Father but be careful not to isolate yourself overall.

You may feel at times just like David did and again yes like Jesus even did that God has abandoned you. "But God" – we must fight on knowing who God is and who we are to Him. Feeling that God has abandoned you is a lie from Satan, and we need to fight off his lies and his half-truths. Replace Satan's lies and half-truths with the full truths of Scripture. The Holy Spirit is at work and in the process of reviving us, refreshing us, sustaining us, establishing us, providing for us and driving us on. There are also blessing from God. Lean upon the Lord and surrender to Him. Let us remember and not set aside in our thoughts and hearts all the many and abundant blessings that God has for us and has in store for us. Remember that God has His Checed love for us and all that that entails.

Remember – one of the great blessings that God has for us is that we can be in and experience His presence in our lives. We always have His presence with us in the Holy Spirit residing in us at the moment of salvation and then never leaving us. However, we don't always "experience" this blessing of feeling God's Presence – but we can as we pursue Him!

The Presence of God is such a wonderful blessing that each believer has for now and eternally. This is what David was experiencing as he went from spiritual depression to spiritual revival in Psalm 142 and in what we just looked at in Psalm 13. I hope that as we looked at Psalm 13 and the end of Psalm 142 how God was active in His work in David's spirit and heart that he will also do this for us too.

For me. For you! Plus, how David was active in the process of refreshing in the Lord as well.

As we close out this section of the "Solution – Found in God" and beginning our next section "Solution – Seeking God's Presence (David's Part)" we will see how the two blend together. God being God and leading the way and being the causative action, He also calls us to be involved in the process. I've heard that saying to "sit back and let God do it." That is true but only partially true. Yes, we sit back and trust in God but that does not mean that we just sit around doing nothing. I agree there are times when we are so depleted that we crash but even in the crash times we are called to lift our eyes to the Lord. That is our active participation in this process of spiritual revival.

With all of that in mind we can now focus on what did David do to participate in this process. We are going to do this by walking verse by verse through Psalm 142 and see what he did. Let me give you a little "spoiler" –David's main battle ground armor was to focus on and seek the Presence of God. Let's explore that more now.

IV) SOLUTION – SEEKING GOD'S PRESENCE
(DAVID'S PART)

Before we begin our verse-by-verse study of Psalm 142 to see how David fought back I would like to do a brief overview of what God's presence is. This should then flow right into verse 1 and verse 2 as we will see how David sought the Lord's presence. With the Lord's presence David was unable to fight back against the enemies' relentless pursuits of him both in the physical realm and spiritual realm. Seeking God's presence was the key for David's spiritual revival and is also for us.

Seeking God's presence does not mean that we as believers could ever lose His presence in our lives. I agree that even for a believer there are moments when we "feel" that God's presence is not with us – but that is simply not true. We cannot let our feelings rule over what the truths of Scripture so clearly tell us. Seeking God's presence is more for a believer of "experiencing or living" in the sense of His presence. Since as believers we are always in His presence yet there are times when we can feel we have lost that. For emphasis here as a believer we have not actually done so but rather have lost the sense of His presence which is different. For a believer then a seeking of God's presence is more of a seeking to experience His presence, to sense His presence and to live in His presence.

In the book of Acts we see the Holy Spirit come to indwell every believer at the moment of salvation. The Holy Spirit is not a secondary blessing of God but comes upon – into a believer at the very moment of salvation. This is a Scriptural truth to accept and believe because that's in the Word. The Holy Spirit is always indwelling a believer at the moment of salvation and will not depart from them even though again it may "feel" like He has in actuality He has not.

Let me give an illustration of this. In one of my visits to Estes Park, Colorado I had a hotel room that was right on the edge of town near the entrance to Rocky Mountain National Park. My room had a view right to the front range of the mountains. It was as if they were right there, and I could reach out and touch them. I had no doubt that the mountains were there as I could plainly see them.

One day the clouds rolled in, and the view of the mountains became obscured to the point where I could no longer see them at all. I did not ever think for a moment that the mountains had picked themselves up and left and that I would never see them again. I simply knew that at this time the clouds made it impossible for me to see with my physical eye, but my mind knew that they were there because I had seen them with my own eyes before.

That afternoon once again the mountains became visible as the clouds rolled away. This can be with us at times in our humanity that even as believers there are days when the clouds of our despair or troubles "seem" to make God disappear and that He has left us. Even David fought this at times and would cry out to God as to where He was and that he didn't feel Him. When those times hit us (and they have hit me too many times I sadly must confess) we need to fight back with the truth that we know that we know that God's presence never leaves us – even when we don't "feel" Him near us.

Once a person is saved, they immediately receive the Holy Spirit, The Spirit of God is eternally with them. Jesus said this very truth in John 14:16 the He (the Holy Spirit) will be with us forever. The word forever is interesting. Do you know what it means? It means "forever." Forever does not mean one day there and another day gone depending on if we did something "wrong" as a believer. God is the One who saved us, and God is the One who keeps us. Here are just a few verses including some truths in the Old Testament as well.

"It is the Lord who goes before you. He will be with you; He will not leave you or forsake you. Do not fear or be dismayed."
– Deuteronomy 31:8

"Keep your life free from the love of money, and be content with what you have, for He has said, I will never leave you nor forsake you."
– Heb 13:5

"For the Lord loves justice; He will not forsake His saints (believers). They are preserved forever, but the children of the wicked will be cut off."
– Psalms 37:28

"When you go out to war against your enemies and see horses and chariots and an army larger than your own, you shall not be afraid of them, for the Lord your God is with you, who brought you up out of the land of Egypt."
– Deut 20:4

"For the Lord will not forsake His people, for His great name's sake, because the Lord has been pleased to make you a people for Himself."
– 1 Sa 12:22

As a side note to this truth of God's eternal never leaving presence with a believer those verses also reveal that as we live in that truth it can influence our fears. Fears can sometimes begin to rule over us and take us on a drive into depression. But as these verses tell us as we realize and hold on to the truth of God's presence in our lives then this can be fuel for the Holy Spirit to drive out the fears of our lives. Knowing this truth of God's presence in our lives and then the seeking of Him in a deeper sense can affect our drought times and revive our spirits.

God's presence with a believer is eternal and it is guaranteed by God Himself who puts His very name on the line in saying this. He does this because He loves us so much and once in His hand no one including ourselves can deliver us out of His hand which also means His presence. Once truly saved – always saved. Once given the eternal presence of God in the Holy Spirit – we are always in His presence.

Those verses we just looked at reveal that the Holy Spirit is always with us eternally. They also show that He is with us in our daily battles as well. When we step out into battle – God is with us. When we are afraid Jeremiah 1:8 tells us that we are not to fear as God is with us. God said the same thing to Joshua when he took over for Moses. In Lamentations 3:57 we see that God is the One who pleads our soul's cause and redeems our lives and when we call upon Him. Thus, our fears can move away just as the clouds move away from the mountains.

Our anxieties can be lessened and tossed into the sea as we see in Isaiah 41. All because we live in the truth that through God's presence, He can filter out our fears. He doesn't stop there but then says that He will strengthen us, help us and uphold us by His power. Experiencing God's presence is to wait upon Him.

The word for "wait" in Hebrew is Qavah (kaw-vaw). It means to rely on, completely rely on, put hopes in, look for, expect, to look eagerly for, to bind together as by twisting. That last part is very revealing. Waiting upon the Lord is not just sitting in a chair waiting for a bolt of lightning to come down out of heaven. Waiting upon the Lord – to experience His presence – is to bind ourselves together with the Lord more and more and twisting together our spirit with His spirit.

Spending time with Him and getting to know Him deeper and who we are to Him is waiting upon the Lord. This will greatly enable us to know that we know that we know that even when the clouds obscure our previously clear view of God that He is always there. Again, this is not always the easiest thing for us to do when we are amid a trying time or depressing episode but the more we train ourselves in this truth the more fuel the Holy Spirit has in us to move us beyond our doubting times and into the truth times.

This is what David did to fight back against spiritual depression. This is the pathway we need to take as well. As we walk verse by verse through Psalm 142 it will give us some more insights as to how David practically applied this truth of seeking God's presence into his life. David progressed on a journey to see God for Spiritual refreshing and revival during his emotional and spiritual depressions. Through it David was personally involved in the process with God as he was seekig out the Lord fo deliverance.

As I was styuding Psalm 142 I saw a list of 10 "action steps" that David had or developed which helped him to reach out and also experience God's presence within his troubles of circumstances and troubles of soul depression. Following is the list of 10 "action steps" of David that he used to fight back.

DAVID'S ACTION STEPS TO FIGHT BACK

1) David starts out by saying "I cry out"
2) David developed an "Upward Focus"
3) David "Surrendered" to God's Presence
4) David "Keeps on Keeping on" seeking God's presence
5) David "poured out his sorrows and pain" to God
6) David "Knew Right Theology" – Truths About God
7) David "Waited" Upon The Lord
8) David "Personalized" His Relationship With The Lord
9) David knew the phrase – "But God"
10) David was motivated to "Give Thanks" to the Lord

Let's begin now our journey into how David fought back as we walk through Psalm 142 verse by verse and see how there 10 "action steps" flow from it.

~ Verse 1 ~

"I cry aloud to the Lord; I lift up my voice to the Lord for mercy."

"I cry out desperately that we – You and I Lord – can gather (in Your presence) that we can be joined together as I shriek from my anguish caused by my dangers. My heart is disturbed within me, and I am directing my cry to You Lord. Let us join together as I cry out loudly as if it was thunder being heard as I speak and listen to You. Unto You O Lord I beg for your generous favor as You graciously stoop down and bend down from Your heavenly thrown to be together with me. You are the King of kings and Lord of lords while I am just a man, yet You stoop down to be and gather with me in these circumstances of my life and troubles of my soul." (EHGV)

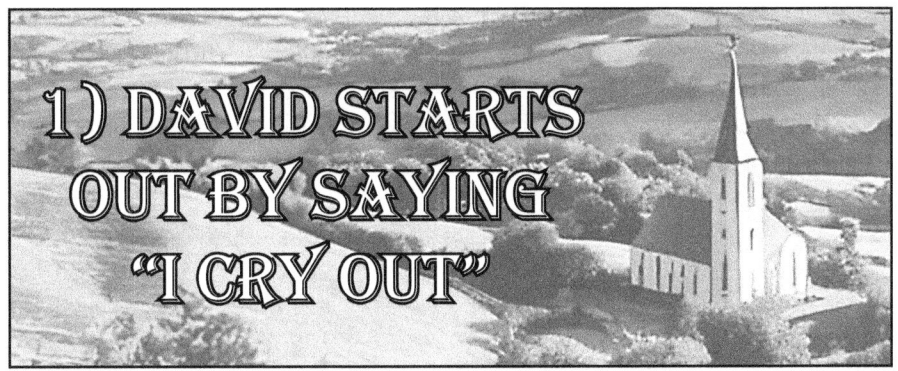

1) DAVID STARTS OUT BY SAYING "I CRY OUT"

In Verse 1 we see David's journey of his personal footsteps he took to participate with the Holy Spirit to move from spiritual depression to spiritual refreshing/revival. Perhaps it might be a phrase that could be overlooked because it seems so simple in nature but can be a great starting point for us to fight back – cry out.

The Hebrew word for "cry out" is Zaaq (Zaw-ak). It has the obvious general meaning to cry out, ask, complain, pray, call for help. Complain does not mean here to be like what we would normally associate the word with. We might feel that to complain is to be winning about something. But it means here more of a lifting up of one's circumstances and how things are going in an honest way without the sense of "winning" about it. It is not like what we feel a little child might do when they don't get their way or even an adult who acts like that. I've had some obvious rough days and at times I will share that with some and at times I was told to stop complaining. That was not my heart, but it made me feel as if I was wrong in sharing what was happening or how I felt. My heart was "usually" not in that respect of complaining but simply more of an unloading of my heart and feelings to someone or various people to help me to download what was inside me.

To unload what is piling up inside of us, especially for someone fighting PTSD or depression can help us. It is much like we might call clearing the air. This can be therapeutic at times if it does not flow into the woe is me and murmuring about what is going on. This is more of what this Hebrew word contains in that aspect. It is an unwinding of what is piling up inside of us that needs a way out.

Zaaq can also carry with it the meaning to shriek from anguish or danger and to cry aloud or out for help in times of distress. It is a cry from a disturbed heart in need of some kind of help. Anguish and distress are closely connected when one is experiencing excruciating or acute agony, grief, heartache or misery. It is a great pain and anxiety with either physical or mental (emotional) suffering. There is an ache inside of someone where it just does not seem to go away.

David was not embarrassed or ashamed when he felt like this. In fact, this was just the opposite as it was his honest heartfelt cry out to God with how he was feeling inside. One is not less a Christian when they get to this point or seem to live in these emotions for a period. Some "believers" can even look down on other believers who go through this as if they were less a Christian for feeling like this and that they simply did not trust Jesus enough to just get over it. I am sorry for those who have experienced this additional pain of rejection from those around them. But take heart… God says, "I am near to the brokenhearted, and to those who are discouraged."

The word "near" speaks of a personal relationship. God won't abandon you or look down on you or consider you less a believer when you are struggling in this area. He won't push you away out of dislike or fearing you might say something wrong biblically about Him while you are in this state. He stands with you! He is your personal ally and friend.

The word "brokenhearted" is in reference to those who feel they have been smashed down, shattered to pieces, injured, broken down, rejected and thrown away, shipwrecked. The seat of your emotions, passions and very being have gone through so much pain and suffering. Many of those around you may not understand and may even walk away instead of being the helping hand of the Lord to you. But God – He is always there. To those who are discouraged – Jesus is there.

As I circle back to the word "zaaq" there is also another meaning in the Hebrew besides the action of crying out to the Lord. It also means to be called together and to be joined together in your time of anguish, danger or despair. Our times of distress physically, emotionally and spiritually can be some of the greatest times for us to encounter the Lord in a deep personal way that we never would have without the trials we were facing.

It could be compared to hanging on for dear life to Jesus and that is good. It is in these troubling times where we can feel His hand and presence with us in a deeper way. I am sensing that right now as I am writing this. One purpose of this book was for me to preach to myself and to sense God's presence in me directly and this is happening right now for me.

As I am typing this, I'm watching a video of Jerusalem. I am feeling out of sorts and depressed this morning and right now I sense the Lord is meeting with me. He also sent a phone call from a friend who has also experienced some deep pain lately. Together we have been endeavoring to help each other and that was a blessing from the Lord too. God hears our pain inside. At times we literally cry out for help and at times our spirit cries out. God hears them both. David cried out to the Lord from a desperate heart that was in deep pain and agony. If no one else would hear, then David knew that at least the Lord would.

David did so as we see here in verse 1 literally with his voice. He wept loudly as if thundering. Again, the word voice carries with it the meaning of being together. Bound together with the Lord who is the Creator of the Universe and loves us literally to death. This is not a bad place to be in our joining closer together with Him in our times of times of anguish and pain. Sometimes we can keep all of this bottled up inside ourselves and that is not good. Crying out to God with your literal voice or spirit is a way you can release the waters of your pain to be refreshed by the Lord in a special way.

2 Chronicles 20:9 sums up this truth of crying out to God in our distress, "Should disaster, trouble, evil things, ruin, adversity, distresses, dangers, depression, evil strongholds come to pass to us in a form of a military attack and battles from those who are wielding swords at us violently or judgments or destruction and even dying of starvation due to these attacks we will still stand, remain, endure and rise up to be caused to stand with the Presence of God whom we can depend upon as we are aligned with him. God puts His reputation on the line to be with us. And we will Zaag – cry out to God and be joined together with Him in all our troubles, distresses, sufferings, anguishes, afflictions and tribulations. God is listening to us and paying attention to our troubles. Let us Zaag – cry out to God in prayer that He will be our Jehovah Yasha to deliver us, help us, protect us, bring us victory, enable us to prevail (no matter the outcome), to be delivered and saved in this battle." (EHGV).

What a great rallying cry and that is also a cry we can shout up to the Lord and be joined together with Him as we face our battles. The person who was doing this crying out to Lord in that verse was Jehoshaphat. That can be our cry too. The word used there for evil when he says, "if evil comes upon us" can also mean depression, evil strongholds, great wickedness, sinful practices, evil schemes. That specific meaning or part of the meaning of evil might not have applied there to Jehoshaphat but it can be applied to those who are suffering from those things.

I have more recently concluded that PTSD and subsequent episodes, depression, fears, anxieties can have their roots and strength from the spiritual realm. Peter tells us that Satan and his demonic forces are in constant spiritual battle against us. They attack and scheme as to how they can trip us believers up. I don't see demons behind every little corner, but they are real and are fighting against us as God says they are.

In our battling back as we should we need to see that this spiritual battle we are in requires spiritual weapons. Crying out to God is an act of prayer. Whether it is silent or shouting it from the rooftops. This crying out to God was a powerful piece of David's arsenal to fight back against his spiritual depression. This helped him to enter an experiential presence and awareness of God in his life amid the battle that was raging around him and inside of him.

We must also FIGHT BACK! We must not let the enemy have the high ground and victory in this. We already have our victory in Jesus Christ eternally and we can also live in the victory that He has for us in our daily walk too. A very good first step to fight back is to "cry out" to the Lord with all your heart. This is a prayer offered up to God.

2) DAVID DEVELOPED AN "UPWARD FOCUS"

I see this second point of David's participation as one that could also be somewhat overlooked. It is vital that we like David develop this Upward Focus to God. Who is David crying out to? It is the Lord! David's first go to person was God. This is also very much connected to my third point of David's participation in seeking and or surrendering to the Lord's presence. However, I wanted to touch on this point #2 first as a segue into what is I see as our focus here – God's presence. For here let me introduce this topic by looking briefly at how David's focus was upward.

As David was facing so many troubling situations and then subsequently troubles of his heart and soul he first went to the Lord with his troubles. This reveals an upward focus that David had here. David did not always have this right upward focus. David, like all of us, can struggle with letting our focus be turned inward, outward or downward instead of upward towards the Lord. David in Psalm 142 reveals this upward look to God. Here are just a few areas that I saw:

1) Vs 1
I cry aloud ——— TO "the Lord."

2) Vs 1
I lift up my voice ——— TO "the Lord."

3) Vs 2
I pour out my complaint ——— BEFORE "Him" (In His Presence)

4) Vs 2
I tell my trouble ——— BEFORE "Him" (In His Presence)

5) Vs 5
I cry ——— TO "You" Lord

6) Vs 5
I say ——— YOU are my refuge
YOU are my portion

6) Vs 6

I cry for help ——— Listen Lord

7) Vs 6

I need rescuing ——— Listen Lord

8) Vs 7

Set me free from this prison my soul is in ——— YOU are the causative action to bring this about Lord!

When David was faced with seemingly insurmountable problems, he had this upward pursuit and looking to God. He floundered at times but fought back by resuming this upward pursuit of God. Psalm 56 which was probably also written right during this time period as when Psalm 142 was written by him David says in verse 3, "When I am in this journey of life there are times when I become much afraid and even terrified of events surrounding me. When those times come, I will trust in You. I will feel secure in You. I will have confidence in You." (EHGV) This reflects David's upward looking at God from the valley that He was in. When you are in a valley of life – Look up to God!

David echoes that same thought and action in verse 11 when he says, "In God – Elohiym – I will put my trust and have as my source of security. I will not be afraid. Since I have Elohiym as my God and security what can man do to me? Nothing!" (EHGV) When David had as a driving purpose in his life to look upward to God he was in reality seeking God's presence. This seeking of God's presence is one of the most vital cornerstones of our active participation in fighting back against our PTSD, depression, anxieties and troubles as they come and at times surround us. This is my third Participation Points that David did. Let's look at this – Seeking God's Presence or even better than building on that and Surrendering to God's Presence in our lives.

3) DAVID "SURRENDERED" TO GOD'S PRESENCE

First of all, what is that I mean by surrendered? Surrendering to God is yielding to Him and His power. It is a giving up of ourselves over to Him. To give up all of ourselves over to His sovereignty. I also see very strong that surrendering or yielding to God also involves a deep and persistent seeking of God. Surrendering to God is yes for sure a "giving up" of ourselves to Him but it is also a major step in "fighting back" in our battles with spiritual depression.

Surrendering is Seeking God's Presence! This is the heartbeat of this whole section of how David fought back against his spiritual depression. Surrendering to God's Presence. Experiencing God's Presence. This can be done even during dire circumstances and inner soul depression. This was David's focus and desire. To seek God's presence, surrender to God's leading presence and to experience God's presence.

The topic of God's presence is all throughout Scripture. God's presence is so wrapped around everything that the Holy Spirit even used a multitude of Hebrew words to keep getting the depth and importance of this to us. Let's spend some time exploring some of the Hebrew words that express the importance of seeking, living, and experiencing God's presence. We have already just looked at one of those Hebrew words – Zaaq.

ZAAQ

A) Zaaq – just as a brief reminder as David was crying out to God, he was in essence seeking to be in God's presence – to be gathered with Him. As the storm was swirling all around him David desired above all things here to be gathered with the Lord. Flip back just a few pages if you desire to review what we studied there about "zaaq."

YASHAB

B) Yashab (yaw-shab) another Hebrew word of God's presence. Psalm 27 is another Psalm written by David when he was also in a time of being actively pursued. Scholars don't know for certain when this Psalm of David was written. However, it was certainly not written when David was on the seashore enjoying a restful vacation. David had evildoers coming upon him who wanted to kill him. These enemies he described that were surrounding him made him feel he was in a besieged city with no apparent way out. War was raging against him. In this Psalm like David wanted in Psalm 142 was to be in God's presence.

Verse 4, "The one thing above all things that I urgently request of the Lord and one that I will search for, chase after, and desire is to be in Your presence Lord. To dwell and abide with You. To remain with You. To spend time with and rest in You. I desire this all the days of my life. I want to gaze at, perceive and personally experience Your kindness, beauty and splendor. I desire to seek You out and search for You deeper and deeper. To examine who You are and to then meditate and contemplate all that You reveal to me about Yourself. Amid being in this besieged place that I am in – You are who I desire." (EHGV).

I hope that portrays the depth of David's heart that even while in such dire straits his one thing was to be in and experience God's presence. David did not want to just know about God and study God for the sake of study, but David wanted this to bring him to a place of deeper intimacy with God. A deeper relationship that no matter what storm is raging around him that he could always know and have an inward sense and reality of God's presence. David didn't first ask for all of his problems as serious as they were to be automatically taken away but rather David first desired God's presence! He wanted above all else to gaze upon God and who He is. Following in verse 8 we see how he would then be lifted up over his enemies. Seek God's presence first.

David would slip at times and as we have looked at. He even occasionally wondered where God was and why had God abounded him. Although in truth God had not but he still felt that. At times we might also sink to that depth, but our driving passion needs to be here where David was in his upward pursuit of experiencing God's presence. David wanted as he said in verse 5 in Psalm 27 in his day of trouble to be in God's presence and His shelter. God's shelter is a reference to obviously being in His presence. Not just to be in His presence but under the protection that His presence would give. That was what David wanted to experience. He wanted God first and above all because He was God. He sought God to simply be in His presence and then there were blessings that went along with that. One such blessing as we see here was to be under God's protection in a deeper way.

Being in God's presence allowed David to look down from the perch of God towards his troubles and enemies which then gave him a whole different perspective on things. David was rising above his circumstances and troubled heart not on his own initiative or by his own doing and strength but by God's causative actions on His part to David. David's participation here – diligently seeking after the prescience of God. This seeking of God's presence is Holy Spirit fuel to move forward.

This pursuing of God's presence by David is not a ho hum thing that you do once every month or two. It is not a special occasion type thing that we do. It is a relentless pursuit daily – even moment by moment as we walk through the day. This is what David was saying in Psalm 63 when he was in a wilderness time.

Even in the wilderness times he would seek after God. Diligently seek God. Earnestly seek God. Rising early in the morning before the day starts in order to seek God – to thus experience God in a deeper way. When our souls are overwhelmed by whatever is hitting us what and who we need above all things is God Himself. Again, as believers we always have the presence of the Holy Spirit in our hearts but at times we don't experience Him. This can be simply because we are not doing this diligent and earnest pursuit of Him. God's presence is what we need. God's presence is what we should desire to then experience Him in a deeper way.

C) Paniym (paw-neh) – another Hebrew word for expressing the presence of God. Going back to Psalm 142 verse 2 we see David using the phrase "Before God." This is the Hebrew word paniym – "I pour out my sorrows BEFORE God…" This is probably the most common Hebrew word people refer to when thinking of God's presence. In many places in the OT, it is translated as "face." It's like saying "the Face of God." Paniym meaning in essence the Presence of God.

It is not just being in God's presence, but it also refers to God's power. Thus, experiencing God's presence is to experience His power. God's power is characterized by His rule overall. God's sovereign rule. The Hebrew word paniym goes even deeper as it also means to intercede. To intercede with His presence using His sovereign power. God's presence does not mean that He is just hovering about watching all things happen. Paniym strongly reveals God's sovereignty in that He intervenes with His powerful presence.

So when David was in great soul depression he was pouring out his sorrows in verse 2 surrendering to God's power, God's sovereignty and God's loving intervention into his soul and circumstances.

When we feel we are alone and abandoned by God's presence we need to have the truths of this word etched into our hearts and minds. God can and will intervene for us as we seek Him out. And even when we are too dried up to even seek Him then God is still here to raise us up and protect us through our troubles. It is not dependent upon us for God to intervene in our life but our participation in surrendering to Him and the seeking of His presence enables us to "experience" His presence more.

God's presence is His active intervening on our behalf especially when we are living in difficult times through the circumstance in life. This also includes the trials of an overwhelmed heart and soul. This is exactly what David was experiencing in Psalm 27 when he was earnestly seeking God's presence. When David was in great turmoil, he sought God's presence with all of his heart and soul. He then experienced God's intervening power to lift him high above his enemies.

God's intervening on our behalf might not always happen in our timetable but God says He will intervene with His presence and therefore He will. I am experiencing a soul depression today as I am writing this section and I am seeking right now God's intervening presence in my heart. I was feeling very distraught and out of touch this morning as I woke up. This was a day off from work for me and my first thought was to work on things with my baseball cards. I had a card show coming up, so I wanted to get ready for that.

As I mentioned I was not doing very good in my spirit. Yet even in that I firmly felt the Holy Spirit nudging at me to not let my baseball, football, basketball and hockey cards be the first place I visited this morning. I was attempting to place the Lord first as I began my day by getting into the Word. But still as I studied the valley was not turning into a mountain top experience.

I felt like I just wanted to pack everything up and go live by the seashore or mountainside. The depths of my soul fatigue were sinking ever deeper. But at least I was still fighting on. As I kept studying, I kept sensing God's presence more than I did several hours before when I was just starting. I wish it was stronger but at least again I'm not as low in the valley as I was when I woke up. God was lifting me up from the valley of soul depression as I sought His presence.

What is vital for me and us to see is that as I put in the effort and desire to seek Him. Then the clouds began to evaporate a bit. Not fully as I would like but maybe I am seeing some of the tree lines that I know lead up to the mountain top. Some days this is what we face and live in. Not where I would like to be but better than before.

I am seeking the Paniym (presence) of God right now. I am attempting and trying to live out what I am preaching here in this book I am writing. I want to cry out for God for more and to take me higher. But at least I'm better than I was a few hours ago. More than likely a few of you reading this can completely understand where I am at right now. Let me encourage you to keep on keeping on as I am trying to do right now. It's not easy, but I must keep climbing. I need to not only know of the truth of God's Paniym presence of how He will intervene in my life, heart and soul but to trust that He will.

With even a bit more self-disclosure here I even feel like condemning myself for feeling this way with this soul depression and not being able to come out of it. I know some others may say and feel that I must be doing something wrong since I keep slipping into these doldrums of the soul. Maybe I am and perhaps God has not yet revealed that to me, or I am not listening closely enough. I don't know. All I know today I am struggling with being in a valley but wanting to not stay here. I truly desire to hike up into the mountains of God with God but right now it is a struggle. I will keep on writing at this point trying to battle through this rough day I guess that I am in.

When I am studying I usually have a peaceful video playing and this particular morning I have a video of riding in a train and seeing it as the conductor sees it. The train is making its way through the valleys of the Swiss Alps with various stops in towns. The train gets higher and higher as it goes into beautiful scenery as it elevates. I desire to be there so bad right now. I desire to be able to be in Estes Park where I used to be able to visit quite a bit but now I can't even fathom when I'll ever be able to get out there again. I say and feel like I am stuck here. Stuck here in my doldrums of life and of my soul. I desire to climb higher with the Lord.

But I do see that I am still fighting back I guess by studying this morning and seeking God's presence. Today I feel like God's presence is His intervening to simply keep me from sinking further down. It might feel like I am just treading water, but I am still above the waterline. I need to see and preach to myself right now that even in the "just" treading of water days that God is still with me. God is intervening in me to keep me from going under. Just when I almost literally drowned as a young child God sent my cousin Maureen to intervene to save me from going under. So today God is also intervening in my life with me experiencing His presence to keep me afloat.

It just hit me that maybe this is what David felt like at times too. Like he was just treading water and fighting not to go under. Maybe I need to adjust my thinking and see it as not just treading water to survive but climbing up the mountain. I might be at the base of the mountain but at least I am climbing. Better yet it just hit me that maybe I need to see myself not at the base of the mountain but rather that I am already way up on the path and some clouds have simply rolled in that makes me seem like I'm in the valley.

At one point in my life I was in an active pursuit of becoming a pilot. I wanted to be able to go to Alaska and be a bush pilot. I was at a flight school in Colorado and while there I got two ear infections. Having ear infections and flying in a non-pressurized small plane do not go together. Because of that I was not able to keep flying and I had to leave that dream for a time. Or I thought it would be just for a time, but I never got back into that path of being a pilot.

However, while I was there at the school that I was attending I did learn a lot. One thing was that on cloudy days when you are flying, and you can't see anything out the window that you are not to focus on what you see out the window but rather on the instruments in front of you. If you focus on the window and all you can see are clouds, then at some point you will become disoriented and lose control of the plane. What a pilot needs to do is trust his internments which can guide him through the clouds.

That is in essence I guess what I am feeling right now today. This morning I feel like I am flying with clouds all around me and it is hard to navigate my way around. Even as I am attempting to fight out of it by studying God's word and spending time seeking Him the clouds are still there. Maybe not as thick as when I woke up, but they are still there.

What I need and must do at times like this is to trust my instruments. My spiritual instruments of truth of who God is and who I am to Him. All the truths of God that we have looked at even in this short book are full of truths of God that right now I need to trust. I need to trust in God and who He is more than my feelings right now. Are my feelings real? Yes, they are. My feelings of despondency are just as real to me now as the clouds are real to a pilot on a stormy flight. But I need to trust in God. I need to trust in my spiritual instruments when I can't see so clearly with my eyes. Trust in knowing the truth that Jesus' Paniym presence is here with me intervening in my circumstance and my spirit – even when I "feel" He is not because He is. I need to trust my instruments right now. The instruments of truth.

This sense of disorientation, lack of direction and focus along with a sense of being alone can come and go but God always remains. God's presence always remains even on the cloudy days. I can't know obviously what your cloudy days are like. But I can experience with you the effects of the clouds. The clouds that I have are different from yours along with some of the results but whatever they are they can have similar devastating results in our lives and in our hearts. They can push us into a deep dive of soul depression.

I have shared some of the clouds that have come into my life that have obscured my spiritual and emotional vision. From my battles with PTSD, I have experienced the cloud of abandonment by some. There have been close people to me who have said that they simply cannot handle some of the ups and downs I have due to my PTSD episodes and so they have left the participation of my life. Another cloud for me is that some have said that they are not psychologists and therefore can't help me, but I didn't need another counselor I just wanted their friendship.

I could go on with some more clouds that I experience but it would just end up being a ranting rave on my part and I'll save you from all that. Just to say we all have our clouds that can at times prevent us from seeing clearly around us. Trust in the Lord even more so in those times. Even when friends and family pull away their presence in our lives God will not. Jesus is ever present with you as you are His child.

As we have been seeing, David had many clouds in his life. Clouds of circumstances and clouds of despair. David also knew one of the paths to be able to navigate while in the clouds was to know the truth of God's presence in his life - even while in the clouds. God's intervening presence in his life was there for him to experience even while amid the clouds.

Psalm 18:4-16 reveal how David experienced God's intervening presence. Those verses give a great and "poetic" way to see the sheer power, majesty and depth of God's innerving paniym presence in his life and ours and especially during our times of great troubles and soul depressions.

We can see in Psalm 18 how desperate David was plus how he fought back by seeking out God. Verse 7 shows how God responded to David's situation and his pleading for help. The following briefly shows God's responses back to David as David was calling out and reaching out to God in his deep distress. In somewhat of a poetic way here is God's responses to David.

Vs 7 – The earth shook and quaked.

The foundations of the mountains trembled.

Because – God was angry at what was happening to David.

Vs 8 – Smoke came up out of God's nostrils.

Fire came out of His mouth to devour.

Vs 9 – God bowed the heavens with thick darkness under His feet.

Vs 10 – God rode upon the cherub and flew.

God sped upon the wings of the wind.

Vs 11-12 – God's brightness passed through the darkness and around Him came hailstones and coals of fire.

Vs 13 – The Lord thundered in the heavens.

God uttered His voice and again hailstones and coals of fire came out to David's enemies (even the enemies of his soul depression)

Vs 14 – God sent out His arrows and scattered David's enemies.

God's lightning flashes came in abundance and routed David's enemies.

Vs 15 – At the Lord's rebuke the foundations of the world were laid bare from the His rebuke and the blast of His breath and nostrils.

Wow, if you can fully explain all that to me, please get a hold of me and share. It is so amazing and so full of God's power and love for David that can't fully be explained and even understood by us. But the truth is He is there for us with His presence in our times of deepest darkness. God will thunder forth from heaven and do whatever He needs to do in order to intervene into our lives. What was the result of God's intervening paniym presence in David's life?

Vs 16 – God took David and drew him out of his many waters to be on high.

Vs 17 – God delivered David from his strong enemy and from those who were his enemies and who were too strong for him (but they were not t too strong for Almighty God!)

Vs 18 – The Lord was David's source of security in his day of trouble.

Vs 19 – The Lord brought David into a good place of rest for him.

Vs 19 – The Lord rescued David - BECAUSE God delighted in David.

God's paniym presence is for us as well as it was for David. God will intercede and intervene in our troubles. God's desire is for us to look up to Him and cry out to Him and to seek His presence. Gods' presence is with us.

I am reminded of how Jesus after He rose from the dead was walking along and talking with two of His followers on the road to Emmaus. Those two travelers that Jesus connected with were experiencing a great sense of confusion. Their leader Jesus had just been crucified and they felt that He was now gone and what were they to do and become of them. During that time Jesus came up to walk along with them. To talk with them. This story from the Bible is a great example for us to hold on to in our lives. Jesus is our constant companion walking along right with us even in times of great confusion that we might be experiencing.

Jesus is directly interceding for us. Jesus is directly intervening for us. Jesus is walking along right beside us and with us! Jesus does this because He loves us. Jesus is committed to us. The word commit means to do, perform, or pledge oneself to a position, issue or a person. I am – you are – and all believers of all time are God's issue. Jesus' desire to bond more together with us is not just observing what is going on with our lives but to rather be personally active, present and engaged with us. Extremely so when the storms hit us. Mark chapter 4 reveals this that Jesus was not only in the boat with the disciples but that He also directly intervened for them. Jesus' love is not just in words but in actions of love. That is what the two travelers on the Road to Emmaus experienced. This is what Jesus' disciples in the boat expereienced when He calmed the storm. That is what David experienced. This is what we can experience.

When God Yatsaed the Israelites out of Egypt along the journey He led them by His active presence exhibited by a pillar of fire and cloud. God reveals Himself in so many ways as to His active paniym presence in our lives. I am praying this today that I can experience God's paniym presence in my life in a deeper way. I know this is a journey of healing, recovery and revival. Just as the Israelites journey from Egypt to the Promised land took 40 years with some difficult times, I know that this journey I am on to spiritual recovery and revival might take some time. While I am on this journey, I realize I will be experiencing moments, days and even seems like years of this constant battle of my soul. Yet through it all I need to keep my eye on the instruments of truth that point me to God and who He is and who I am to Him. The truth is that His paniym presence is always with me.

David knew the importance of living in the Paniym presence of God and living under His sovereign rule. David writes in Psalm 21:6, "Lord You store up blessings, favour and special presents for ever and all time for those who seek and live in Your presence. These blessings, favour, and special presents to us from

You are continual. They are enduring. They never end and last forever and all time. They are eternal in You. In Your presence You give me great joy and make me glad. In You through Your presence I rejoice. In Your presence O Lord is joy, happiness, pleasure, delight, enjoyment, celebration, joy everlasting is in Your presence." (EHGV)

D) Panah (Paw-naw) – another Hebrew word for experiencing the presence of God. This Hebrew word is very similar to Paniym as Panah comes from it. Panah is again to experience God's presence. Which as we have seen is what David was doing here in Psalm 142. In Psalm 25, which was also written by David roughly during or just preceding the time of Psalm 142 we see David in great troubles there too. Psalm 25:16 reads, "I am very lonely and feel deserted and in solitary confinement as I am oppressed and weighed down by my thoughts, feelings and circumstances that are heavy on my mind and spirit. I feel distressed, helpless, burdened, shaky, distraught, afflicted and depressed in my mind and spirit due to my circumstances. Lord, let me Panah You –experience You as I seek help from You. I ask that You accomplish deeds of great mercy for me. I turn and look to You to experience this in my heart, mind, soul and circumstances as You intercede for me." (EHGV)

God's presence expressed by David through the Holy Spirit is not just God observing David's circumstances and his resultant depression It's not David just seeing God but rather to go beyond that and to experience God's intervention on his behalf. Let us be so bold as David was and ask God to intervene for us. God is the same now as He was then. We are told that we can come before the throne of God with boldness. Let us do so. Let us fight the good fight and not let the enemy have the high ground.

PALEL

E) Palel (Paw-lal) is another Hebrew word for experiencing God's presence. Palel means to intercede, pray, intervene. Intervene means to interfere with force. Interfere is to oppose something. Remember Jonah? He disobeyed God and attempted to run from Him. Jonah was just like Adam and Eve when they were caught doing what they were not supposed to do, and they also ran from God. With Jonah God being who He is was not going to give up since He wanted Jonah to go to Ninevah. God was in opposition to what Jonah was doing and so God was going to intervene. Jonah was not going to thwart God's plans and since Jonah was running in the opposite direction in opposition to God's plans God intervened with His presence into Jonah's life – in a powerful way. Jonah's running from God would be a short one. Besides whom can outrun God? Sometimes maybe we think we can too. Better to seek His presence than to run. Jonah learned this the hard way.

Jonah must have felt that if he could just get on that boat then God would not be able to find him and send him to Ninevah. Instead of being on the ocean Jonah found himself in the ocean. Literally swallowed alive by a whale. What did this swallowing up cause Jonah to do? He came running back to God. Actually – he came floating back to God inside the whale. Jonah 2:1, "Then Jonah prayed (Palel)." That was Jonah's part as he prayed inside the belly of a fish. Palel means to pray and a sense of deeper prayer with a pleading for God to directly intercede into his situation – even in the one that he himself had caused.

Jonah knew that without God's intervening presence that he was done for. Jonah would not make it without God stepping into the situation. Let me emphasize this point. Jonah was the one who caused this problem by disobeying God. Jonah was now on the receiving end of God's loving chastisement due to his disobedience. However, this clearly shows that God still loved him despite his disobedience. If you sense or know that your current situation and subsequent depressions are a direct result of your running away from God don't despair as God has not walked away from you. God is like he did with Jonah still coming for you even if you feel He is not. God loves you and He will pursue you. He will pursue you even if the trouble you are in is a direct result of your initial running away from God and not doing what is right.

In a brief look at Jonah chapter 2 we see how Jonah was in deep distress due to his running away from God – which is disobedience to God. As a result of Jonah's disobedience God out of His love for Jonah would not let him stay in his disobedience and because Jonah would not listen to God and follow God this moved God to have to take more drastic actions. This is seen in verse 3 where

Jonah admits that it was God who threw him into the ocean. Yes, it was the other people on the boat who did the physical action of picking him up and heaving him overboard but that was all out of God's moving them to do so. When God has to step into our lives in a radical way in order to get us back on track He will do so because He loves us too much to let us keep going on our own pathway.

Due to Jonah's disobedience, he was engulfed with the currents of the sea and God's mighty waves of chastisement swept over him. God had a plan for Jonah and God is sovereign so He would get Jonah going back in the right direction. It might have felt like to Jonah that he had stepped out of God's presence but, he never did. God's presence was with Jonah even in the being hurled out into the sea. God's presence was with Jonah even while being hurled about in the great tempest waves of the waters. God's presence was with Jonah even while he was being swallowed up by the whale and hurled about inside it. Jonah's right response to all this hurling about – he cried out to God. Jonah through all this turmoil was his desiring a fresh experience of God's presence in his life.

Jonah 2:4 is very revealing to what she should do if we ever sense or feel that God has left us. Jonah through his own wrong decisions had felt God had deserted him and taken His presence from him. When Jonah felt this what did he do? Let's see in Jonah 2:4, "I thought that I had banished and completely driven out of Your presence God. I thought that this was a thoroughly completed action of being thrust out of Your presence by my own wrongful decisions and action. Yet in spite of there feelings and wrong thinking I will once again gaze at and look intently at You God. I will so gaze intently and seek You to be joined together with You and Your holy dwelling place were You reside – I will see Your presence God." (EHGV)

When you feel God has left you and abandoned you - which He obviously has not since Jesus said that He will never leave us or abandon us. (Heb 13:5; Deut 31:6; Josh1:5; 1 Ch 28:20; Mt 28:20.) But when those feelings come upon you know that truth that He has not and do what Jonah did – Seek Him even more so!

Verse 6 of chapter 2 reveals that as Jonah sought God's presence in the middle of a whale's belly his renewed seeking of God was having an affect in him. Just as God was the direct causative action for Jonah being thrown into the ocean, we see that God is also the direct causative action for Jonah being rescued from that dire circumstance. God sent a whale to rescue Jonah, but God was the real One rescuing him. Then God had the whale deliver Jonah onto the dry land. That must have been a great Holy Spirit experiencing moment for Jonah.

When you feel like you are in the whale's belly and in your most dire of circumstances cry out to God to intervene with His presence and actions. God did not abandon Jonah when he ran from Him. Even in his disobedience and subsequent running from Him God ran to him. God will not abandon you either. Cry out to God from your own whale belly circumstances and seek God's presence to intervene and to turn you back to Himself through it all. Even in one's sinful, disobedient paths of actions God is greater than our disobedience! Do again what Jonah did in verse 7 when he was in great trouble and distress – he remembered who God was and he sought God through prayer.

God's presence is His being with us always and forever. God's presence is Him interceding on our behalf directly with His great power and force even when we mess up as we run back to Him. God's presence is Him associating with us as our companion and friend and ally. God's presence is for Him to commit to us to do and perform actions for us as He has pledged to do. We are bound together with Him on clear days as well as on horrific stormy days. God's presence brings us into His security to prevail in and through our troubles. God's presence is sufficient and adequate for any need we have. God's presence is abundant in all His greatness and all His unlimited resources. All of this is God's presence in our lives.

The Holy Spirit continues and gives us other Hebrew words for the depth of meaning of God's presence as we discover more here.

F) Matsa (Maw-tsaw) is another Hebrew word associated with God's presence. Psalm 46:1, "God is our refuge and our source of safety. God is our hope and our shelter from the rain, storm or dangers. God is our powerful stronghold who makes us secure. God thunders down loudly and boldly for us. God is absolutely and continually present with us as our One who helps us and supports us. God is the one who delivers us from troubles, distresses, calamities, problems, afflictions and our subsequent anguishes." (EHGV)

God's presence. The Hebrew word here for presence is Matsa. It has a rich depth of meaning to add to what we have already seen about God's presence in David's life and our lives. Matsa means to be found, encountered or gathered. In essence what we've already discovered that at the root it is for God to be with us and us to encounter Him. This is especially true as this verse says when we are in trouble.

This word Matsa also means that through the troubles God's presence will cause us to prevail. Even if the troubles do not automatically disappear that through God we will prevail. With God's presence we are secure. With God's presence we will be spared. With and through God we can prevail with His presence even while we are in the midst of our troubles. Through God we will win out and find victory even in what seems like defeat. Even if death is the trouble one is fighting through God we will prevail. This great defeat of death is a believers ultimate victory – our eternal victory. Through Jesus Christ whatever our present darkness is we must know that God is still our light.

God shines through any darkness even through the darkness of death. God reigns therefore, we can be triumphant even in our storms of darkness and despair. Our depressions don't have to dominate us as we can abound in Christ's victory.

Some of you might be experiencing this darkness of depression and rough times right now and you may not be feeling victorious now. Perhaps it has been like a constant battle raging in you and around you. Let me encourage you to Keep on Keeping on. Keep on fighting back. The mountains might feel like they have gone away because some clouds have obstructed their physical view, but they are still there. The dark clouds that can seemingly make it feel like God's presence has left you are not the truth in the matter. God has not left you as His child. God's presence is still there with you. Keep fighting back to experience His presence.

I have gone through these same battles repeatedly. It's where I experienced several long days of depression and PTSD episodes, and it seems like it is never going to end. At times during it all I don't "feel" God's presence with me but I'm learning to keep on reminding myself that God's presence has not left me. I can't be ruled by feelings that are simply not true. God's presence has not left me even in the storms. God is gathering me together with Himself and through the Spirit I am enabled to prevail. It is not easy when those times hit but I must continue to fight to sense and experience His presence. I pray this can be true for you as well.

God is sufficient for us. God is adequate for our every need – even in the need of deliverance from depression, anxieties and PTSD episodes. God is all sufficient in all His abundance and love for us. We are richly supplied through God's unending and unlimited riches. We are filled to the top and can overflow to others even in our storms because of God's abundance in us and for us. That is God's presence in our lives that we can experience even in the storms. Know these truths and fight to live in them.

At times our storms can seem to never end. Our battles with depression and anxieties caused by whatever troubles we are in or have encountered may have been going on for some time. They seemingly have no season of breaking or rest. David felt this and experienced this for sure. As you read through David's Psalms you will see how loaded they are with this same theme time after time after time. David was in an almost constant state of battling with his enemies outwardly. These then in turn produced the inward battles that kept him running spiritually with subsequent battles with his PTSD and depressions.

The underlying truth in all his victories over his battles was David's realization of God's continual presence with him. God kept on revealing this truth to David time after time and with many varied Hebrew words. I firmly believe the Holy Spirit wrote about this truth of God's presence with us so often because of the deep truth that it contains for us in our battles. God doesn't repeat things just for the sake of filling up space. When God repeats a truth repeatedly then we must sit up and take notice.

With that in mind I have one more Hebrew word reflecting God's presence with us in the storms. It is found in Psalm 69. David wrote this Psalm which also reveals his deep depression with the overriding desire for God's presence to outshine the darkness that he was experiencing. This is our next Hebrew word revealing that God's presence is always with us and is found in Psalm 69.

G) Qarab (Kaw-rab). This Hebrew word used by David also carries with it this need and desire for God's active presence in his life. It means to be near, present, be there, draw near, draw closer, got closer, approach. It is the most near and intimate presence of the person and entails actual contact with that person. It is entering into battle together as an active helper for the other one. God being the One helping us. As we see it means to approach. Yes, God approaches us, but this also implies that we are to be in the process of approaching God as well.

Psalm 34:18 tells us that God is near to those who are or feel broken, shattered, destroyed, shipwrecked, crushed, cut off and broken hearted. This verse goes on to say that God is near to those who are discouraged and crushed in their spirit. Through it all God is nearby. The Hebrew word used there is Qarowb and is associated with Qarab as it comes from it. That Hebrew word Qarowb expresses with it to have a personal relationship with the other person. God's active presence in our lives is derived from our personal relationship that we have with Him through Jesus' saving power at the cross. Through Jesus' sacrifice at the cross and the forgiveness of our sins we have an active and intimate relationship with God. This is what David was seeking to experience with the Lord during his time of trouble in Psalm 34.

In essence the circumstances surrounding David when he wrote Psalm 24 are a precursor to Jonah's story that we just touched on. Psalm 34 was probably written by David just prior to his writing of Psalm 142. Psalm 34 revolve around the time when David was fleeing from Saul and ran for protection to Achish King of Gath – the Philistines.

Do you remember who the great enemy of Israel was when David was just a shepherd boy? It was Philistines! Do you remember who David defeated in the great encounters he had? It was Goliath. Do you remember who Goliath was? He was a Philistine! And when David killed Goliath he took along with him the spoils of war – his gigantic award. This same sword of Goliath David was now carrying with him and some people Gath (the Philistines) discovered it. How do you think the Philistines felt towards David? Not very highly!

David knew this and along with running from Saul he also now feared Achish the King of Gath – the Philistines. Not a good position to be in. David should have been trusting in the Lord as he ran from Saul but instead he ran to his countries enemy – the Philistines. Not a good idea to run from one enemy into the hands of another enemy for safety. Run to God! Jonah ran from God too and felt the consquences. Then Jonah turned and sought God again. Psalm 34 is also a reflection of David seeking after God after his mistake too. Read Psalm 34 as you can with this in mind. Now let us continue to Psalm 69.

The other Hebrew word Qarab then flows us into Psalm 69. Psalm 69 jumps right into this theme of being in trouble with its title of "A prayer of distress." Looking at the context of the Psalm we can see that David felt like he was drowning. He was exhausted in his search for help. I have felt this time after time in how distraught I have felt after or during a period of depression with a sense of helplessness filling the air around me. It is exhausting. It is exhausting living in that and exhausting trying to fight out of it.

I have learned that this is why I can feel so drained for days after I have walked through an episode. Most cannot understand what it is like to be triggered and enter an episode that can last for a short time or stretch into days and then as you fight your way out to then feel drained for days after that. Then at times to be almost immediately triggered by something else to begin that cycle all over again. It is like fighting to come up for even a short breath to be able to keep on fighting from drowning. How can one fully explain this to someone who hasn't experienced this and to then be understood by them. If others cannot we can know though that God does. And that God also will never leave us or abandon us through it all. Even if others might God will not.

David experienced these in and out episodes as we see all through the Psalms that he wrote. As we said we see this also in Psalm 69. David right after the title then in verse 1 says that the waters which in the Hebrew expresses that they are floodwaters. Floodwater can bring great destruction as they move along their path and David was directly in their path here.

These floodwaters as a result were beginning to attack and overtake his emotions, passions, desires and the very depths of his soul. It had devastating results in his life in every way. These outward disturbances were affecting his heart and soul in a major way. He had, as we see in verse 2 of Psalm 69, fallen into the depths of a slimy mire where he could not get a foothold. He had wearied himself out with crying and his spiritual eyes were fading. Ever feel that way yourself? What to do?

This could also be a whole chapter or more in a book itself, but we will jump in and take a jet tour of some things that David did to fight through this turmoil around him and inside him. Verse 3 is very insightful to what David did and what we should also be doing in these times. David said that while experiencing these floodwaters that he continued to wait upon the Lord. Wait here does not mean to just sit around wallowing in our despair. It means to trust in God through the pain and suffering. It goes on to the idea of waiting in expectation for the Lord to act on our behalf in one way or another. It is a looking for and expecting God to intervene and for us to experience His presence through it all. Jonah stayed in the whale's belly for three days. Probably not a pleasant three days but Jonah waited upon the Lord also then with this same expectation that God had his best interests in mind.

In the Hebrew the bottom line from this word for waiting upon the Lord is to be patient. That is so easy to do when the floodwaters have lifted all around us right? No, it is not easy. But this was David's heart and desire, and we must strive to make it ours as well. I'm preaching at myself right now to better live in this patient endurance with an expectation for God to move in and through it all.

In verse 9 we see that even while living in these floodwaters of circumstances and the subsequent spiritual sense of drowning David did not give up. He did not let the floodwaters that were engulfing him to fully overtake him. David turned his attention and heart and pursuit to be in the presence of God. This was his zeal as we see there. Zeal is to have an intense devotion towards and for something or someone. It is your passion. David's focus shifted from the floodwaters to the One who controlled the waters swirling around him. An outward focus from his circumstances to an upward focus on God. To experience God's presence in the storm.

I have found out personally that this is such a key weapon in my battle when a trigger happens that could send me into an episode. I carry with me a pack of index cards with names of God on them. If I can react quick enough when a trigger happens, I can reach into my bag of index cards and thumb through them till the Holy Spirit rests me on a specific name/epithet of God that He uses to help me fight off this initial trigger attack. This has helped me out so many times that I see its powerful effect in me. This is that upward focus to God replacing the outward focus of the circumstances around me. I'm not always successful in reaching into my bag of index cards as I would like but I am gaining ground in this area. I would consider this a part of having a zeal for God especially when the floodwaters are beginning their course towards us.

David then continues his active pursuit of God's presence in other ways as we see in verses 13-15. David prays to God in verse 13. This is an active pursuit for God's presence. He then in verses 14 and 15 david cries out to God as he reaches out to Him for help. David does not want to go under but feels like he is just about to. He appeals to God's love for him which he knows is real and forever. David has the right theology and then he appeals for God's presence.

David goes deeper with this desire in verse 17 as he appeals for God to not let His presence go away. Then in verse 18 he cries out with this Hebrew word Qarab for God's presence again. This is very key that David wants God's presence in his life for his soul to persevere through these floodwaters. David wanted to experience God's presence in the seat of his emotions, passions, mind, appetites – his inner self his soul. David was in the depth of soul depression, and he so sorely wanted to experience God's active presence in his soul to revive him and to keep him going. There was no other way David knew by which he could overcome this soul depression except through God's presence and experiencing His presence. Friends are great when fighting through soul depression, but God is the ultimate soul pleaser and reviver.

Our PTSD episodes and depressions are spiritual in nature. Our anxieties and emotions come from within even if ignited by outward circumstances. The battle front in our spiritual depressions and our soul depressions is ultimately rooted in the spiritual realm. They arise from such varied things and even to possible chemical imbalances some have but clearly here David was seeking God's divine intervention in his spirit for his ultimate help.

In a previous section we saw how all of David's circumstances had affected his emotions and spirit to the point of him developing PTSD and the subsequent episodes and frequent bouts with anxieties and depressions. David realized how his spirit had been so affected by his circumstances that he now reaches out to God for help. Let me repeat – knowing this is such a key point in our battle plan against the enemy. I am not saying to stop going to a counselor or to stop taking any medications that a doctor has prescribed but what I am saying is that God must be at the core of our battle front and plan. God is the key ingredient to Yatsa us out of it all. Without God nothing is a permanent solution. Without God nothing has the deep effect for lasting impact. We need God's active involvement in our spirit in order to properly be in the battle like we should be and to be victorious in this battle. David knew this and so must we.

David knew that he had an active part in this as well. He was to draw close to God (Ps 119:169). Jeremiah says this also in Lamentation 3:54-58. When the waters were overflowing in his life, and he felt cut off Jeremiah cried out to God. He knew God would draw near to him and so he fought to draw near to God. Jeremiah and David were in a battle for their spiritual lives. Let this be our example to follow in our battles and ask God to invade even more so in our heart as we draw near to Him.

Draw near to God. The Holy Spirit who is residing in us and living with us will fight for us. He will fight for us in our spirit to combat our soul depressions. This is such a vital truth to know and live in as we do this battle. Draw near to God. This includes so many areas in which we can be engaged in. We can read and study the Word. It includes our times of prayer and worship. It is a meditating on God and who He is plus who we are in Him and to Him. It is meditating on His truths. It can be memorizing these truths so that the Holy Spirit can then retrieve in us when needed. It can be taking a walk with God talking and listening as we go. There are so many ways we can draw near to God and experience the Spirit's presence in our spirit. The Holy Spirit lifting us up closer and closer to Him.

As I have said before, but this also deserves repeating that as we draw near to God it will not mean that our circumstances or even our depressions will automatically disappear into the night. Jesus still went to the cross after a fervent night of prayer with the Father. God's plans may include our being in the storm for reasons I don't know but God does. Remember that Jonah was in the whale's belly for three days. God did not immediately "vomit" him out right away. There are things to be learned while in the belly of our own whales. There are things to be learned while sitting in the cave. Continue in your seeking of God!

Whatever or however God decides within His sovereign plan for us know that God is there for us and with us to strengthen our spirit. To revive our spirit. To refresh our spirit. To quicken our spirit. To teach us and guide us through it all. And at times to simply survive in and through the storm.

Whatever the need the Holy Spirit is able, ready and desiring to help us with His active experiential presence with us! I need to be open to Him and draw near to Him. I need to talk with Him and listen to Him. This was David's theme in these first few verses of Psalm 142 as we swing back to that Psalm.

We have spent time here looking at many Hebrew words to get us to see God's active presence in our lives. I still feel we have not scratched the surface of this topic. Let me challenge you to dig deeper in your own private study on this truth of God's presence in your life. This could activate more of the Spirit's power within you by which you can do battle with the enemy in your battle with PTSD, anxieties and depression. Ultimately it is God's battle and through it He calls us to be active participants in it with Him and through Him.

This awareness of God's presence is the main theme of how David was able to fight off his soul depressions. His rough circumstances bringing on to him his soul depressions were a constant battleground for David. Yet he fought back. A huge part of his arsenal was this truth of God's presence with him. Seeking and surrendering to the Presence of God. This is what we need and must do as well in our battles for soul revival and soul refreshment.

Let's continue on in our journey through Psalm 142 as we discover more action steps that David took as he fought back in his battles of spiritual depression.

~ Verse 2 ~

"I pour out before Him my complaint, before Him I tell my trouble."

"Lord, I am bringing to You the full weight of my grief, sadness, fear, and discouragement – I am dying inside. I have nowhere else to go but to You as I pour out my heart – my emotions to You. I am here completely pouring out my soul – the seat of my emotions and all that I am. You are the only one who can help me. All my anxieties and distress and troubles I am coming to You with. I ask that as I am pouring out my soul to You that you will change me – change me to trust You more. I need Your heart guarding peace. Let me sense Your presence as we meet in this prayer. While others may hear I am praying specifically here to an audience of one – You! I come into Your presence to be lifted by Your presence.

As You know I'm surrounded by trouble. These dangers and adversities make me feel like I am in a strait which is being pressed in with nowhere for me to go. The storms are raging all around causing great turmoil around me and inside me. There is such distress and anguish in my soul. I am therefore pouring myself out to You. I am empty inside and so I empty myself into Your hands - into Your presence."

David does not hold back when he goes to have time with God. He pours out with intensity what is in his heart. What did David pour out? Some translations say it was his complaints. I don't really like that word complaint here as I feel it is not the best translation for the Hebrew word that is being used. When we think of complaining it's more of finding fault or dissatisfaction with someone or something. Complaint could also mean telling one's pain which is what I sense was David's heart here. With looking at the context and such I just see that David was not coming to God and finding fault and murmuring about his situation. We will look further into the Hebrew word used here in just a bit but let me do just a brief overview of the entire verse before we break it down further.

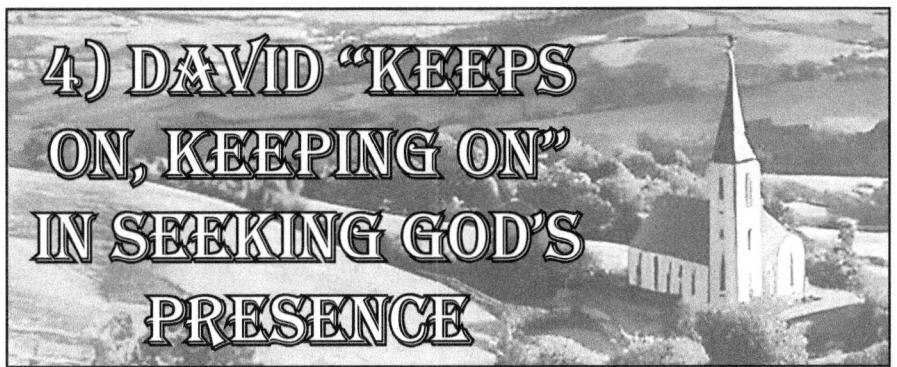

4) DAVID "KEEPS ON, KEEPING ON" IN SEEKING GOD'S PRESENCE

In verse 2 as we are discovering our fourth step into how David himself fought back against his spiritual depressions during his dire circumstances. In this I see three more Participation Points he had put into practice that we can learn from to help us fight back as well. One is the reminder of what we have already studied from verse 1 and that being to seek God's Presence. The other two Participation Points are wrapped around this major truth of seeking God's Presence. David keeps bringing this up so we will keep looking at it as well. Obviously, the Holy Spirit sees this as a point to keep drilling into our hearts and spirits.

Let's look again at the Hebrew word that David uses again here in verse 2 on seeking the pretense of God that we looked at earlier. I bring it up here again just as a reminder and review. The Hebrew word used again here is Paniym. Most translations use the word "before" and that is a good translation and is ok but as we looked at that Hebrew word Paniym it carries with it a deeper meaning.

If you are before someone you could say that you are in their presence and be accurate. But what if that person you are with does not care if you are there or even acknowledge that you are there? Then to be in their presence to impact you does not matter too much. It is of no or at best limited benefit or blessing to you. I worked in Washington D.C. for a little over a decade in my earlier years. The company that I worked for had numerous gatherings or parties on Capitol Hill that our office held in order to connect with Congressmen(women) and Senators to try and voice our thoughts concerning issues we felt were important for us. As with all other staff I was able to attend these gatherings. Did the Congressmen(women) and Senators care at all that I was there or come over and talk with me? Absolutely not and I did not even expect them to. I was virtually nonexistent to them.

I do remember one time back in my DC conference days on Capitol Hill where our head legal counsel was attending one of our gatherings and he came over to talk with me. At that time, I did not even know that he knew my name or that I even worked with the same company as he did. He did not have an office in our building but worked elsewhere. But here he was with all the "important" people he could reach out to and connect with to talk with, but he took the time to come over and talk with me. I was somewhat surprised by this in a good sense and felt important that in a room full of "important" people that he came over to talk with me. He approached me. Here I was from a small town in Illinois at a gathering of vital people who were making huge decisions and our head legal counsel sought me out to come and talk with me.

My encounter with our head legal counsel reminded me of what our relationship is with the Creator of the universe. A bit of an analogy of how our heavenly Father is with us. As He is holding all things – ALL things –together and orchestrating ALL events and guiding ALL believers He is also connecting with me and seeking me out!

God's presence though differs from the encounter I had with our head legal counsel. God's presence goes so much deeper. The Hebrew word there signifies that in God's presence we are overwhelmed. Overwhelmed with His presence. Overwhelmed with God Himself. The word means to take care, determined, approach, advisor, come alongside, constantly, interceding. God is involved in my daily life, my daily needs, my daily problems and concerns and then does something about it.

God is approaching us. God as He is holding the whole universe together and orchestrating all things, He is also taking the initiative in approaching us! There are times when we simply get wrapped up into our own daily events that we don't seek out God like we should. We have a game to go to. We need to get to the store. We need to take a nap. Connecting with God can be put way down the priority line. We've all been there. For those living in depression simply don't seek out God because we are just overwhelmed inside and are not in the right place or state of mind. Unfortunately, we then don't pursue the One who can help us out.

Thank God that He pursues us! God approaches us! Then in the power of His Almighty power He moves on our behalf. David knew this and so he raised up his voice and attention and prayers to the One who could help him and understand and care and do something about it. David knew that God could either alter his circumstances or strengthen his spirit to help him overcome or prevail through his circumstances. This is the blessing we have as God pursues us and we step into His presence seeking to encounter Him. Keep on keeping on entering God's presence.

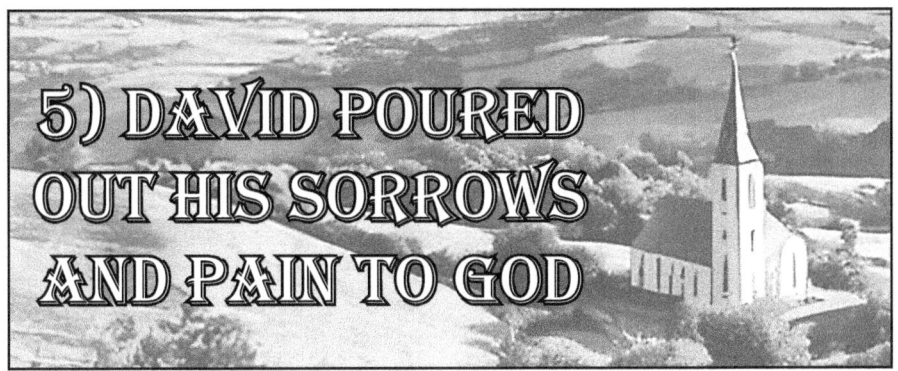

5) DAVID POURED OUT HIS SORROWS AND PAIN TO GOD

A fifth step by which David takes to keep fighting back for spiritual revival is seemingly a simple one – he pours out his sorrows and pains to God. David poured out his "complaints" in God's presense (Paniym). There are several key words there that we will look at individually and then see how they flow together. First let's look at the phrase "pour out". That's pretty much what it means in what it says. They Hebrew word latterly means to pour out, spill out, dump out, gush out. This is all done with intensity. It also has a deeper sense to put out one's heart and oneself. It's passing from one container to another. We are the one container that is pouring out, spilling out, dumping out, gushing out with intensity to the other "container" – God Himself.

This is where the meaning of Paniym comes into play. God is not a passive stand by person who then gets overwhelmed when all His children all at once pour out their souls to Him. Quite the opposite. He listens to each one of us. He cares for each one of us. He intercedes and moves on behalf of each one of us. Each one of us are His beloved children. God is there for you individually wanting to have that personal connection with you. Or better put wanting you to experience that personal connection with Him. Pouring out our hearts and troubles to Him is a way for us to do this connecting with Him.

This is the connection that David is seeking to have with God here in Psalm 142. He is in a troubling situation which is impacting his heart and soul. He knows he needs help, so David turns to the One who cares for him. David turns to the One who he knows can intercede for him. David turns to the One he knows who cares for him and can carry him through these difficult times. David is not just whining about his troubles, but he is taking his sorrows to the One who can do something about it.

When Jesus was in the Garden lifting His deep prayers to the Father He was not complaining or whining about the difficult task of what laid ahead of Him in the coming hours and days. Jesus was pouring out of His heart to His Father in heaven whom Jesus knew cared for Him and was there for Him. We can apply this to our lives and our situations. Pour out your heart and soul to the Lord above who is there for you and cares for you.

I believe God also gives us friends and families here by whom we can pour out ourselves to as well. God gives of Himself to us through such friends and family. Things in life can pile up on us. Those who are struggling with anxieties and depression these everyday "pile ups" can have such a negative impact as to trigger us into something deeper.

This reminds me again of what a close friend has tried to tell me when I get triggered. Mike (my friend) tells me to try and "Pump the brakes." Pumping the breaks for me is being able to pour out verbally to someone else when I am triggered or having a bad day. Something suddenly happens or someone says something to me that triggers me. At times it is hard for me on my own to "pump the brakes." This is when I really need God to help me to do so. Many times, God enters this by using other caring people around me who are willing and able to simply listen to me as I pour out my struggles.

When I am in desperate need or simply in need of some relief, I don't see this "pouring out" as complaining. What I am doing is just sharing what I'm going through. I am being hit with something that is triggering me and I am simply trying to pump the breaks by releasing them to someone else.

It is a blessing to those who struggle with depression to have that friend who can be there in these times. One who can simply listen when we are struggling and need a caring set of ears to just hear as we pour out our sorrows. Not as a complaint but to release. This helps us to reconnect and move past it. We always have the Lord to run to and He also gives us each other to do this with as well.

This is what David was doing with the Lord. David was pouring out his heart to the Lord by simply stating the truth of how difficult his circumstances were and how they were impacting his soul. The Hebrew word for complain here is siyach. It means to be deep in thought. It can also mean to be distressed, in pain, filled with anxiety or troubled. It is to lament, which is to express one's feelings of excessive sorrow, grief or pain. It is to mourn deeply. It is like a deep spiritual groaning that naturally flows out of us when our hearts are troubled. We should not keep that inside of us. It is not good to store up that in our mind, heart and soul. It can start to corrode us within our spirits. Pouring out of our heart and soul to the Lord and to others who are there for us is a good thing. David practiced this time after time with the Lord.

The Holy Spirit encourages us to follow David's example in our own prayers. We are to bring all our inner sorrow, pain, grief, turmoil and troubles to Him. Bring it all into His presence. It is not noble to keep things all bottled upside us and never pour out to God. In fact, this bottling up works entirely against what God wants us to do. He desires us to bring all of ourselves to Him. Our joys and our struggles. If we keep it all inside, we are basically telling God that we can handle it all on our own. That we don't need God's intervention into our lives or His presence when troubles and distresses hit us. That's so wrong. If we don't share with the Lord (and yes with others too whom God has given to us) then it becomes an inward focus that "you" can handle it all. That "you" can juggle all your situations and struggles alone. That "you" don't need anyone when you get distressed or troubled in your spirit and soul. You don't share because people might think you are a weak Christian. Don't let yourself get into that pattern. Bring all your struggles, fears and troubles to the Lord. What a blessing it is to then also have a trusted friend or friends with whom you can also safely pour out your heart, soul and mind when needed.

David was a man after God's own heart. David took on the giant Goliath when no one else would. David took on lions and bears single handed in order to protect his sheep. This same David would break down and pour out his inner soul in deep desperation to the One who could and would help him.

This participation point that David did for his inner healing is also a vital one for us to participate in as well. Pour out yourself to God. He already knows what's going on around you and inside of you. He wants you to connect with Him through it all. Connect with God! Pour out your struggles to your loving and caring Father who is there for you. He is waiting for you to come near to Him. What a privilege we must do so. What an honor we must do so. God is our ultimate answer so let us run to Him and pour out our hearts to Him.

Verse 2 of Psalm 142 continues with this same thought and action pattern. This says to me that the Holy Spirit desires for us to get this truth drilled deep into our hearts. It says that David "declared his troubles" in God's presence. Again, the Paniym (presence) of God and all that this entails.

The Hebrew word for trouble used in verse 2 is the word Tsarah (Tsaw-raw). We have already looked at that word, but it needs a review here as this word encompasses so much of what the Holy Spirit is trying to convey to us as we encounter struggles in our lives. The word for trouble here is more than just having a bad day. It's more than just being late for work and saying you are in trouble with your boss. This again is where our English words can't fully convey what is being said here. This Hebrew word Tsarah (trouble) goes so much deeper.

The trouble here that David was expressing to the Lord and experiencing is one of excruciating or acute distress, anguish, adversity, calamities, afflictions, suffering and pain. A calamity could be described as a great misfortune or disaster. It's like a flood which can wipe away everything in its path. It can also be related to our lives as well when seemingly all is lost, and all has been rushed away in a moment's notice. It feels like we have been hit by a surging and destructive flood raging through our lives. It is catastrophic in nature and can be widespread. It affects all areas or most areas of your life.

These outward floods of troubles can result in bringing on an inward sense of agony, misery, grief, sorrow and torment. This can then affect a person physically, emotionally and spiritually with great intensity. Confusion and disorientation can manifest themselves along with it as a result.

I have been told that the brain's neuropath ways got all jumbled around and they are not connecting like they should. If someone receives head trauma and they suffer from some of these same effects most people around them understand and rush to try and help them. But I've found out that if our neuropath ways of the brain have gone astray due to emotional trauma then people are not so quick to understand and reach out a helping hand.

This is so unfortunate, and I have personally experienced this as probably some of you have as well. But God is still there even if all others or most walk away because they simply don't get it or even try to understand. David even experienced this "people walking away from him" at times. It can be devastating to someone who is suffering from this emotional and spiritual flood that has hit their lives. Instead of being there for someone it is easier for some to just walk away or fade away from the one who is suffering.

One thing that David did to help him reconnect his damaged brain neuropath ways is by repeatedly bringing his troubles to the Lord. The Lord also brought to David during one of these difficult episodes was his friend Jonathan. We talked before of how Jonathan traveled a great distance in order to help David encourage himself in the Lord. We need more Jonathan's who are there to help people through these difficult troubles of the soul. There is a help wanted sign out there for God's soldiers to help those of us who struggle at times just to get through the day. God is there! God send us your foot soldiers as well.

David's first steps of racing into the throne room of God are seen here in verse 2. He boldly declares before God this deep anguish that he was in. This heartache, grief, sorrow, misery and the suffering of his soul that he was experiencing due to all his troubles surrounding him. More so than the troubles of his circumstances were the trouble within his spirit. He brought it all right into the presence of God. David knew that God was there not only to listen and understand but also willing to act intensely and directly on his behalf.

David wanted and needed the Lord to intervene first in his spirit. David wanted to sense and experience God's presence to help his spirit to fight back against it all. Then the surrounding circumstances can take on a different perspective. This is a good pattern for us to follow as well.

The word "boldly" also hit me as I was studying this out. To come boldly before someone is to come without hesitation. To go immediately to God with your inner soul depression and anxieties. There are no rules here in how to pray when we are in such deep distress and in need of God's intervention and presence. There are times when everything around us and in us seems so chaotic that we just need to run fast into His presence and pour it all out. Boldly come into the throne room of God we are told. On your knees, standing or walking. Crying out to the Lord with your voice or in silent inward talking with Him.

Coming boldly to God also means you are not worrying about the opinions or judgments of others. You are in desperate need of help from God, and you know it. When I was literally close to drowning when I was a kid, I was not casual about my reaching out for help. I didn't just say well ok I guess I will go under. No, I yelled out as best as I could, and I kept throwing my hand up out of the water as I was going down and coming back up. I knew I needed help, and I was yelling for help as best as I could. Come before God with what is in your heart.

Reach out to Him with the desperation of how much you need Him and His intervention in your heart, soul and life.

God is the One who will never reject you. God is the One who will always be there for you. God is the One who truly understands. God is the One who has all the power, love and desire to be there for you. God is the One who can help you in the very best way. God is the One who does this in His right and perfect timing. David knew these truths about God, and he then runs to God and pours out himself to God. A good and solid pattern for us to follow as well as we keep on fighting in this battle, we are in.

~ Verse 3 ~

"When my spirit was overwhelmed within me, it is You who watch over my way, in the path where I walk people have hidden a snare for me."

'Lord as all of these troubles is happening all around me and to me, they have caused my spirit to be overwhelmed. My strength and desires have dried up and have led me to become greatly discouraged even to the point of spirit depression. My thoughts, emotions and energy of life have become so troubled as my life feels like it is uncontrollable. Darkness has enveloped my spirit. I am fainting away with exhaustion and my life is ebbing away.

However, when all this is happening, I also know that You, Lord is paying attention to me. You fully understand from all these trials, troubles and dangers my spirit has slipped into this depression. Through this all You will reveal Yourself to me in a deeper way that I have never understood before. I hang onto this truth. My very footsteps I know are ordained by You the Sovereign One. My path is under Your care, compassion, guidance and control. Yet I feel even now – even knowing these truths about You and my relationship with You – that my spirit is still slipping away. How can this be? My focus is slipping back again to my enemies and my situations. My enemies have intensely and intentionally with repeated actions have hidden traps for me to fall into. They are planning adversity and hardships for me. They desire to bring multiple distresses into my life and bring me down. They are a source and the agents of calamity to me. They want to simply wreck my life as I know it.' (EHGV)

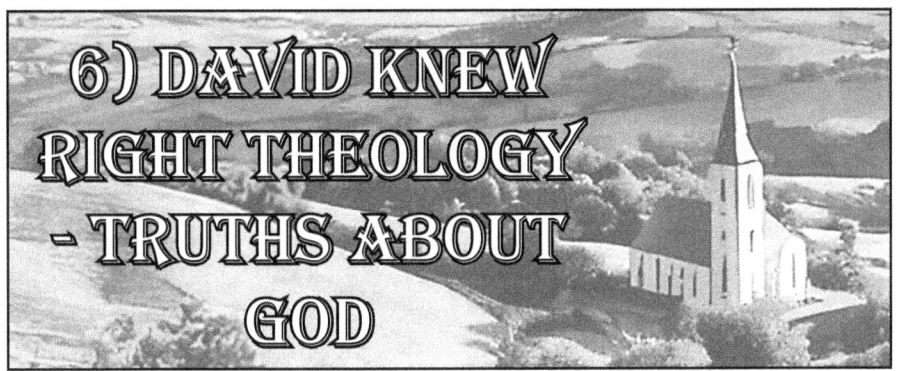

6) DAVID KNEW RIGHT THEOLOGY - TRUTHS ABOUT GOD

David's spirit, his strength, his life's breath was struggling and sinking into the pit of discouragement and depression. David was in despair and overwhelmed in darkness. He felt like he was feeble and fainting away. This is not a guess on my part, but it is exactly what the first two words here in the Hebrew in verse 2 mean – Ruwach Ataph. David was in a dip pit of despair.

However, David did not sit in the pit and wallow there. He fought back to climb out. David put into action and used some more spiritual armor here to fight back. Here in verse 3 we see how David leaned upon right theology in order to fight back. David leaned upon the truths of God that he already knew.

We get this from the Hebrew word Yada. I have felt drawn to this word from the first time I studied it out many years ago. Yada declares that even though David was in dire circumstances and that his spirit inside was overwhelmed into depression he still held onto the truths of what the word Yada reveals. Yada reveals that God fully understood how he felt. Yada reveals that God was still fully determining precisely David's path in life even while he was in the deepest darkest valley. Yada reveals that God is loyal to us even when our hearts are so overwhelmed that we can't think straight. We might slip in our loyalty to God at times, but God will never ever slip in His loyalty to us.

This truth that David held onto here in order to fight back his spiritual depression is seen in other passages of Scripture too (all in NASB here):

Psalm 1:6 "For the Lord knows (Yada) the way of the righteous…"

Psalm 31:7-8 "I will rejoice and be glad in Your lovingkindness because You have seen my affliction; You have known (Yada) the troubles of my heart and You have not given me over into the hand of the enemy."

Psalm 106:8 "When the Israelites kept being unfaithful to God God sill remained faithful to them…" Vs 8 – Nevertheless He saved them for the sake of His name, that He might make His power known (Yada).

God desires for us to see who He is. In His love. In His power. In His faithfulness. Even in the days of our unfaithfulness to Him. This same truth is seen in Psalm 109:26-27. David wanted God to intervene in his life so all could see who God was.

In one of my favorite Psalms 139 verse 1-2 we read, "Oh Lord, You have searched me and know me. You know when I sit and when I get up; even from far away You understand my motives and my thoughts." Verse 4 continues, "Before yes even before what I am about to say You already know it, Lord."

My Mom memorized Psalm 139 before she passed away. I still remember lying in bed and hearing my younger brother, Ted, helping mom to memorize it in the next room. Mom would be in bed and Ted would sit next to her as she worked on memorizing Psalm 139. It wasn't easy for her as the time period in which she was taking on this memorization of Psalm 139 was not the best. In fact, it was probably the most difficult time of her life. She was battling cancer which eventually took her into heaven.

Even while she was memorizing Psalm 139, I could hear her at times even struggle with keeping on going with it. It was a struggle to memorize yet my brother, Ted, helped her to persevere and keep going with it. Was it just to memorize it? No, but it was to pour the truths of what Psalm 139 contained about God into my mom's spirit. Holy Spirit Fuel!

My mom, even though she was literally struggling for her life did not give up. She kept on pouring into her mind, heart and soul the truths about God. Truths about God that she already knew were rekindled in her heart and new truths about God that the Holy Spirit revealed to her as she memorized Psalm 139.

She held onto the truths revealed about God in Psalm 139. "Yada" – God knew my mom and even when she was fighting off cancer my mom knew that God was still divinely sovereign and in charge of her life. My mom took these truths about God that she knew and fought back with those truths. Storing up truths about God is giving the Holy Spirit fuel to help us fight back the soul depressions that can hit us from our circumstances of life.

This is what David did in his participation point – action step – with his ongoing battle to fight off the enemy of his soul depression. Psalm 9:9-10 is so powerful for us and drives this truth home. "The Lord is a refuge, stronghold, defender and protector. The One who provides for our safety. He does this for those who are oppressed, feel crushed and afflicted. God also does this for those who on a regular basis are in danger, distress and suffer from adversity. For those surrounded by calamities and various storms of life that can cause anguish." (EHGV)

Verse 10 continues that even while those who are in such calamities of life that there is a turnaround for the crushed spirit. It is seen again in the Hebrew word "Yada," "And those who KNOW (Yada) You Lord by experience and see who You are we will put our trust, our confidence and our security in You. You make us feel secure in who You are. You are our hope for You will not desert us. You will not abandon us. You will not leave us. You will not let go of any who follow You to seek your guidance. You will not let go of any who search for You." (EHGV)

The Holy Spirit will keep moving us forward as we keep on seeking out the Lord. Seeking out the Lord and getting to know Him deeper and deeper even while we are walking in the valley. Psalm 31:7 says that as we do this in the valley that we can even rejoice and be glad in Him. Even while the storms are raging around us we can still rejoice in the Lord. Is this easy to do? I admit it is not! When we are down in the valley it is not easy at times to even attempt to get up let alone praise and rejoice in the Lord. But with His power we get back up again – and again – and again – and again. When the storms of depression hit, we need to lean on the truths about God and who He is and who we are to Him. To keep looking up. To keep on fighting back. To Keep on Keeping on!

This is clearly seen in Is 40:27-31 which is also one of my favorite passages to lean on. Beginning in Isaiah chapter 40 through chapter 66 we can see an overall theme of God's consolation and comfort to His people as He reveals truths about Himself. He is the God of all comfort (2 Co 1:3) and these chapters in Isaiah have as their aim to reveal this truth about God to us. Our ultimate comfort is in the Lord and Isaiah 40 speaks of Him as our comforting Shepherd. We can be comforted as we know these truths about Him and what He does for us.

Isaiah chapter 40 talks of God's greatness and who can compare to Him (vs. 18). Then verse 21 gives us the first of the two "Do you not know and have you not heard?" phrases. Then verse 28 repeats that. It is like Isaiah is almost saying, "Come on, don't you know (YADA) who God is? Come on!".

Isaiah also gives to Israel and to us this plea to know God – Yada God. The plea to experience God firsthand is seen in verse 9, "BEHOLD your God." Behold here means not to just look at God but to take note of who God is. Pay attention to who He is. Observe who He is. Take a good look at who He is and not just a casual glance. Examine and take the time to see who God truly is. Discover who He is. Watch closely to see who and what He is like. It is imperative that we do this now as well! Come quickly and behold your God!

In verse 28 after Isaiah gives us his second "Do you not know?" as he lists off several truths about God to his readers. This is for us here and now too!

* God is the Everlasting God
* God is the Creator God
* God does not become weary
* God does not become tired
* God's knowledge, intelligence and discernment is unsearchable yet still is worth all our effort to examine them
* God gives strength to the weary (same strength He used in creation)
* God increases the power to those who lack might and strength

Then Isaiah gives us our part – our participation point – our action step. Our first participation point or action step that Isaiah gives us is to know (Yada) God. To behold our God! This is what David was doing and thus giving us the example to follow when the stroms of life hit us. This is the truth that Isaiah was giving to the people of Israel and to us as well. It is a truth the Holy Spirit desires to drive into our spirit. To seek to Yada God. To know who He is and who we are to Him. This is more fuel that the Holy Spirit uses to enable us to Keep on Keeping on through the storms of life. Another participation point or action step that Isaiah gives to us is seen in verse 31. This is also an Action Step of David as well. Let's look at both Isaiah and David's call to our next action Step.

7) DAVID "WAITED" UPON THE LORD

Would you like to more fully experience God's power flowing through you to revive your soul? Take this next action step – Wait upon Him. Exactly what does this mean to "wait upon the Lord"? Let's first look at Isaiah and the Hebrew word used there for "wait." In Isaiah 40:31 it is the Hebrew word Qavah (kaw-vaw). It means to wait with patience. But it goes much deeper than just to sit back and wait for God to do something. It also means to prepare as we are waiting. It means to completely rely upon the Lord while we are waiting. Our hope is in God, but He does not want us to just sit back and do nothing.

As we are in the valleys of life we are to eagerly look for and anticipate God's moving in our lives. These times are also a time to prepare for whatever journey the Lord is going to take us on next. It is a time of opportunity to grow deeper in our relationship with our Lord Jesus. This word Qavah also means to bind together with perhaps by twisting.

That is interesting. As our struggles and circumstances are whirling around us and twisting us up inside it can also be a time and should be a time that we twist our souls tighter and tighter with the Lord. We have already studied out this Hebrew word earlier in our study but since it is so vital it deserves our review here.

Waiting upon the Lord and trusting in the Lord are closely related to each other. Psalm 37:5 tell us to "Trust in the Lord and do good." The word for trust there is the Hebrew word Batach. This is closely related to waiting upon the Lord. It is to have full confidence and dependency upon God. Trusting God is to rely on His integrity, strength and ability. Those are all wrapped up in His love for us.

It is easier to "wait" upon the Lord if we "trust" in the Lord. Trusting in the Lord is built upon getting to know Him more and developing a stronger relationship with Him. Knowledge simply for the sake of knowledge is not our end game. Allowing that knowledge to move us into a deeper relationship with the Lord is a goal we should have.

This is a conviction fueled in us by the Holy Spirit as we get to know God deeper and deeper. Then as we are seeking out God and knowing Him better and developing a deeper relationship with Him, we begin to trust Him more. This is waiting upon Him.

As we are waiting and trusting God, we are then called to take another action step in there and to "do good." The Hebrew word for good there also reflects the truth of "waiting upon the Lord." It is the Hebrew word, Asah. Asah means to prepare, to accomplish, to grow, to advance, to bring forth on the journey as we proceed onward. To do good things.

This "waiting upon the Lord" is a readiness on our part, As we are in the valley we are to get prepared for God to move us up the mountain side and out of the pit of the valley. Get prepared for the next step in the journey that God has already planned out and sovereignty ordained for us – for you – for me. God may keep us in the valley for a period but that is even within His sovereign plan for us and possibly for us to reach out to others as well. We are to wait upon the Lord by preparing for whatever else He may call us to do within the valley or while on our journey out of the valley.

Waiting as we see then is not just sitting around on the front porch waiting aimlessly for God to roll down bolts of thunder on our behalf. Although He does do this at times as we can see in Scripture and hopefully within our lives "waiting" is usually though not a passive event on our part. In out waiting God does not eliminate the reality of His desiring our participation in the process.

I will stress here as well that our participation in the process of waiting up to the Lord does indeed require times of us just sitting down and listening to Him. Am I just contradicting myself here? Let me flow these two truths of action and being quiet before the Lord together.

Jesus slipped away from the disciples often to spend time alone with the Father. Going away from it all to spend time with the Lord in the quietness is also waiting upon Him. There is a combination and balance of these truths here. Spending time alone with the Lord is waiting upon Him. This is a part of the preparedness that we are called to. Usually out of those quiet times we are moved by the Spirit into action. Jesus prepared "to do" by being with the Father. Then Jesus went and did. Being still before the Lord and acting are all connected with "waiting" upon the Lord.

As I stress the times of getting prepared and the doing part, I am also stressing the truth of spending those quiet alone times with the Lord. The doing and quiet times are both in the "waiting" upon Him. There is a balance and a mixing of those truths together to form our waiting upon Him.

I am speaking out of personal experience on this right now. Just this last week or so I had a great experience with the Lord on a night before I was doing a card show. I got a hotel room in the city the card show was in and that night I spent most of the time seeking Him out through spending time in the Word. Through that time, I felt an experience of His presence with me in such a strong way. It was a time I wish I could live in all the time.

But the reality is that eventually I needed to go to bed and the next day get up and do the card show followed by another night of travel to do the next show the very next day. While doing that show an older man came up to my tables and we began some conversation around a vintage Bible card I had out. It was from the early 1900's. It was in German but from the picture it could be seen what the Bible verse was about. From that we got to how he was a retired pastor and I then shared how I was also. It became a time of encouragement for us both.

I hope I am connecting the truths of waiting upon the Lord here with these stories. On one night at the hotel, I spent in quiet as I was seeking the Lord. This was an action step on my part. The following day I was at the card show connecting with a fellow retired pastor encouraging one another. This was also a part of waiting upon the Lord as I was doing action as well. The combination of being still coupled with the going and doing. This is the combined truth of waiting upon the Lord that I feel Isaiah and David had and were trying to pass on down to us.

Moving forward on our journey to fight out of the valley can be a difficult journey for sure. As I wait upon the Lord, I know that since I am still breathing that He has plans for me. He is not done with me yet. It is hard to believe that at times, but I must. As I wait upon the Lord, I must also get prepared for what He is calling me to do along my journey of moving forward. This is hard to do while in the valley. We must also try and maintain our upward focus on Him. The Spirit can, will and does move me forward and upward and with our soul revival.

I don't know yet what is next for me on my journey here but since I am still breathing then God must have plans for me – His sovereign plans for me. And I must fight to get prepared. Part of that preparation for me I believe is in writing this book. As it is helping me as I am writing I pray and hope the Lord will use this for His kingdom as well when it is all done.

There is a mixture of getting prepared and being still before the Lord. Being still is also connected with and a huge part of getting prepared. If we don't take enough time and yes energy to be still before the Lord, then we can slip into doing it on our own. So those two truths are essentially wrapped into one. Be still and get prepared! The two can and do go together in our battle for soul revival.

During this period or periods of "waiting upon the Lord' we are to bind ourselves deeper and deeper with Him as we get to know Him more and more. Baseball has its spring training. As the players are eagerly waiting with expectation for opening day, they are not just sitting around doing nothing. They are going over areas they already know to get sharper in them. Pitchers know they are to cover first base when the ball is hit to the right side. Yet during spring training they do this repeatedly so that it becomes a natural thing for them to do when the season starts. Muscles are being brought up to speed again from the wintertime of not playing perhaps every day. Injuries that happened last year are being carefully watched as once again players are being built up and getting ready to play on opening day.

I would say that there is also a bonding that a team develops and rekindles during this time period. Revived friendships as they gather again after being away from each other since the last season. New players, coaches, or managers come in to learn this new group of teammates. This is all a process of waiting for Opening Day. It is not a wasted period and if used properly can make Opening Day more enjoyable and productive. Players, yes, do take days off to rest. So is God's pattern for us to actively participate in our soul revival we need both rest and preparing. Ask the Lord for this correct balance for you in your life.

This Qavah waiting upon the Lord was not just a random thing that David did and called us to do in Psalm 142. As David fought the battle in his own spiritual depressions, he saw this truth of Qavah in the Lord and repeated it in many of his other Psalms.

* Psalm 40 when David was in the pit of destruction and miry clay that weighed him down, he waited (Qavah) upon the Lord. God then brought him out of this spiritual dungeon that he was in and didn't stop there but He set David's feet on the rock and put a new song in his heart and mouth. David's trusting in the Lord had results.

* Psalm 25 when David had enemies pursuing him, he had this upward focus toward the Lord (vs. 15) as he also took refuge in the Lord (vs. 20). David Qavah (waited) upon the Lord (vs. 21).

* Psalm 39 when David felt or thought he felt God's pressing in on him (for refining purposes but David didn't feel that then) David kept on praying (vs. 12) and he waited (Qavah) upon the Lord.

* Psalm 52 which was written around the same time as our Psalm 142 we see how because of David's visit to the city of Nob as He was fleeing from Saul how Saul used that to murder and destroy the whole town except for the one who escaped to tell David. In verse 8 David trusts in God's Checed love. His loyal, faithful, devoted love for him despite this dire circumstance and news about the town of Nob being destroyed along with everyone in it. Through it all David Qavah (waited) upon the Lord (vs. 9).

David knew how vital it was especially during severe troubles of circumstance which can affect our spirit to wait (Qavah) upon the Lord. David knew how important this participation point was for him to do. David had this ongoing spiritual depression that battled against him, and he realized this truth and challenged us to also Qavah - wait upon the Lord.

Psalm 27:14 echoes these truths, "Wait upon the Lord, rely on Him, put your hope fully upon the Lord, rely completely on the Lord. Bind yourself together with Him as you walk through your troubles and situations and subsequent despair of your heart. Be strengthened and encouraged and be courageous in the Lord as you regain your strength. Trust in God to repair and revive you in Himself. As God establishes you, strengthens you, emboldens you, makes your heart steadfast, makes your emotions and your passions steadfast wait upon Him. Yes, I say again – Qavah – wait upon the Lord." (EHGV)

The same calling that the Holy Spirit gave to David is the same one to us as well. This is hopefully your desire. We have been somewhat talking in generalities about our need to wait upon the Lord. How does this come about or work out in our daily lives? Let me put forth a few areas for us to consider. Some of these ideas you simply might not be able to do yet depending on where you are emotionally and spiritually now. Your journey to being able to Qavah wait upon the Lord might be in the beginning steps. Don't be discouraged with the ideas and thoughts you see here that you cannot do yet – it's ok! Simply do attempt to strive for those areas and do the ones you can do now. Remember it is a journey. At times it seems like baby steps and at other times it feels like we are in leaps and bounds. Plus, at times it can feel like we are falling stagnate or even falling backwards. Remember that it's a journey. What I am sharing here is not in any special order of importance so progress as you can in the Lord.

* Waiting Qavah upon the Lord is learning to trust in and lean upon God's sovereignty. His sovereignty over the whole universe as well as in your life. Study the topic of God's sovereignty. I know this can help to strengthen you. Knowing that God is fully in control and bringing about things in His perfect timing can be comforting. In John chapter 11 we come upon Lazarus who was a friend of Jesus. Lazarus became ill so Mary and Martha went to Jesus to seek His help. Jesus waited three days before going to Lazarus. In that time period Lazarus died. Jesus knew Lazarus would die and his death was all in the sovereign plan and timing of the Lord.

Jesus did not have to go to Lazarus to heal him as Jesus could have done that right wherever He was but He chose not to heal him. Lazarus' death though was all a part of God's sovereign plan to show forth Jesus' power over death. As Jesus traveled to Lazarus most of us know the story as to how He raised him from the dead. Thus, showing to those there and to us as reading it now the power that Jesus has over the grave. Nothing is too difficult for the Lord. The Lord always has His perfect timing to accomplish His purposes.   Mary and Martha and the people there questioned as to why Jesus had not healed Lazarus. Perhaps causing some doubts in their minds? But then they saw the greater miracle that God had in store and that was to raise Lazarus from the dead. We normally want things in our way and in our timing but as we study God's sovereignty this can help us to develop this waiting upon the Lord spirit in us.

We need to train ourselves to keep on trusting God even when the storms hit. When the prayers and desires that we wanted to have not yet come to pass. We don't know best but God does. Perhaps the storms that we go through are meant for Jesus to show forth His strength, love or power on a grand scale to you and to others. Just like Jesus did with Lazarus. This does take a committed and repeated effort on our part not to cave into the wrong thinking of blaming God when He does not act in the way we thought He should or in the timing that we thought He should act. Keep on praying. Keep on asking. Then also trust in the Lord through the storms and situations.

Remember Mark chapter 4 and the great violent storm on the Sea. Jesus could have sent the storm away sooner or not have it come at all. But through that storm that the disciples' thought was threatening their lives Jesus revealed

Himself to them in a powerful way. Due to the storm the disciples got to witness an incredible act of power from Jesus. It also revealed His care and love for them too. God is sovereign over nature. God is sovereign in your life – the good and the rough times.

Studying the topic of God's sovereignty can build up your spiritual ability to wait upon Him.

      * Seek the Lord. This is a consistent running theme throughout the whole Word of God. Psalm 27 again when David was in dire straits the one thing that he desired was God's presence – seeking God. Psalm 63 and 42 shares that when your soul is in a spiritual dry wilderness to spend more time with the Lord. Read your Bible. Memorize passages that relate to your specific situation. If you are not sure what verses apply just Google it and I'm sure you will be directed to some sites to help you in this. Seeking the Lord is also taking the time to worship Him. This is especially done with music. Whatever your style is, play it. Let it lift your soul to the Lord. Seeking the Lord also takes time to think about Him – meditate upon who He is and what He is like.

* Get a list of God's attributes and read through them or study them out. In the addendum I have given a list that you could use to get you started in this. Look up the verse related to them. Maybe take one attribute of God a day or one a week and think and ponder on that truth about God.

* Do the same above with names/epithets of God. I have also put in the addendum a list of all the names/epithets of God that we have looked at in this book. What I have done further with this for me is to get index cards and write out the various names/epithets of God and I take them with me wherever I go. I have a whole big pile of cards that I take with me especially to work. If I am struggling, there I can usually take out one and let my mind focus on that truth of God even as I work. This has helped me to settle down any number of times. I believe it even makes me more productive at my job as well since my mind becomes clearer. When I do card shows and the crowd starts to get to me a bit, I take out one of those index cards of God's name/epithets and it helps me to get through those times too.

* Start a prayer journal. Then along with that try and have some sit-down prayer times with the Lord. You can pray anytime and anywhere but having a list and a specific undistracted prayer time can help in your developing this Qavah wait upon the Lord strength. This can also help you to see how God has moved in your life. Prayer is for sure a way that Scripture says to bring our requests, concerns and hopes before the Lord. Prayer is asking. Prayer is listening. Prayer is a bonding relationship time with the Lord.

* Fight off fear. "When I am afraid, I WILL put my trust in the Lord." (Ps 56:3-4). This develops into a determined mindset and then to action steps of doing it (with God's ability). David gave through the Psalms a lot of "I will" statements. We need to also develop this "I will" determination and along with that a "I will NOT" attitude as well. This I agree is not an easy thing to do. I will

say that this participation point or action step for us to take or strive after will more usually just start to flow from us as we are pursuing the Lord. It becomes an overflow of our upward pursuit of God. But there are times when we simply need to say, "I will" or "I will not" and take a stand.

* Expect God to act. This is a part of the meaning of Qavah as we wait upon Him. Pray with confidence. Knowing that God cares for us and has our best interests in mind. When you pray don't just leave it there and walk away. Keep your spiritual eyes open for how God answers. This can be a fun exciting time as we keep waiting with great expectations of how God will answer. Again, knowing that He knows best and always has our best interests in mind.

* Know that our trials here of circumstances and of our spirit are only temporary. I know this is not much comfort as we walk through our problems, but the Lord does call us to have a heavenly mindset while on earth. We have a heavenly home awaiting us with our Lord. Take hope that we are secure there. This is what Jesus was teaching the disciples in John 14.

Jesus told them to not let their hearts be troubled. The Greek word for heart there is "kardia." It denotes the center of not only our physical lives but also our spiritual lives. It is the soul seat of our emotions, affections, desires, passions and appetites. It is also the seat of our intelligence. What we know to be true can guide our emotions and desires.

Jesus tells His disciples there to not let your soul-heart be troubled. The word for troubled there in the Greek is "tarasso." It means to NOT be distressed, disturbed, confused, agitated, shaken, alarmed, terrified, stirred up or perplexed. It specifically means to not let our outward circumstances be allowed to cause us inward commotion. Don't let the outward take away the calmness of the spirit. Let me get a little more specific here and say that this word in John 14 was written in the Imperative Mood in the Greek. What does that mean? It was written as a command from Jesus to His disciples which flows down to us as a command as well.

Basically, this is not an option that we have to just simply give in and let our emotions rule over us no matter what is happening all around us or to us or to the ones we care about. Easier said than done? Of course, it is but God is calling us to fight in this battle as well. What is the fuel that Jesus then gives the disciples to help them fight this inward commotion that was happening to them? Jesus begins to teach them about their heavenly home. This is one of the first bibles verses I ever memorized. When my dad passed away when I was 16 years old this verse was on a handout sheet. I filled my mind with this passage as it brought me great comfort knowing where my dad was. Now later in life it brings me comfort to know where I am eventually headed to. No matter how bad it may get here I can know that Jesus is preparing a place for me in heaven that no one can take away or tear down. Knowing our future home is secure can be fuel that the Holy Spirit can use in the here and now when we walk through the fires of living.

Try and put into our mindset that the timeframe by which we arrive there is also in the Lord's hands. This is a somewhat weak analogy but when I was in ministry full time the pressures were there day in and day out. At times it was very rough going, not only dealing with getting the regular lessons out and filling in with my other duties but also the pressure of trying to be used of the Lord in youth and adult lives that were very severe at times. Then add on to that it seems like ongoing issues from within the church itself. I needed time away at regular intervals to regroup. My main big time get away was in Estes Park, Colorado. When I had a planned time off even the making of reservations was a joy to do. Then looking forward to the travel time out there was relaxing for me. Being in the mountains themselves gave me something to look forward to which would help me get through some of the rough times that occurred within the ministry.

This is what Jesus was telling His disciples as He was preparing them for His departure from earth to heaven. He knew that this could have a radical affect upon them, so Jesus was equipping them with how to fight back. Part of this waiting upon the Lord is to fight back knowing the truths about God and about our heavenly home with Him for eternity. To know is not just an intellectual knowledge of the facts but it is a conviction of the truths and in our relationship with God. It is to entrust one's spiritual well-being to Christ and what He did at the cross and in conquering the grave.

This is where the command part comes in with regards to our role in this fight to spiritual revival. We must have this mindset of not letting the feelings and emotions of our present circumstances rob us of our joy in the security of the Lord that we have. All things are under His control. I know that this is a great challenge to do in not letting our troubles overrule what we know to be true. It is very difficult at times, and I struggle in this area. I'm not there yet in mastering this but I am trying. I know I can frustrate people around me when I fall into an episode, yet I am still trying to have this focus. If you struggle in this area don't give up. Keep on keeping on in this pursuit of allowing our heavenly home truths to invade our present circumstances to be Holy Spirit fuel to keep us going. It may seem like at times that we are walking in the thickest mud but keep taking the steps forward even if the boots come off from the mud keep on going!

There are times when I am writing things like this that I feel like I'm doing what I am preaching. There are certainly times when I can't seem to even get out of bed. Some may even be reading this who know me and what I've been through and my continual struggles and be thinking that I am not putting into practice what I am writing here. Unfortunately, that is probably true and true too many times. What I would like to say to myself so that I don't get too discouraged is that I'm on a journey in my revival. I go from one oasis in the desert to another. Trying to get up enough courage and strength to try and go through the desert again.

My journey to revival is probably going to be a lifelong one. If that is my journey, then I must keep on going from station to station. If I frustrate those around me because I am not progressing at the speed that they think I should be then I must accept the fact that there is nothing I can do about that. I've lost so many friends to this because it seems I simply could not at the time fulfill their expectations of what I should be doing or progressing. I am sorry for that, but it is what it is. I'm on a journey. It's a rough journey through the desert. I am not alone as I know I still have a few close friends left and always the Lord. I assume some reading this are also experiencing this as well in their lives. Keep on the journey through the desert. Let the truths of our heavenly home take root in our hearts. Let this be used by the Spirit to move us forward to the next oasis in our journey of revival.

Our looking forward to our heavenly home can spur us on here during the rough days. That's why Jesus was teaching to develop this heavenly mindset. It's good to ponder what heaven will be like. Study out heaven as much as the Lord has given to us about it. Realize that just being with the Lord forever is enough and yet there are so many add on truths as well awaiting us there. No more pain and suffering. No more tears. Joy inexpressible. Knowing these truths can be used by the Holy Spirit to get us through some of our dark hours here which in essence are only temporary and fleeting. Again, I know that this can be hard to do when you are right in the middle of the storm but when there is an eye of the hurricane time prepare yourself for the storms by studying what awaits us in heaven. It can help. It's Holy Spirit fuel!

* Know that waiting upon the Lord and trusting in Him and seeking Him will not automatically take away all of our troubles. I might be battling this depression and PTSD episodes the rest of my life or God could heal me instantaneously. What I need to try and keep on remembering is I need to keep on keeping on – even if a miraculous healing does not occur. I need to keep on seeking the Lord even in the dark hours. Jesus in His darkest hour was in the Garden seeking the Father in prayer. So, we must continue. I need to keep on connecting with my counselor and trusted friends who understand and can help me through some dark hours. There are times for sure when I am simply tired of being tired. Tired of fighting all the time just to keep my head above water, but I need to keep on keeping on. The "I will" keep on fighting even if my troubles don't fly away like I want them to.

* This next thought is a tough one for sure I know but here goes. We need to learn to ride the winds that are blowing against us. To soar to newer heights with the Lord through them. I love it when I see an eagle soar as it rides up on the winds blowing against it. What comes natural to an eagle is not for us. This isn't easy and I'm for sure not there yet in this myself. I desire to be able to do this and at times I can, but it is difficult. Study out some on Google how an eagle uses the down and up drafts to soar to new heights often without flapping its wings but just sailing along with the wind. I had a bad day yesterday and I am still struggling a bit right now as I am writing this. This part right now is hitting me to try and ride this downdraft that came yesterday and allow the Holy Spirit to use this to take me higher. Let the winds that seem to be going against us to drive us down be used by the Holy Spirit to lift us up.

There is a John Denver song that I like called "Looking for Space." One of my favorite videos of this song is with a man soaring with a parachute type thing like a hang glider as he goes from place to place. This video right now is in my mind to try and ride with the downdrafts that I can get and allow the Spirit to use them to ride further into healing. I'm trying. Keep trying.

* This next thought is one that really works for me. I have index cards (which I have mentioned) that I have written out a name/epithet of God on each card. Right now, I am experiencing especially how ones from this book that are helping me. I have a whole handful of them that I try and carry with me especially into situations where I know I could be triggered. I am getting better now at recognizing when I've been triggered. When I can realize this has happened, I will grab my index cards and thumb through them searching for the one I sense will help me at that moment. Time after time this has calmed me down almost immediately. As I focus on a particular truth of God the Holy Spirit uses that to calm me down. Maybe you can do this with Bible verses. Whatever might be good for you let me encourage you to try this.

* Learning to wait upon the Lord can be strengthened as we read stories in the OT and NT of where the Lord moved in people's lives. Do character studies of people in the Bible and discover how God brought them through some very difficult situations even when they themselves brought on the troubles. Just one example would be of Jonah and how God did not abandon him even when Jonah ran from the Lord. You can see how in the darkest hour Jonah turned back to the Lord. See how Noah had the courage of the Lord to build an ark while being I'm quite sure criticized and ridiculed as no one even knew what rain was then. At the time the earth was more of in a canopy which supplied the water. The people around Noah must have thought that he was crazy for what he was doing. See how Peter, even after denying the Lord three times, was brought back to be so strongly used for the Lord's kingdom. The widow who we don't even know her name in her giving of what she had to the offering is still used as an example for us today. The list can go on and on. God still moves today in our lives as He did with the people in the Bible. Same God just different times. Let the rough times that many went through in the Bible be used of the Spirit to see how God never gave up on them and He won't on you either.

* Know that your story isn't over yet. People have said this to me numerous times when I have gotten to the point of feeling that my usefulness for Him was over here. But if we are still breathing then the Lord has plans for us for His kingdom's use! When our appointed work from the Lord is done here then He will take us to be with Him in heaven. If you are still here and since you are reading this, then you are still here – then the work the Lord has for you to accomplish with Him is not yet done. You do have a purpose here even in the times when you feel you don't – you do! Keep on keeping on knowing that God is not done with you yet. Even in the storms God can use you. Not only to mold you more into the image of Christ but for others too. Perhaps Elijah had thoughts that God was

214

done with him when he was staying by the water and ravens were feeding him. He probably did not feel very useful for the Lord, yet he didn't know that just around the corner was a woman in need whose son would die – and God used Elijah to bring him back to life. Your story is not yet done! We don't know what the Lord has waiting for us just around the corner to do for His kingdom so keep on moving forward!

* See a counselor. See a doctor. The Lord can does use them to work through them in your healing process. God can use them to help you to better wait upon Him. I used to resist both avenues of God but now I see how they can be God's ambassadors for me – and for you.

We could go on and keep adding to our list of ideas by which we can strengthen our abilities to Qavah wait upon the Lord. I'm sure you also have some of your own that will help you. Take what works for you and attempt to put into practice this waiting upon the Lord into our lives. Do what you can and keep moving forward.

As we close out verse 3 here with our 7th Participation Point, I think that it's important that as the Lord moves in us and as we participate with the Spirit that there will be blessings and results that go along with it. Let's go back briefly once again to Isaiah 40:31 and we can see a list given to us by the Holy Spirit which shows us some blessings we can receive as we walk along this path of waiting Qavah upon the Lord. I see in that verse four blessings can be ours.

Let me list them out and then briefly talk a bit on each one:

We will:
* Be given new strength
* Mount up with wings like eagles - soaring above it all
* Run and not be tired
* We will walk and not become weary

1) We will be given new strength. The Hebrew word for renew here in Isaiah is Chalaph (khaw-laf). It means to change, sprout up, grow up, renewed, find renewal, continue, sprout again, to go on from whatever has happened, spring up like from a cold hard winter, go on forward, strike through. This renewal in us is not just simply limited to coming out of the wintertime and be springtime like renewal but it also enables us to move forward. It is almost like the Hebrew word Yatsa that we have looked at which has layers of meaning and one building on the other. In the Yatsa God took the Israelites out of Egyptian bondage TO the Promised Land. It was yes, a journey but a journey forward even when the Israelites wanted to go backward and return to their Egyptian bondage when it got rough God said NO and that they were to move on forward and keep on moving forward. Keep on Keeping on!

He is the same God now for us and will do the same for us too. Enabling us "To go on from whatever has happened." As I was typing this in from my notes this part of the meaning hit me very strongly. I feel like I am stuck in the situations that happened to me and it is so difficult to do this moving forward. I need to keep remembering this Hebrew word Chalaph and I'm going to try and do a deeper study of it for me.

I sense right now even the Holy Spirit is trying to get through to me that I can find renewal from all of this. Things won't be the same but maybe renewal can bring a new Promised Land for me. For you! Keep this Hebrew word Chalaph in your mind, heart and spirit. God can move you forward from whatever has happened to you. Maybe you are reading this book because you have a friend or a loved one who is going through depression, and you desire to be able to help them better. Keep encouraging them to keep moving forward.

As I mentioned, this is a journey. This journey at times can seem very slow and even taking steps backwards. But we must trust in the Living God who says He is there for us and wants us through Him to move forward no matter what the circumstances you went through or are going through. God is the causative action behind all this too. He created the entire universe in a mega-second so He can create in us a new and renewed heart and spirit as well.

Isaiah says here that God will renew our strength. God can move us from exhaustion to energy. God can move us from instability to being stable. God can move us from being attacked to being a warrior for Him. As Isaiah said in verse 29 God will give this renewal of strength to the weary. He will give it to us who lack might. He will increase power to us and through us.

2) We will sour like the eagles do. Renewed strength to soar. You might be saying like I do so often in my mind that there is no way this can happen to me. Maybe Moses said this when God called him to his various journeys. Maybe Peter felt this right after he denied Jesus three times and felt it was all over. I would say that Peter was renewed and mounted up like eagles did and soared for Christ.

It is not God's desire to pull us out of our pits to just let us lay there at the top of the pit hole. God does not leave us there to then fend for ourselves. Peter was a broken man after he denied Jesus and even went back to his regular job of fishing. What Peter needed was a renewal from Jesus Himself and this is what we all need and can get from Him. The Holy Spirit is there getting us to move forward with His renewed strength to soar.

An interesting thing I found out about eagles was that when they build their nests, they put thorns in the bottom of it. You may feel that seems cruel. You know how it works, I found out? Then the baby eagles have been nurtured in the cozy little or big nests that they build it comes a time when they need to get going and fly. That was what they were made to do. But they have a reluctance to do so as it is so cozy in their nests and all their needs are provided for them. When the nest finally starts to wear down (right at the right time!) The thorns in the bottom are there to push them out of their comfort zones and to mount up with their eagle wings to fly. God at times does send or allow tough situations into our lives for His various sovereign reasons which we may never know about while we walk this earth. But God is there orchestrating every event of our lives to His good and our ultimate good.

Examine where you are now. Ask the Holy Spirit to give you wisdom as to how God is trying to move you forward. I don't know your situation so I can't venture to say what is going on and for what reason and what to do and when to do it – But God does. Seek Him out on this. Let what we feel in the downdraft to be used by the Spirit to send us to the updrafts and soar anew!

God wants us to move forward past our circumstances that have put us into our pits. God wants us to come bursting out, to move forward, to invade and soar to new areas of service that He has for us. As God restores us, He soars us. This is a blessing that can be an exciting time instead of a depressing time as the Holy Spirit renews us to launch us out. God enables us to survive within the storm. God draws us out. God brings us up. God renews us. God trains us up as He is renewing us. What a blessing.

3) We will run! The Hebrew word there in Isaiah for run is Ruwts (Roots). Ruwts has lawyers of meanings depending on the context of which it is being used. As it applies to this passage it means – messenger. Back then to get news to someone a distance away was to get a runner. A runner had endurance and boldness. The runner was not going to be stopped. He had a mission and was going to fulfill it. Suffering Christians can sometimes have difficulty getting out of bed let alone walking and then let alone running. But God –

God is our source who can and enables us to turn things around. With God there is hope for the struggling believer in what the Holy Spirit can do in us. This runner or messenger back then also had a sense of urgency. It might be a long run that requires endurance but long runs even taking a long time can come with a sense of urgency. I believe one thing the Holy Spirit has been drilling into me lately is this sense of urgency. Not necessarily a sense of rush, rush, rush but urgency.

To be urgent means more to have a strong imperativeness to it. It is necessary to do something. It is critical to do so. It is essential. I have felt that in my spirit these last few weeks in continuing to write this book. I have felt the urging of the Spirit to keep going with it. As I am typing it in from what I wrote maybe weeks or months ago it is helping me out on the day I am typing it in.

So perhaps one of the urgent, critical, essential purposes for me to do in finishing this book was for me. I believe that. I hope it is also helping those who will read it too, but I do sense that the Lord is pushing me forward to finish this book for my sake. This book has become part of my journey in revival of my soul so that I can run again. To be running again for the Lord. I don't like this sideline life I feel I have been trapped in due to what happened and then leading to my PTSD and depression battles. I want to run again. I want this blessing in my life again. God says He can and will do this for me and in me. I must believe that and then participate in ways that I can. I want to run again with and for the Lord.

4) We will walk and not become weary. We just talked about running and now we're back to walking. Walking here doesn't mean we slow down. Walking here means to lead. To proceed and to keep on going. In other words – Keep on Keeping on! Such a recurring truth that we see. This Keep on going type of walk that then becomes a manner of life for us. To be in our upward pursuit of God which results in the Spirit's inward renewal day by day. Then we are better prepared and trained for our outward serving of the Lord. Also then accompanied by a stronger desire to do so. The stronger we become in Him will result in the Lord moving us to keep on moving forward.

We can't look back to where we were but to where He is taking us. We cannot let the wrong thinking that the Israelites had at times when they hit rough times. They cried out to Moses as to why did he take them on this journey out of Egypt to die in the wilderness. They wanted to go back to being slaves in Egypt. Not the right thinking. Don't look back – look forward in the journey to revival. There is a song that has helped me that has the line in it of "yesterday is dead and gone." No matter what you have been through God is greater than what happened, and He desires to get us going and then to lead even others out of their darkness.

Let God use the deep dark pit you are in or have been in to be a way by which He can use you to help others. The Lord has been pulling you out, renewing you and preparing you to help another struggling Christian. God can now use you to help them get out of their own deep dark pit. You know firsthand what it is like to be in that deep dark pit, and you have been finding your way out through the Lord. So now you are better equipped to be used by the Lord to help guide them out. It becomes a cycle of our spiritual journey here that as the Lord renews us, He will use us as His messenger to help others. It is God doing the work and He has decided to use us in the process. This is one of my hopes again that the Lord can use me for His kingdom to help others who are struggling.

Those are the four-fold blessings from the Lord found in Isaiah that can happen in our lives as we also wait upon the Lord.

Let's keep moving on with Psalm 142 as we keep on exploring how David participated with his part of seeking for spiritual renewal.

Here again is verse 5 of Psalm 142 in the EHGV.

~ Verse 5 ~

"I cry to You, Lord; I say, You are my refuge, my portion in the land of the living."

"In my desperate need Lord, I am again calling out to You for help. With no one coming to my aid or even seems to care enough to try I am reaching out to You. I am desperately crying out to You. I look to others and there is no one who cared enough to help me in my deepest time of need. They are always around yet run away when I try to share my hurts and my pains. Friends and even blood family keep me at a distance. They say that they are there for me yet hide when they see me coming as I reach out for help. I asked for help, and they disappeared. This has brought me to look to You, my Lord. You are my God who cares and Who cares for me. You are my God of refuge. You are my shelter in these storms that I am in that don't seem to go away. However, I see that You will not go away even in the darkest of storms and will stand with me and by me.

Let me be joined together with You – You who are Jehovah the Sovereign Almighty One. You are my portion – my stability. My flesh and my heart may fail me. My flesh which represents my blood relatives who have forsaken me and failed me. My own heart as the seat of my desires, emotions and courage fails me. I also fail myself time after time as I try and work through these depressions of mine. Yet I know that You are my strength. I know that You are my portion. I know that You are my stability for ever. I know that You will not fail me. Join me now Lord or better put help me to join with You. I need You Lord now more than ever." (EHGV)

There are two Participation Points that David is revealing here in verse 5. One we have already studied a bit and that is for us to "Cry out to God." When a truth is repeated in Scripture then it certainly is something we need to pay attention to, and this is one of those truths. A reminder to us to be constantly crying out to God. Calling out to God. Praying to and with God. This is such a vital Participation Point that we need to keep on keeping on with. The other participation point that David exemplified here for us becomes our 8th "Participation Point from David." Our next Action Step.

8) DAVID "PERSONALIZED" HIS RELATIONSHIP WITH THE LORD

Another major Participation Point here is how David personalized his relationship with God. We see this repeatedly here in verse 5 and in so many other of David's Psalms. He uses the word "my" quite often. It is almost as if he is reminding himself that he has this personal relationship with the Creator of the universe – God Himself! I have studied through David's Psalms at various times just looking for when he uses "my" regarding his relationship with God. This we can also do.

Have you ever had this untrue thought that God loves and takes care of all His children – except you? That is, as I said so, untrue but when we struggle with abandonment issues we can even fall into this false view. We need to constantly remind ourselves just like David did to the truth that God is MY God and all the other truths and blessings that go along with that.

This is so vital for us to have in our arsenal of defensive and offensive weapons. So vital that in the addendum I have given this truth a bit more emphasis where I have listed out a number of these "my" statements of David throughout his Psalms. Reading through and meditating on those verses can fuel us up from the Holy Spirit to keep on fighting and moving forward.

Just in this one verse here David refers to God as:

My Lord

My God

My God of Refuge

My Shelter

My Portion

My Stability

My Strength

What a list to ponder with just those seven truths that David knew he had in his relationship with God. In that verse David only uses the words refuge and portion but from those two words come all the other ones listed here.

Likewise, we also have those same truths and blessings with our personal relationship with God. As a reminder let's look at just two of those truths/ blessings we have in our own personal relationship with Jesus.

We looked at how God is David's and our Jehovah Machaceh. God is our shelter, refuge, safety, source of safety and source of our hope. God is our shelter from rain or storms or danger. For those who feel hopeless God is your hope. For those who are in a deluge of a violent storm God is your shelter. For those who are surrounded by danger God is your source of safety. God brought these truths home to David's heart. This enabled David to declare that God is MY Machaceh – My refuge.

Now carry this over to God being David's and our Jehovah Cheleq. We have also looked at the Hebrew word Cheleq (portion). David realized this this truth and could say and know that God was his Cheleq. David could say with confidence that God is "MY" stability. God is "MY" portion.

Just like David we can also say that. God is my ration and the One who provides my provisions that I need. This is all coming from Him to me. He is all I need and provides all that I need. He is MY Jehovah Cheleq. God is for us too just as He was for David.

Look at all the truths that we have studied here in just this one book about God. Now place the word "my" in front of all of them for yourself. David does this time after time in so many of his other Psalms. It could be that David was constantly reminding himself of this truth. It probably brought David to stand in awe of this tight relationship that he truly had with God. Let me encourage you to take a walk-through David's Psalms yourself and see all the various "my" statements he makes.

If I could I have here a little assignment for you to do that can help drive home this truth of your own personal relationship with Jesus Christ. I have made just a short list here below of some truths that every believer has in their relationship with Jesus. Let me challenge you to in front of every one of these truths to fill in the blank with your name. This can really help you to fill up your mind, heart and spirit with this truth of your personal relationship with God.

Jesus IS

——— Refuge   ——— Salvation
——— Source of Safety   ——— Help
——— Shield   ——— Security
——— Strength   ——— Comfort
——— Rock   ——— Friend
——— Fortress   ——— Hope
——— Deliverer

I think that we can at times lose sight of these truths of our personal relationship with Jesus. Jesus went to the cross for ME. Jesus is building ME a special place in heaven where I will dwell with Him forever. The list goes on and on.

In Psalm 94:17 as we see with the EHGV that knowing these personalized truths with God can affect us in our daily living. "If the Lord had not been MY help, MY deliverer, MY support, MY ally, MY one who helps then my emotions, my passions, my appetites, my mind and my heart could have easily wasted away and been caused to be destroyed." (EHGV)

Do you see the deep significance of knowing and living in the truth that unless God Himself had been all of that to you personally then you would have been lost and destroyed or felt that way. Don't live in the falsehoods that say you can't be helped. Don't live in the falsehood that says you have no more hope. Don't live in the falsehoods that say what you have been through there is no recovery from. Don't live in the falsehoods that say it is all over.

Allowing those falsehoods to take root in our heart, mind and soul can have a very devastating effect on our emotional and spiritual lives. We need to anchor our souls into the truths of who we are in Christ and our deep personal relationship we have with Him by what He did on the cross for us. The cross was just the beginning as we also now have the Holy Spirit residing in us enabling us to be revived in and through Him. The work that Jesus did at the cross brings into this "MY" relationship with the Father, Son and Holy Spirit. Know this and live in this.

We can then better be able through the Spirit to fight off our periods of loneliness, hopelessness, insecurities and depression. We again give the Holy Spirit fuel to help us fight the good fight and to keep on keeping on. This can be one tremendous way that we like David can stem the tide of our emotional and spiritual depressions and insecurities. Participate in this with the Holy Spirit. Know and live in all these "MY" truths that we have with and through Jesus Christ!

Let's move onto to final verse 7 of Psalm 142. In this verse we will discover our final 2 of David's 10 Participation Points or Actions Steps that he took with the Lord to fend off spiritual depression and fight for spiritual renewal.

~ Verse 7 ~

"Set me free from my prison, that I may praise Your name. Then the righteous will gather about me because of Your goodness to me."

"Lord, bring me out of this deep dungeon of depression and dangers that I am in. My emotions, my passions, my will and my mind need rescue. Energize me once again Lord. Not only rescue me out but take me forward to green pastures. Take me out of this dungeon to go forth with purpose and for results for You. Take me from this dungeon and proceed to something great. Just like you took the Israelites from slavery in Egypt You didn't just take them out of there, but You also took them to the Promised Land. Make this a great "coming away" to a great "going to" event. Let this be another source of praise and worship that I can freshly raise up to You as You do this. Let this also be seen by others so that then we can gather as one to praise You for what You have done for me and simply for who You are. Lord, take me out from this dungeon and take me to something great."

Bring my soul out of prison! What depth of despair David was going through. David's battle with this spiritual warfare seemed so up and down at times or better put a lot of the time. David could go from the Pit of Despair to Praising God and then back again. David did not like being in this pit that he was in. David pleads with God to YATSA me! We've looked at God being Jehovah Yatsa and our main example of this was how God drew out and rescued Israel from their bondage at the hands of the Pharaohs in Egypt.

David obviously had been taught about the depth of despair that the Israelites had suffered at the hands of the Pharaoh of Egypt. David knew this same depth of despair. David also knew the meaning of Yatsa and what God did for the Israelites. David knew that God was the One doing this for the Israelites back then.

The Hebrew word Yatsa here also clearly indicates that God is the causative action for this to happen for David. David could not simply just pull himself up by his own bootstraps as some people try to tell those in this kind of distress to do. Others may say to just snap out of it. David knew that he could not bring himself out of this dungeon of situations and subsequent depressions that he was in. David needed God to do something and to do something in his soul which was the seat of his emotions, passions, appetites, mind and heart. David was so to speak at his wits end as how to get out of this soul pit of despair and depression. He did not know what to do anymore and was crying out to the Lord for help. Good move David! Again, we see David in his calling out to God as his source of being able to come out of this.

Several of the reasons that I am writing this book is for me in my battle with PTSD and depression. I felt doing this deeper study of how David fought could help me. Another reason is I desire to be used by the Lord to help others in their own spiritual battle against depression and other anxieties. For me this depression and PTSD related things is an ongoing battle.

Even today as I am studying verse 7 here, I am once again struggling. I am trying to get some more insights into how I can fight this off. I feel like David must have felt when his soul was in a deep dark pit of a dungeon with no apparent way out. It does get hard to fight this day after day and the emotional and spiritual draining that is involved from it. It feels most of the time that no one really understands except those who have and are currently going through their own battles. Talk about feeling alone. David felt this way and so do I.

Jesus felt this way too in the Garden that night when He was about to face the most difficult battle of all eternity. Yet his own very close disciples and friends could not even stay awake with Him to pray. Jesus felt alone. Jesus as we have mentioned from the Greek language used there also felt like He was in a deep dark dungeon. Jesus knows how we feel even if no one else around us does.

Bring my soul out of prison. The prison and dungeon of PTSD. The prison and dungeon of depression. The prison and dungeon of anxieties. The prison and dungeon of my emotional and spiritual decay that I am in. This is what David was in as he wrote Psalm 142.

The word dungeon carries with it the truth of a deep dark dreary no hope place of despair. The Hebrew word for dungeon means to be locked up, shut up, captured, abandoned, calloused as becoming insensitive or indifferent. Have you been feeling this way? This is how I feel when my episodes hit with like a gale force wind. Some say it's just having a bad day, but it is so far from just a bad day. It feels like the depth of despair with no way out! This is how David felt here and he felt this way time after time. Don't condemn yourself if you fight this fight repeatedly. David was declared to be a man after God's own heart, yet he struggled in this turmoil of despair time after time. Like David we don't want to live in the dungeon of despair and there is a way out. I'm not saying the climb out is easy as it can be a tough road to climb. But this climbs out can happen as we pursue our Lord through it.

How can I personally find and fight my way out of this? How did David fight to have his soul released from this dungeon? How can you fight out of your own dungeon of soul depression? Let me give a few thoughts that are helping me that I hope can help you as well. Verse 7 gives us some more insights that we can use in our arsenal. Verse 7 is where David is completely honest with the Lord.

David knew God must be the causative action to release his soul from the depths of this deep dark despair. He knew he could not be the cause and lifted himself up with his own bootstraps. How false that is. In Psalm 3 David was fleeing from his own son Absalom. His own son was after him! It also says his enemies were taunting him saying that no one could save his soul now. They were saying to him that no one could deliver him and even God would not deliver him now. What did David do with all those negative forces coming at him? We see in our 9th Participation Point – Action Steps what David did.

9) DAVID KNEW THE PHRASE – "BUT GOD"

When all this was being flung at David in Psalm 3, he says in verse 3, "But You, O Lord…" When the world is throwing its junk of despair on you, and nothing seems to be going right – "BUT GOD"! When you are feeling like you are sinking lower and lower with no way out – "BUT GOD." This needs to be a rallying cry for us. One that certainly needs developing and focusing on. We can like David become "But God" people during our struggles and despair. The depths of our situations or emotions are no match for the depths of our God! But God! In view of your struggles and pain keep in mind who our God is and who we are to Him.

Some more truths to weave together with having a "But God" mindset.

David began to weave together some of the other truths that we have looked at with this "But God" focus. In verse 3 David knew that God was his shield. David knew that the Lord was the one to lift his head up out of the mire and unto Him.

* To come out of this prison and dungeon of soul depression we see in Psalm 3:4 how he cried out to God. He had this upward focus to God. Calling on the Lord to take his soul out of the dungeon. There is a John Denver song that's coming to my mind right now with some lyrics that go something like this as Denver sings, "I'm doubtful deep in despair. My heart is filled with impossible notions could it be you no longer care?" John Denver wasn't singing to the Lord here but honestly those of us who suffer in this way can at times be drawn to the notion that maybe God no longer cares for us. David even felt this way at times. Jesus cried out at the cross, "My God, My God why have you deserted me." God won't desert you if you are His child. Hang on to the upward truths of how much God loves you and cares for you – even when it is dark outside amid a storm.

When it seems like the darkness has surrounded us remember **"But God."** His light can outshine any darkness that tries to invade our soul.

* David's soul dungeon. Psalm 6:3-4 we see how David's soul is greatly dismayed. David said his soul was in severe panic mode. David felt dumbfounded, shaken, anxious and dismayed. We see in this verse how David pleads with God to refresh, restore and repair his soul. David does this as he appeals to God's

Checed love for him. He knew God was faithful to him. David knew that God was loyal to him. David knew that God's love for him was unfailing, steadfast and never moving away. David hung on to those truths of God and his relationship with God as if he was hanging on to a lifeline. A lifeline that would keep him from sinking and drowning in his dungeon of despair.

These deep truths of God of who He is and our own personal relationship with Him due to what Jesus did for us at the cross can get us through the storms. Our lifeline at times is hanging on to these truths and holding on for dear life. When great thunder and storms grow against us and in our souls, we must hold on. Hold on! Hold on! Keep on keeping on!

When it seems like our lifeline is about to be cut remember – **"But God."** He is still there, and we are eternally secure in Him.

* David's dungeon of his soul despair. Psalm 6:7 we can see how David's circumstances had affected him – "My eyes grow weak with sorrow; they fail because of all my foes." Dire circumstances had a great impact on David's soul. But God – God heard David's weeping and "the Lord accepts my prayer." God pays attention to our prayers and engages with us through it. Psalm 6:9 teaches us to pray, pray and pray some more – even when we apparently don't see the answers or the answers that we want. David's heart and soul here was at its wits end. So as David remembered who God was and his relationship with him, he prayed to God for help.

Our Psalm 142 is also an example of how David constantly reached out to God for help. As a believer I'm sure we all know prayer is key but are we praying as if our lives depended on it? If your soul is in a deep dark dungeon pray up to God relentlessly seeking His help and intervention as only, He can do!

I have a little bit of a story that is one that I joke around with this person now but at the time it wasn't very funny. I was once standing in the alley behind a friend's house, and my friend slowly started moving the car forward and accidentally was driving the car over my poor defenseless foot – my toes! When he did this, I did not casually say to him as he was sitting in the driver's seat if he could possibly move the car and get off my toes. No! I appealed quite loudly and emphatically to the driver to move off my foot!

I'm sure you see the analogy here that I am trying to make. When your soul is in a deep dark dungeon of despair, and it is riding over you we must not take a casual ho-hum approach to it. Look up to the Lord first and if need be, like I did in the mountains in Colorado on several occasions scream out to the Lord for help. He is the One who can get the huge vehicle of soul depression off our soul. He is the One who can direct us to the person or people that He desires to use to help us through it all. Let us not be casual and half-hearted when the storm hits. When we are being rolled over on cal out vehemently for the Lord. Let the Lord know your pain! Ask Him to intervene and help you!

By the way if you are wondering – my foot was not hurt at all in the incident of the rolling over on my toes. That seems to me right there to be a miracle of

God! How could a heavy car roll right onto my toes and I come out unhurt? God is in the miracle business!

When you feel like you are being run over by circumstances around you and/or the heaviness of your soul remember – **"But God."** God moved a car off my toes and God can move mountains for us.

* Psalm 17:13 – David asked God to rescue him and to bring his soul into safety from the wicked. The word "deliver" in this verse means to bring into security. David's soul – his emotions, passions, desires, mind and heart were under attack. David says that the wicked were after him. This whole Psalm 17 has this theme as a prayer of David. David needed and asked God for protection against his oppressor – the wicked. Oppressors here can mean those who were seeking to destroy him and you! Those who might assault you physically, emotionally or spiritually and sometimes multiple of those things. Your enemy is bent on destruction so that they attack and attack relentlessly.

Oppression is the sense of being weighed down and pressed heavily upon. This attack of oppression can invade our minds which then can hit us physically, emotionally and spiritually. David here was overwhelmed with persecution, affliction and beat down. One could be harassed or picked on in a variety of ways. Verse 11 of Psalm 17 says that they surrounded David and desired as their goal to cast him to the ground. Ever felt that way?

This is the rescue that David was seeking God for and speedily. David's soul in this Psalm was in a struggle to survive. Whatever it is that is oppressing you go on the counterattack with God in prayer. Our enemy Satan is always on the prowl trying to hunt us down through his many varied means. Peter says this that the Satan is so much against us that he is ever seeking to devour us. I firmly believe that this is a great part of my spiritual battle with depression. It is obviously spiritually based as we see in this with so many of David's battles with his own depression battles.

I don't look for demons under the bed or around every corner I take as that gives them too much credit and authority. But this spiritual battle is real, and our enemy is real. We first need to recognize it and then fight it spiritually through the Holy Spirit's power. Scripture clearly says in Eph 2:1-2 how Satan is at work in the unsaved. So many who are not in Christ according to Scripture are probably unknowingly being used to try and bring us down in one way or another. Someone might say to me, "how can I say that"? I don't say that, but God's Word does therefore I must also say it. We must be aware of this reality and truth found in Scripture and go to war with prayer as one of our weapons to fight back with.

I would recommend doing a deeper study as you can of this spiritual battle that we are in. Study out Ephesians chapter 6 on how to do battle in this area.

We are under spiritual attack **"But God"** is greater than what the enemy throws at us.

* Psalm 17:5-7 – "Hold me fast Lord. Seize hold of me O Lord. Let us take hold of each other together. As I move along this path and journey help me to obey Your commands. Enable me to not deviate from Your ways. I cry out to You and summon You through Your various names which reveal who You are. Hear me O Lord and let me hear Your response. Bend down from Your throne on high as You and I gather in my prayers to You. Show me special favor and make a difference in this situation that I am in. I ask this knowing of your Checed love for me. I will with intensity look to You, run to You, flee to You for protection as my harbor of safety".

As we are doing this seeking out the Lord to help us in this battle, we also see how David is playing a role in this battle as well. David had as a goal and lifestyle to live a godly life. We know how he failed at times and at times very badly. God still forgave him as the Lord does with us when we fail. God's love is not dependent upon our getting up each day and living a perfect live as none of us can ever do that – and God knows that. But we are still called to pursue righteousness as our lifestyle.

David's Participation Point here is to run to God as his refuge. David lifted his prayers to God, and he trusted in the Lord. Pray with trust in mind. Trusting that God knows what is best for us and how He will accomplish His ways for us.

David also specifically asked for blessings from the Lord. It is ok to ask God for this. Ask Him to shower upon you His wonderful awesome expressions of His love for you.

When you sense that your lifeline to and with God is slipping away remember – **"But God"** and how much He loves you and desires to bless you.

* Psalm 23:3 – Probably the most known Psalm. Even though David was walking through the valley of the deepest darkness that he was experiencing then David still in those times turned to the Lord. David relied on the Lord for his soul restoration. No matter how dark it seems to get we must keep our focus and pursuit on the light of Jesus. This is also what David is saying in Psalm 25:1 when he lifts his soul to God. Lifting is looking up. It's to gaze intently at the Lord.

David said in Psalm 27:4 that even amid being surrounded by the enemy his gaze was upward. This upward gaze is such a huge part of our spiritual recovery and refreshing. David refers to this upward gaze often in his Psalms. When one is in the pit it does no good to look down. It takes courage and determination when in the pit to look upward but just keep reminding yourself that is where our help comes from.

When you feel that you are in the bottom of the pit remember **"But God"** and keep your focus upward to Him!

* Psalm 17:10 – "Guard my soul. Protect my soul. Keep my soul. Oversee and be the watchman of my soul. Be careful to keep my soul. Surround my soul. Maintain my soul. Put a hedge of protection around my soul as You deliver and rescue me. Through Your doing Lord cause, me to not be distressed, disappointed and to be just the opposite. Be my help as you see fit to send it. Help me to not become dried up spiritually. I will take shelter and find my safety in You as I look to You, run to You, flee to You as my refuge. In You, O Lord, I will trust and

find my hope." (EHGV)

When we are in some rough dark times it can very easily move us to become spiritually dry inside. We get so tired of the constant battle raging on around us and in us that we simply begin to dry up like an old rag that was left out in the sun too long. We need to recognize that this spiritual dryness could sneak up on us and to then depend on the Lord to help us fight this battle as well.

When spiritual dryness seems to be entering into our hearts and souls remember – **"But God"** and that He can restore us as we take our spiritual refuge in Him.

* Psalm 63 – This is a tremendous Psalm which ties in the above Scripture as well. Psalm 63 is such a great Psalm to study for those who are in a spiritual fight with depression, PTSD, anxiety and such. As David felt like in Psalm 63 that he was in a dry and weary land where there was no water. This is when we need to seek God relentlessly. Seek out who God in all His glory and majesty as David does in Psalm 63. From this seeking out of God David found his soul satisfaction. God was his soul satisfaction even in a dry and weary land where there was no physical water. God was his refreshing spiritual water.

God is the ultimate ONE who can supply our ultimate needs. God is our ultimate provider and sustainer. Even when we are sensing that we are falling into the dark pit again God is there making sure you don't fall out of his loving hands. We may at times feel like we are, but we are not. For us to experience His presence in the dark and weary land times we must be on our active pursuit of God. Don't allow the dark hours to engulf you. Seek out the Lord's light. Seek out the refreshing spiritual water of God's presence. Experience His touch.

Have as our goal and pursuit to find our soul satisfaction in the Lord. In Him and Him alone can have spiritual enjoyment, pleasure, relationship, fulfillment, contentment or ease of mind even when surrounded by dire trials. Even in the desert times we can find refreshment in the Lord. Jesus Christ is our all and all who is there to meet all our needs and desires and satisfaction (Col 1:13-29). In Jesus we are made full when we feel empty. In Jesus we can find contentment even when our world seems out of control. As we feed and depend on Jesus He does and will supply our every need.

This Soul Satisfaction grows as we grow in our relationship with Jesus. Seeing who He is. Meditating upon those truths as we let them sink into our minds and spirit. When we see who we are to Him. When we see how He will never desert us or forsake us. Clinging to Jesus with all our might as God is clinging to you is a great combination to fight our battles. The same God who created the entire universe and beyond is the same God who knitted you together in your mother's womb. He is the same God who also holds you up. Unlimited power to you and unlimited love for you.

When you are in a desert time of a dark and weary place where there is no apparent water remember – **"But God"** and that He is there for you to refresh you and to give of His waters of delight.

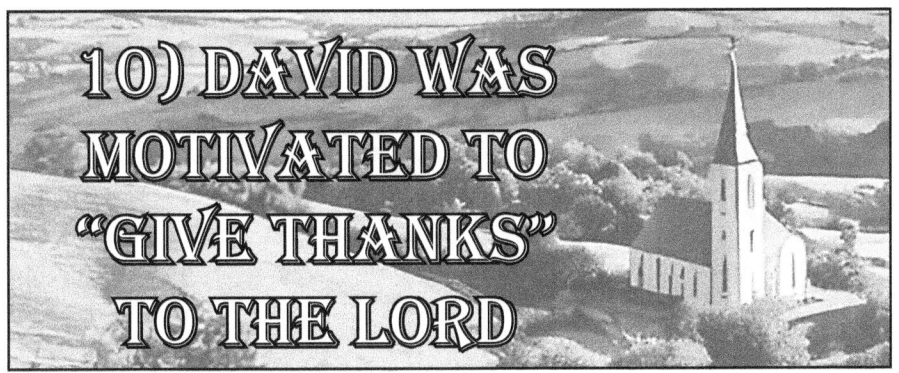

10) DAVID WAS MOTIVATED TO "GIVE THANKS" TO THE LORD

As we begin to close out this section of seeing David's part in the process of spiritual soul revival/refreshing let's look at the end of verse 7 of our Psalm 142. What was David's motivation or goal for asking God to take his soul out of this spiritual pit of darkness of a dungeon? It was so that he could give thanks to God for who He is!

In Psalm 35 when David was sending up prayers to the Lord for rescue from his enemies, we see in verse 17-18 there that his goal, motivation and reason for asking the Lord to deliver him was so that again he could give thanks to Him with the others around him. David desired a congregational time of thanksgiving and worship unto the Lord.

David also echoes this same theme of thanking God, praising God and worshiping God when God delivered him from his enemies in Psalm 30:1-4. This is also where God delivered his soul from the depths of despair and kept him going. This caused David and moved David to thank God and sing praises to Him.

This was an overriding reality in David's life even in his obvious and almost constant battle with his soul, depression brought on by all the varied circumstances. Yet through it all David's heart and desire was to thank the Lord and praise God – to worship Him. This was David's desire not only when God delivered him from his enemies and depressions but also when he was in the midst and surrounded by his enemy as we see so clearly in Psalm 27. This is also seen in Psalm 7:17. It is a pattern of David's life.

A defining passion in David's heart was to worship the Lord. The Hebrew word here for thanks in Psalm 142:7 is YADA. This reveals a very expressive giving of thanks, praise and worship to God. This event directly talks of lifting of the arms in an open expression of worship. This is not a casual thank you to God with expressionless worship. To add weight to this it occurred during one of David's many times of experiencing an aching heart of soul depression.

David here in Psalm 142 wanted to have his soul freed up from his spiritual depression in order to be freer to openly and more fervently praise the Lord. If you have personally experienced this deep soul depression perhaps you have also experienced how difficult it can be to openly praise the Lord. It does not mean that your heart and soul does not want to praise God so don't beat yourself up on this if you are in a worship vacuum. Since we were saved to worship God it does reveal though how much these spiritual depressions can wage war against our soul. It is a battle. It is a spiritual battle of mega proportions.

If you are struggling to bring your heart to worship, then try to listen to others who are and let the Spirit fill you up through their worship. This has happened to me more than I can say. Before the main thrust of my spiritual depression hit me, I can honestly say worship was one of the main purposes of my life. I used to get in the car and immediately have worship music playing. I play the guitar and any time I could, I would play it and worship the Lord. I write praise and worship songs and have two CDs of my songs that I wrote for and to the Lord. Worship flowed from my heart.

Through the deep and dark pit of my spiritual soul depression this worship up to the Lord has been hindered. My soul has been so impacted by the darkness through my circumstances and subsequent battles that to my dismay my worship has also suffered. For me this is one major way that I know that I am in this battle for my soul revival and refreshing as I want so much to have that desire back. I leave my guitar on my bed every day and at night I must take it off and I put it on the floor. Then each morning I force myself to get it and put it back on my bed so that at least I am handling my guitar. I hope this is a way I can get back into this lost part of my life. Maybe one day I will stop moving my guitar back and forth and play it. Sometimes I pick it up and play and write but unfortunately not very much. But I am not giving up. I hope this return as this for me will signal a huge upward swing in my revival. My music and worship music were a way for me to lift my thanks and worship to the Lord. I pray this return for me and soon.

I am unfortunately in league with David here where his troubles and soul depression had such a bitter and horrific negative effect on his personal worship to the Lord. David saw this and realized this was happening and hated it. David desired to be rescued by God in his soul depression so that he could once again praise the Lord more deeply from his soul that had been so battered and sea tossed by wave upon wave and torrent upon torrent of thunderous storms in his life and inner soul.

I say all of this as I'm sure some of you reading now are currently struggling with your praising and worshiping to the Lord due to the deep underlying spiritual battle that you are in. You desire to have that desire back again, but it simply is such a battle to even desire to worship. I get it. David would get it. Don't lose hope. Don't give up. Keep on keeping on amid the storm. Try and fill your home, car and life with worship music even when you can't worship yourself. Let the worship of others fill your spirit and life. Let this be used of the Holy Spirit to revive and refresh your spirit. Let the fuel of others refuel you.

There are some planes that when they are low on fuel can be refueled by another plane flying above them. They get refueled and they keep on going. This is where the body of Christ needs to and must step in for the ones who are struggling. Don't wait for the struggling person to ask for help. Due to their struggling I know by experience they will crawl up inside themselves and begin to stop reaching out for help. Reach out even if you get rejected and keep reaching out to them. I wish so many had not stopped reaching out to me.

I realize in looking back how much darkness I was in and still am in that darkness that I pushed people away and some just simply didn't want to deal with me anymore – much to my dismay. We don't turn our back on someone who has a broken back and tell them to simply stop hurting and to get up and walk again. Let us as a body of Christ not give up on the spiritually broken and tell them to simply snap out of it and get up and get going again.

It takes time and effort to reach out to the spiritually broken this I know. But are we not supposed to be the arms and legs of the Lord while we walk this earth. Are we not called to at times to put ourselves out on the limb in order to save those who are about to fall off. I wonder how our churches today would handle David with all his soul depression and weaknesses. Would he be rejected or reached out to? Sadly, I feel David would experience a lot of rejections from our "modern" churches who look the other way at those who are struggling like he did.

Now with all that said on how we do need others to help us in these times of spiritual depression we can also see that David did not just sit back and did nothing. We have already seen many areas of how David participated in his own soul revival. We can see this again in verse 7 of Psalm 142. Not only here but in so many other places in his Psalms he did not wait for others to reach out to him, but he also was an active participant in this process as we have seen repeatedly.

As David was pleading with the Lord to bring up his soul from this pit David was also personally seeking the Lord. David, as we have seen, knew so much about the Lord as he expressed them in all the various names/epithets that we have seen and studied here in this book. David knew that like he said in Psalm 30:11-12 how God is the One who would turn his mourning into dancing. David knew that God would be the One to gird him up again in gladness and thus leading him to a heartfelt worship.

In fighting off his spiritual depression David was continually seeking to experience God's presence. David was continually reminding himself of his personal "MY Lord, MY provider, MY portion for ever and ever, MY protector, MY faithful friend. David continually sought to know who God is through all His various names/epithets of which we have seen just a few of here in this book. David continually reminded himself of God's attributes and the works of His wonders all around him and in his life. David continually sought to trust God even when his trust was as it seemed on thin ice and ready to cave in. Let this be our continuous seeking of the Lord be as well.

All these truths just listed above I see woven together in another of David's Psalms. Psalm 9:9-11 these separate truths come together to keep us going and provide the spiritual fuel the Holy Spirit can and does use to keep us going. Even when we feel we are on the edge let us try and keep these powerful verses for what the Holy Spirit is saying to us.

Psalm 9:9-11, "The Lord is a refuge, defender, protector and provides safety for the oppressed, afflicted and crushed in spirit. The Lord is a refuge, defender, protector and provides safety for those who are in a time of trouble, distress, adversity, suffering, in anguish and in the midst of storms. Those who know You. Those who seek to find out more about you and to discern Your ways and who You are will trust and depend on You. You will make them feel secure even in the storms of life. You O Lord, will not forsake, abandon, desert, neglect or reject those who seek You and follow You" (EHGV).

I see this verse as a pattern in David's life that he attempted to live in. For sure as we have seen David had his many moments of despair and even the "where are You God" times but he came back to the truths of those verses we have just read. This should be our drive as well during our troubles, anxieties and depressions is. Know these truths about God in those verses and to seek God's presence personally. To experience God personally in a direct one on one way. Studying out His various names/epithets as we have done here can be a key ingredient for victory in this battle of soul depression.

Even in our storms we will begin to see Jesus is still with us in the boat – with us. Jesus never leaving us or abandoning us. Even when we feel that He has – He hasn't. He is My Lord, My Savior, My protector, My deliverer, My help, My friend who is always there for me and with me. This is fuel for the Spirit to move us to be revived and have a refreshed spirit. Moving us to a heart of fresh worship flowing from our revived hearts. This was David's heart, desire and pursuit. Let it be ours. Even when you are struggling to even desire to do this let what my dad used to say so often it seemed – "Keep on, Keeping on".

As we end our study in Psalm 142 and other Psalms of David let me share two more things. First is a personal story that still hits home to me and one that I still remember back from my high school days. This still impacts me in my spiritual battle with soul depression today. Then I will close by repeating what I feel is such a great sum up found in Psalm 9:9-11 that we just looked at. Repetition I have found is a great piece of our battle gear to use.

First in closing is my personal story and how it still helps me to this day. In my freshman year of high school (way back when) my older brother, Tim, was a senior. It was springtime and thus track season. Tim was a star on track in several events. Ones that I remember now him doing are the high jump, hurdles and I believe it was called back then the half mile run or 440-yard dash, I think. It is probably now called a meter run of some length now. I did track just because it was the thing to do to keep in shape from the basketball season waiting for baseball. I was ok at the sprints, and I did the hurdles and high jump mainly because Tim did them. Longer runs were not for me.

One meets we were in and for some reason I still don't know why the coach had me run in one of the longer relays. And to top that I was the fourth runner which was the end runner. This end runner was supposed to bring it home with all the glory! There I was waiting for the baton to be passed on to me so I could go flying off to victory.

I think the event was the 880-yard dash. To me 880 yards is not a dash, but I guess when it's divided up with four runners it could be considered that. To me the 50-yard dash was attainable and one that I did. The 100-yard dash would have been pushing it for me. To say that I was supposed to bring it home in 220 yards of "dashing" was not something I relished doing. But there I was chosen to participate so I participated.

The race (dash) got started and as my fellow track mates did their part the third runner was getting closer, so I got ready to take the baton and I was off and dashing. I still so distinctly see in my mind rounding the corner of the track and heading for the final stretch and I felt like – "Is it over yet." But it wasn't as I just mentioned I still had the final stretch before I would be allowed to lie down in a stretcher. The finish line still seemed so far away coming around that final bend in the track.

As I came around the bend, I saw my brother Tim running up to me on the infield part of the track and yelling out to me, "Keep going, Keep going, push myself, keep going." It's bringing tears to my eyes even now as I am writing this. Even in that short distance of 220 yards I was already running out of gas and getting exhausted. But for my brother Tim this kind of run and dash he would do for a whole half mile yet here I was struggling with 220 yards and only so far completing 110 yards of it.

Tim's encouraging words of cheering me on and pushing me to keep on going was what got me to that second gear and to keep on going. I still remember how my arms started pumping harder and I picked up some speed and dashed to the finish line. That needed encouragement moved me to keep on going and even to push myself more down the stretch. That moment of time of Tim doing that for me is still so fresh that it seems like it happened yesterday. When I was nearing the end of being able to keep on going Tim was there to spur me on to the finish line. Thank you, Tim, even today I thank you for that moment in my life.

The obvious connection to our study here and specifically for me and to my life is to not give up. Plus, when we feel like giving up what a blessing it is for us to have those special people cheering us on to keep going. I still at times and unfortunately too often have those "I want to give up" moments when it feels like I'm losing my strength and don't even desire to keep on going. Getting more depressed about how once again I'm trying to climb out of the same dark pit I keep falling into.

The deeper hole of despair means a more difficult climb out and it is daunting at times. Sometimes just to get through the day in order to just go back to bed. Then to get up to just struggle again to survive that day. At times it can feel like the "Groundhog Day" movie. I know that I have the Holy Spirit cheering me on to encourage me to keep on going and any believer has the same Holy Spirit there for them too. I still have a few people who are there cheering me on, but they have become fewer and that hurts. That is a sad reality for me with how many have deserted me because they can't handle my PTSD episodes. However, this also makes me appreciate the few who have stayed with me even in and through my bad days and times. Plus, I know I can always lean on the Lord.

That is what leads me to my final thought on this all. This is what David did as a pattern of his life. He leaned on the Lord. Again, he was not perfect in this as he lived a life of a continuous struggle with depression of the soul, but he kept on going "in the Lord." This is what I see in Psalm 9:9-11 which is my close thought for us. It can help us I feel to Keep on Keeping on. In the Lord we can Keep on Keeping on! Let's close with what David wrote in Psalm 9:9-11. This version of those verses is a bit varied from the one we just read but it contains the meanings of the same Hebrew words.

Psalm 9:9-11

"For those who are oppressed — weighed down in mind and spirit. For those who feel afflicted — feeling distressed, depressed, grieved and are crushed in your mind and spirit. For those who are experiencing a season of troubles, distresses, anguish, adversity, problems, calamities and suffering in great turmoil. Take heart. Take heart as the Lord is Jehovah Misgab. He is my and your refuge. He is my and your protector. He is my and your defender. He is my and your stronghold. He is my and your secure height. He is my and your fortress. He is my and your ONE who provides for my and your safety.

You are the Sovereign Lord and You will not abandon me, desert me, neglect me, forsake me, leave me behind, overlook me or neglect me. This is for all who follow You, seek You, thank You, worship You, study who You are and seek You out with care and diligence. This is for all who pursue you. I will Yada You Lord in raising up my thanks to you as I get to know You deeper and deeper and as I get to see You more clearly. You are the One that I lift up my arms to in fervent worship. This is flowing from my heart that has learned to trust in You, depend on You, feel secure in You, have confidence and hope in You. As a result, I become more confident and even carefree knowing that You are there for me and the One who goes all out for me. This comes and flows from the actions of getting to know you deeper and to experience personally who You are and who I am to You. From all this I will intentionally and intensely sing my praises to You, my Lord. I will lift to You along with and among other believers my music and songs of praise." (EHGV)

Selah

ADDENDUM

This Addendum is for you to have quick reference to some of the truths we discovered in this study and to also have as a reference some further study on your part. All with the goal of seeking the Lord in a deeper way and to thus experience His presence in a deeper way.

1) Names/Epithets of God Review
2) Attributes of God
3) Who I am in Jesus Christ
4) Promises of God
5) The Lord is My _____
6) Prayer (A.C.T.S. Model)

1) NAMES/ EPHITHETS OF GOD

JEHOVAH YADA

To know by experience
Personally experience
Understand
Fully Understand
Pay attention to
Acknowledge
Determine
Leading
Gives Instruction
Be wise
Familiar Friend
To make oneself known

JEHOVAH MACHACEH

Shelter

Refuge

Safety

Source of Safety

Hope

Trust

Shelter and Refuge from Rain, Storm,
Dangers or Falsehood

Guardian

Security

Preserve

Sanctuary

Anchorage

Harbor

Retreat

JEHOVAH CHELEQ

Portion
Allotment
Inheritance
Territory
Associate
Enjoy Prosperity
Stability
Continuance Without Change
Steadfast
Constant of Character and Purpose
Sticking Together
Attachment
Security
Strength
Support
Abiding Endurance
Shield
Protector
Selah

JEHOVAH CHAY

Fresh

Flowing Fresh Water

Revive

Full Life

Renewed

Reviving as in the Springtime after a Long Winter

Surviving

Sustenance

Supports Life through Nourishment

Sustains

Life

Living

Alive

Prosperity

Inspire - Ignite - Rekindle

Spur on - Energize

Keep from Sinking

Keeping Afloat

Encourage

Revive

Buoy

Overcome

Strengthen

JEHOVAH NATSAL

Rescue
Deliverer
Save
Escape
Defended
Vindicated
Carried Away
Snatched Out
Resist
Kept
Help
Preserve
Recover
To Deliver from Enemies, Trouble or Death
To Deliver from Sin and Guilt
Involved
Without fail

JEHOVAH YATSA

A	B	C
Remove	Burst Forth	With Purpose
Escape	Traveled	and For Results
Come Out	Go Forth	Proceed from
Draw Out	Set Out	something to
Departed	March Out	something
Carried Out	Lead Out	(Exodus)
	Flows	Intends for
	Proceed Active	Desired Result
	Participation	Impact

MAIN PURPOSE:

To see who God is and to draw closer to Him.

It is a taking 'From' (A) and then to going in a 'Process' (B) with a distinct 'Reason' for Purpose and Result with one of those Purposes to see more clearly who God is and to draw closer to Him.

JEHOVAH CHECED

Loyal Love

Unfailing Love

Steadfast Love

Faithful Love

Fervent Love

Intense Love

Passionate Love

Absolute Love

Persistent Love

Boundless Love

Reliable

Dependable

Tried-and-True

Rock Solid

Dedicated

Loyal

Faithful

Kindness

Devoted

Devotion

Allegiance

Brotherhood

Trustworthy

Mercy

Committed

Faithful Acts

Faithful Deeds

Favor of God

God's Promises

Abiding

JEHOVAH NAHAL

Guide
Led
Got Through
Carried
To Lead
Lead Gently On
Refresh
Give Rest
Place of Rest
Guide to a watering place or station
Bring to a station cause to rest there
To Journey by Stations or Stages
Lead to or Bring to a station or goal

JEHOVAH QUWM

STAGE 1	STAGE 2	STAGE 3	STAGE 4
Sustained	Help lift up	Rebuild	Charge ahead
Survive	Stood up	Get ready	Accomplish
Preserve	Help up	Prepare to go	Succeed
Endure	Woke up	Heal	Action
Maintain	Grow up	Grow into	Went forth
Hold on	Build up	Strengthen	Fulfilled
Be fixed	Stir up	Established	Attacked
Not moved	Recover	To be fixed	Carried out
Supported	Ascended	Set out	Perform
		intact	

JEHOVAH TSHUWAH

Help
Safety
Victory
Salvation
Deliverance – usually by God through a person

Rescue
Recovery – regain something lost or taken away
Repair/**R**estore – to a good or sound condition after decay or damage
Restoration – to bring back to any former state or condition and even better

JEHOVAH RUWM

Snatched	Picked up	Reconstruct	Ready to act
Away	Raised up	Construct	Victorious
Removed	Lifted up	Builds	Confident
Brought up	Grow up		
	Restores		

God, who is exalted and lifted up for Who He is and sits on the throne is ready to act. He can remove us from our problems as He then lifts us up to restore us and causes us to grow and be re-constructed and then ready to act in confidence in the victories that He brings us to.

JEHOVAH ALAH

Delivered out	Brought up	Advance	Charge ahead
	Taken up	Marched up	Shoot forth
	Led up	Continued up	
	Going up		
	Restore	Stir up	
	Recover	Increase	
	To rouse	Mount up	

Accompanied
To Accompany
To join in action
To be and exist in association with
Cause to ascend or climb

JEHOVAH ZAQAPH

Comfort
Lifts Up
Raise
To Raise Up to Life

JEHOVAH PAQACH

Gives sight
Open
Pay close attention
Enabled
To be observant
To open the senses

JEHOVAH DALAH

Lifted up
Draws
Drawing advice
To draw up
Enough

To *let down a bucket for drawing out water*

JEHOVAH GAMAL

Deal bountifully
A benefit
To Good to
To deal bountifully with
Treat a person well
Aid
Relief
Care
Help
Assistance
Encouragement
Abundantly supply
Be in plenty

2) ATTRIBUTES OF GOD

There are simply too many attributes or truths about God to list them all. Here are just a few that can give you a good start towards knowing the One True God and Who He is. Use this little guide here as a starting point for your study on who God is. Let this be just the beginning of your personal study of God.

1) God is Infinite – Self-Existing and Without Origin
Colossians 1:17; Psalm 147:5; Psalm 139:3-10; Psalm 147:5

2) God is Love
1 John 4:7-8; Jon 3:16; John 14:21-23; Ephesians 2:4-5; Romans 5:8

3) God is Omnipotent – All Powerful
Genesis 1:1; Psalm 33:6; Psalm 66:6-7; Psalm 89:6-7;
Isaiah 40:22-26; Mark 14:36

4) God is Omniscient – All Knowing
Isaiah 46:9-10; Psalm 33:13-15; Psalm 94:9-11; Isaiah 46:9

5) God is Omnipresent – Always Everywhere
Psalm 139:3-10; Isaiah 57:15; Acts 17:24; 1 Kings 8:27

6) God is Wise
Romans 11:33; Psalm 37:1-6; Psalm 92:5-9; Psalm 119:97-100
Proverbs 3:19-26; Romans 11:33-36

7) God is Holy
Revelation 4:8; Exodus 15:11; Isaiah 6:1-3; 1 Peter 1:15-16

8) God is Good
Psalm 34:8; Matthew 7:11; Isaiah 63:7; Exodus 33:18-19;
Psalm 107:8-9; Psalm 33:5

9) God is Eternal
Psalm 1:12-13; Revelation 4:8-9; Deuteronomy 33:27; Psalm 9:7-8

10) God is Forgiving
1 John 2:12; Psalm 86:5; 1 John 1:9; Colossians 2:13;
Hebrews 10:17; Luke 23:34; Isaiah 1:18

11) God is Faithful
Deuteronomy 7:9; Romans 3:3-4; 1 Corinthians 10;13;
1 Thessalonians 5:24; 2 Timothy 2:13

12) God is Compassionate
Psalm 111:4; Psalm 145:8; Isaiah 65:1-3; Matthew 23:37-39

13) God is Accessible
James 4:8; Hebrews 4:16; Ephesians 2:13,18; Ephesians 3:12
Psalm 145:18-19; Romans 5:2; Colossians 1:22-23

14) God is Life
Psalm 27:1; 1 Timothy 6:15-16; James 1:17; Isaiah 60:19-20
Luke 2;32; 1 John 1:5

15) God is Patient
2 Peter 3:9; 1 Corinthians 13:4-5; Numbers 14:18; Isaiah 30:18
Romans 15:4-6

16) God is Unchanging
James 1:17; Psalm 119:89-91; Isaiah 40:28; Numbers 23:19

17) God is Sovereign
Psalm 115:3; Romans 9:15; Ephesians 1:11; Romans 8:28;
Colossians 1:16-17; Proverbs 16:13; Job 42:2; Acts 4:27-28
Ephesians 1:4

18) God is Trustworthy
Psalm 33:4; Psalm 145:13

19) God is Protector
Psalm 18:31; Deuteronomy 31:6; Psalm 46:2; Isaian 43:1

20) God is With Us
Isaiah 41:10; Psalm 145:18; Matthew 1:23; Matthew 28:20

3) WHO I AM IN CHRIST

There are times when every believer can forget or possibly not even know who they are in Jesus Christ. These truths, especially for someone who is fighting through PTSD episodes or depression can be used by the Holy Spirit to lift us up and to keep on fighting. So many blessings the Lord has given to us through being In Him as His child. Listed here are some truths that all believers have through being In Christ.

I Am
* Loved for ever and ever – eternally (1 Pe 1:5)
* Forever (eternally) kept in the palm of His hand (Jn 10:29)
* Kept by the power of God (1 Pe 1:5)
* Only traveling through here and on my way to heaven (Jn 14:6)
* Quickened by God's mighty Power available to me (Eph 2:1)
* Sanctified – made holy in Him (1 Co 6:11)
* Not condemned (Ro 8:1-2)
* Protected from Satin (1 Jn 5:18)
* Secure in Jesus Christ (Jn 10:28-29)
* More than a conqueror through Christ (Ro 8:37)
* Sheltered under God's wings (Ps 91:4)
* Am light in this dark world - God will use me (Mt 5:14; 2 Ti 2:21)
* God's possession (1 Co 6:20)
* God's child (Jn 1:12)
* God's friend (Ja 2:23)
* Set free from being under Satan's control and kingdom (Col 1:13, Ep 2)
* Forgiven of all my sins (Col 2:13)
* Given through Christ great promises of God (2 Pe 1:4)
* Given access to God directly at any time (Eph 3:12)
* Complete in Christ (Col 2:10)
* Secure in Christ and cannot be separated from God's love (Ro 8:35-39)
* Secure in Christ and cannot perish or be lost (Jn 10:28, 3:16)
* Secure in Christ and cannot be taken out of God's hand (Jn 10:29)
* Secure in Christ and cannot be condemned (1 Co 11:32)

* Secure in Christ as He is the anchor for my soul (Heb 6:19)
* Secure in Christ and have a hope that is sure and steadfast (Heb 6:19)
* Secure in Christ and at peace with God (Ro 5:1)
* Secure in Christ as I am kept by the power of God (1 Pe 1:5)
* Given a sound mind (2 Ti 1:7)
* Adopted into the family of God (Ro 8:15)
* Kept from falling (Jude 24)
* Given the blessing of being able to come into God's throne room and
    pray at anytime (Heb 4:16, Lk 21:36)
* Given the Holy Spirit who forever lives within me (2 Co 1:22)
* A victor in Christ (1 Jn 5:14)
* A citizen of heaven (1 Pe 2:11)
* Protected from the evil one (1 Jn 5:18)
* Sustained, supported, protected, upheld, refreshed, revived in and by the
    Lord (Ps 3:5)
* Delivered through my anguish, sorrow, distresses and afflictions (Ps 4:1)
* Heard and paid attention to by the Lord when I call out to Him (Ps 4:3)
* One in whom the Lord puts joy and delight into my heart (Ps 4:7)
* One whom the Lord makes me to dwell in His safety and security(Ps 4:8)
* One who can enter into God's presence because of His great love for me
    (Ps 5:7)
* Blessed by the Lord (Ps 5:12)
* Surrounded by God's favors as with a shield (Ps 5:12)
* One who has the Lord as my stronghold, protector, defender and refuge
    in times of trouble (Ps 9:9)
* One who the Lord will establish firmly, fix, reestablish and build up my
    heart, passions and emotions (Ps 10:17)
* One who can take refuge in the Lord, find shelter in Him, find safety in
    Him, look to Him for protection, have my hope in Him (Ps 11:1)
* One who can trust in the Lord, have confidence in Him, feel secure
    in Him, depend upon God's loyal, faithful, devoted, steadfast and
    unfailing love for me (Ps 13:5)
* One who can greatly rejoice and celebrate in god who has intervened into
    my life with the ability to do this for me (Ps 13:5)
* One whom the Lord deals bountifully with (Ps 13:6)
* One who God protects (Ps 16:1)
* The apple of God's eye – protected and cherished (Ps 17:8)
* Satisfied with God's presence (Ps 17:15)
* Heard by God when I call out to Him (Ps 18:6)
* Helped in times of disaster, calamities and distress because God is my
    source of security and support (Ps 18:18)
* Restored, guided, given direction and made by God as I pursue Him and
    His teachings (Ps 19:7)

* Caused by God to endure, persist, be established and reestablished, rebuilt, supported, raised up, stirred up, prepared to do and accomplish God's ordained purposes for me, to move forward, charge forward and spring into action as I get to know and depend upon God's Name and who He is as revealed by those names (Ps 20:7-8)
* Made joyful, happy and exceedingly glad in God's presence as I draw nearer and nearer to Him (Ps 21:6)
* One who when I am suffering, oppressed, afflicted, destitute, needy and depressed in mind or circumstances that the Lord will NOT see me as of no importance or despise me even as others might do. The Lord will also NOT detest me, have no use fro me, look down on me or reject me even if others might do so (Ps 22:24)
* One who when I am suffering, oppressed, afflicted, destitute, needy and depressed in mind or circumstances that the Lord will NOT hid Himself from me even if all others do (Ps 22:24)
* One who when I am suffering, oppressed, afflicted, destitute, needy and depressed in mind or circumstances that the Lord will hear me, listen to me, pay attention to m and be interested in me (Ps 22:24)
* Not in want, have need, be without, lacking or deprived as the Lord is my shepherd, my companion, my leader, my friend who leads, guides and cares for me (Ps 23:1)
* One who the Lord causes to lie down in lush places with new grass (Ps 23:2)
* Led with care to secure resting places where I can be refreshed. God does this for me through stations and stages (Ps 23:2)
* Restored, reestablished, refreshed, preserved, repaired and brought back in my life's passions, seat of emotions and in my mind through the Lord (Ps 23:3)
* Led and guided on the way and paths of deliverance, vindication, righteousness and enjoying my salvation in the Lord (Ps 23:3)
* In God's presence even when I am walking through the valleys of deep darkness and extreme danger or distress (Ps 23:4)
* Comforted by the Lord's compassion for me (Ps 23:4)
* One who dwells in God's presence forever (Ps 23:6)
* One who will receive God's blessings (Ps 24:5)
* One who in the Lord will NOT be so dismayed and distressed as to become dried up spiritually as I rely on the Lord, hope in the Lord, rely completely on the Lord and bind myself together with the Lord. (Ps 25:2-3)
* One who when I am depressed, downtrodden, weak and afflicted that the Lord will guide me, lead me, equip me to march out of it (Ps 25:9)
* One who when I am depressed, downtrodden, weak and afflicted that the Lord will lead me, train me up, diligently prepare me along this journey

I'm in so that even in my oppression and depressions the Lord will use
them in my life to train me and prepare me as He marches me forward
(Ps 25:9)
* Instructed, taught and given reliable guidance by the Lord in the way
of life and journey that I am on as I worship and esteem Him as I
faithfully and loyally follow Him (Ps 25:12)
* One who will receive God's council, guidance and personal thoughts as I
worship and esteem Him as I faithfully and loyally follow Him (Ps 25:4)
* One who the Lord will deliver me and cause me to burst forth to go out
from my enemies attacks as I gaze intently and continually towards Him
– to live in His presence (Ps 2:15)

We have in this section looked at many Bible passages that reveal who "I am"
in Christ and so many blessings that flow from this relationship with the Lord.

I have also gone through Psalms 1-25 in search for so many of these truths
of who "I am" in Christ. Let me encourage you to continue searching out the rest
of the Psalms to discover firsthand more truths of who "I am" in Jesus Christ.
Perhaps get a notebook and write them down as you go. Blessings on this journey
of discovering more and more of who "You Are" in Jesus Christ!

4) PROMISES OF GOD

If you suffer from PTSD, anxiety, depression or are going through any major trial right now or at some time why is it important to know the Promises of God? These Promises of God to us are not just for the depressed or those suffering but for every single believer. Let me give just a few reasons why this section is so important in the process of healing and getting stronger as we journey through our troubles.

* In Romans 4:20-21 we see that Abraham grew strong in his faith in God because of knowing God's promises. He trusted God (faith) that He would fulfill His promises. Instead of focusing on the situations or his own "feelings" which can come and go Abraham focused upward to God and His promises. Filling our minds and hearts with God's promises can be used of the Holy Spirit to get us through our rough times and to also be used of Him to help others who might be struggling.

* Knowing God's promises will also help us to not misinterpret things that might be happening to us. If you are going through a sickness or trial, it is possible our thoughts could gravitate towards "why is God letting this happen"? If we know that God never promised us a life free from difficulties, then we can avoid a mistake in assuming God must not love us if He is allowing these things to happen to us. In fact, God has told us in this world we will have troubles. Knowing God's promises and what He has not promised can keep us from falling off into wrong thinking about God.

* Romans 10:17 tells us that faith comes through hearing the Word of God. God's promises are contained in the Word of God so knowing them and studying them and relying upon them can be a Holy Spirit faith builder for us. As we walk through our troubles the Holy Spirit can bring up into our hearts and minds truths that we have learned about God and His promises that He can use to help us journey through whatever we are going through at the time. Again, He can also then use us to help others who might be struggling as well.

* Psalm 16:1 when David was in a crisis, he took refuge in God and one reason for that is that he knew that God had his back and his best interests in mind. This ties in with some of the other reasons but felt it needed another emphasis.

* Psalm 16:5-6 again we see that while David was in this crisis, he knew God was in charge. A life full of strife and difficulties needs to have the truth that God is full in us and is stronger than those trials.

* Psalm 16:7-8. The more we know and live in God's promises that more we can combat our brokenness. I will not be shaken. It does not mean that we won't have troubled times and rough days but as we grow more and more firm in our relationship with the Lord and His promises for us we can stand strong in the midst of the storm.

* Psalm 16:9-11. Knowing our future home in heaven is secure in Christ Jesus can help us to maneuver through the rough waters in our lives in a better way. These promises of our eternity with Jesus might not take away our temporal problems but can help us refocus upward to Him and what awaits us.

I have written out here 25 promises of God plus some Bible verses where these truths are contained. There are obviously more and more promises, but books are written just for those. So here are a few for you to start with. I hope that you can take some time to read through, study upon and even memorize some of these Promises that God has given to us.

1) God promises to hear our prayers and cries of help to Him (Mt 11:22-25; Jer 29:12-13; Ps 10:17; 1 Jn 5:14-15; Lk 11:9-13; Ro 8:26-27)

2) God Promises His Comfort to us (Jn 14:16; 2 Co 1:3-4; Mt 5:4; Rev 21:4; Lk 6:21; Jn 14:27; Josh 1:9; Ps 73:26; Php 4:6-8; Is 53:4; Ps 27:1; Ro 8:18; Ps 23:4; Ro 15:13; 2 Co 4:17-18; Lam 3:31-32)

3) God promises to give us strength for the journey (Is 40:29,31; Eph 3:14-16; Is 41:10; Jos 1:9; Is 12:2; Php 4:13; Eph 6:10; 2 Co 12:9; Ps 73:26; Neh 8:10; Ps 46:5; Php 4:13)

4) God promises His compassion for us and His care for us (1 Pe 5:7; Is 30:18; Ex 33:19; Is 49:10,13; Is 54:10; Is 63:17; Neh 9:16-18; Ps 51:1; 86;15; 103:13; 116:15; 119:77; 145:8-9; Ja 5:11; Heb 4:15; Mt 14:13-14; 20:30-34; Lk 7:12-15; Mk 6:34)

5) God promises to Bring Good out of Suffering (2 Co 4:17; Ja 1:2-3; Gal 6:9; Ro 8:28; Ro 8:18; Heb 12:11; 2 Co 1:3-9; 1 Pe 4;12-16; Mt 5:10-12; Ro 5:3-4)

6) God promises To Guide Us (Ps 32:8; Pr 3:5-6; Is 48:17: Is 58:11; Jn 16;13; Is 30:21; Ja 1:5-6; Ps 37:5; Ps 37:23-24; Mt 6:33; Ps 25:9-10; Ps 121:8)

7) God promises us Hope (1Pe 1:3-4; Jer 29:11; Php 3:20; Zep 3:17; Ro 15:13; Is 40:31; Ps 39:7; Tit 2:13; Ro 12:12; 2 Co 4:17-18; Ro 8:18; Rev 22:12; Ro 15:4; Rev 21:4; Lam 3:21-23)

8) God promises to Always Love and to Never Leave us (1 Co 13:8; Ps 103:17; Deut 31:6,8; Ps 27:10; 1 Ch 28:20; Deut 4:31; Ge 28:15; Heb 4:16; Heb 13:5-6; Josh 1:5,9; Mt 28:20; Ps 55:22; Ps 94:14; Ps 73:23-26; Is 41:10-13)

9) God promises to Provide for Us (Php 4:19; 2 Co 9:8; Heb 11:6; Ps 81:10; Mt 6:33; Pr 10:3; Ro 8:22; Eph 3:20; Ps 34:10; Jn 15:6; Mal 3:10; Mt 6:25-34; Mt 7:7-8; Eph 3:16-17; Jn 14:13-14; Jn 15:7; 1 Jn 3:22; 2 Pe 3:13; Ps 145; 15-16; 2 Co 9:8; Ps 107:9)

10) God promises to Be our Refuge (Ps 9:9; Deut 33:27; Ps 46:1-3; Ps 91:2; Ps 27:5; Ps 31:20; Pr 14:26; Pr 18:10; Is 25:4; Jer 16:19; Ps 18:2,30; Ps 5:11; Ps 9:9; Ps 14:6; Ps 27:1,5; Ps 31:1-2, 19-20; Ps 34:8,22; Ps 36:7; Ps 37:39-40; Ps 57:1; Ps 59:16; Ps 61:3-4; Ps 62:7; Ps 71:1,3,7; Ps 73:28; Ps 91:2,4,9,10; Ps 94:22; Ps 118:8-9; Ps 119:114; Ps 141:8; Ps 142:5; Ps 144:2; Pr 10:29; Pr 18:10)

11) God promises to Restore Joy to Us (Ps 30:5; Ps 126:5-6; Ps 94:19; Ps 51:12; Jer 30:17; Job 42:10; 1 Pe 5:10; 1 Co 15:22; 2 Ch 7:14; Lam 5:21; Ps 71:20-21; Ps 80:3; Ps 126:4; Deut 30:3; Ps 6:4; Ps 19:7; Ps 23:3; Ps 71:20; Ps 85:6; Hos 6:1; Is 40:31; Jer 17:14; Jn 14:1; Mk 11:24; Mt 6:33; Mt 11:28; Ro 15:13; 2 Co 13:9-11;Ac 3:19-21; Ps 103:1-5)

12) God promises to Be our Shield (Ps 84:11; Ge 15:1; Ps 28:7; Ps 18:2; Deut 33:29; Ps 33:20; Ps 115:9; Pr 30:5; Ps 89:18; Ps 3:3; Ps 138:7; 2 Th 3:3)

13) God promises to Sustain Us
Kuwl – (Hebrew word for sustain) hold, contain, endure, provide, nourish, acquired supplies, survive, provided needs, support, guide (1 Ki 17:4; Neh 9:21; Ge 45:11; Ps 54:4; Ps 140:12-13; Ex 15:2; Ps 73:26; Php 4:19; Ps 84:11; Ps 107:9; Jn 14:27; 2 Th 3:3; Is 26:3; Ja 1:5; Is 12:2; Ro 15:13; Is 41:13; Heb 13:5; 1 Pe 5:7; Ex 14:14; Is 46:4; Ps 55:22; Is 40:28-29; Is 43:2; Is 41:10,13; 2 Co 12:9; 2 Co 13:14; Ps 37:23-24; Ps 63:7-8; Ps 18:35; Ps 89:11; Ps 107:9; Php 4:13; Eph 6:10; Ps 28:7)

14) God promises to Be with Me
(Ps 34:18; Ja 4:8; Heb 13:5; Josh 1:5,9; Ps 23:4; Mt 1:23; 28:20; Jn 14:16-17; 1 Co 6:19-20; Ps 139:7-8; 16:11; 62:1-3; 73:23-24; Ps 145:18; Eph 2:18; 3:11-12; Rev 3:20; 1 Ki 19:9-13; Ja 4:18; Ex 33:13-14; Deut 31;6; Is 41:10; 43:2; Jer 19:13; Zep 3:17; Jn 10:27-28; 14:23; 15:5; Ac 3:20-21; Heb 4:16; 10:19-22)

15) God promises to Answer our Prayers (God does so in His Sovereign timing, wisdom and love for us) (Mt 7:7-11; 21:22; Jn 15:7,16; 14:13-14; 16:23-24; 1 Jn 5:14-15; Jer 33:3; Ps 91:14-16; 50:14-15; 10:17; 102:19-20; 9:10; 18:3; Ps 32:15; 37:4; 38:15; 55:16; 56:9; 65:2; 69:33: 81:10; 86:5-7; Ps 102:17-20; 145:18; Pr 2:3; 3:6; 10:24; 15:8; 16:11; Jer 29:12; Is 19:20; 30;19; 55:5; 41:17; 2 Ch 7:14; 2 Co 10:6; 1 Jn 3:22; Is 58:9; 65:24; Jer 33:3; Lk 11:9; Deut 4:7)

16) God promises to Forgive our Sins and Eternal Life with Him (Jn 3:16-17; 31; 4:14; 6:27; 10:28-30; 17:3; 1 Jn 1:9; 5:11-13,20; 1 Jn 2:1-2; 2:17,25; Col 3:13; 1:13-14; Ac 2:38; 3:19; Is 43:25; 1:18; Mt 6:12; Pr 28:13; Ac 10:43; Is 55:17; 2 Ch 7:14; Ps 32:5; 103:12; Mt 26:28; Ro 3:23; 6:22-23; 8:1; 10:9; 5:21; 8:18; Heb

8:12; 2 Co 5:17; Col 1:13-14; Ps 86:5; Mic 7:18; Lk 24:57; Ac 13;38-39; Eph 2:8-9; Mk 10:29-30; Lk 10:20; 2 Co 4:17-18; 5:1 Gal 6:8; 1 Ti 1:16; 6:12; 2 Ti 2:11; 4:7-8; Heb 5:9; 7:25; 1 Pe 5:10; Jude 20-21; Rev 1:8; 7:16-17; 21:3-4)

17) God promises to Uphold me and Sustain me
Uphold – to support or defend as against opposition; to keep up; to keep from sinking or drowning
Advocate, defend, encourage, side with, vindicate, bolster, boost, brace, carry, prop up, help, sustain, buoy up, pick up, stick by
Camak (Hebrew word for Uphold and Sustain) - holds, holds firm, drives on, supports, provides, maintains, protects, establishes, stay, borne up, to sustain, refresh and revive.
What are we supposed to do?
To lean upon the Lord
To rest upon the Lord
To lean against the Lord
To support or brace oneself with the Lord
To grasp and lay hold of the Lord
(Ps 37:24; 145:14; 91:14-15; 16:5; 17:5; 41;2,12; 51;12; 82:3; 3:5; Is 41:10; 2 Co 12:9; 1 Ki 8:59; 2 Ch 6:39; Is 42:1; Ps 119:50, 116)

18) God promises to Help Me
Azar (Hebrew word for help) – support, assisted, allies, aid, rescue, protect, deliver, to surround (Is 41:10, 113-14; 44:2; Ps 118:1,3,7; 54:4; 28:7; 37:40; 86:17 2 Ch 32:6; Is 50:7,9; 1 Sa 7:12; Ps 46:5; 79;9; 119:173,175; 37;40; 89:19; 121:1-2; 27:9; 22:19; 40:17)
We are to call out to God for help. (Ps 35:2; 44:26; 22:19; 38:22; 22:11; 40:13; 70:1; 71:12; 109:26; Ps 119:173; 39:10; 72:12; 79:9; 37:40)

19) God promises – there is nothing too hard for Him even our troubles, anxieties, PTSD and problems (Jer 32:11,17; Lk 1:36-37; Eph 3:20-21; Ge 1:1; 18:14; Mt 19:26; Job 42:2; Php 4:13; Is 41:10; Ps 147:5)
We need to focus in more on God and who He is and how much He loves and cares for us and not on our problems. (Mt 21:22; Jer 33:3; Mt 17:20; 2 Ki 3:18; Lk 18:27; Is 59:1; Ps 90:17; Ps 46:1; 146:8; Php 4:19; Nu 23:19; Ro 8:32; Heb 1:3; Is 9:6; Php 4:6-7; Eph 1:19; Heb 4:12; Ro 4:21; Ps 73:25; Josh 4:24;Ge 18:9-15; Nu 8:10)

20) God promises that I can do all things through Him (Php 4:12-13; Ps 18:28-29; Hab 3:19; Ps 23:1; Ja 1:2-4; Eph 1:13; Mt 6:32-33; 1 Ti 6:6-7; 1 Co 15:5-7; Jn 16:23; 2 Co 5:17)

21) God promises that we can have victory over depression (Ps 42:6-11; 31:24; 4:7; 71:19-21; Hos 6:1; Jn 16:3; Ro 8:35,37; 1 Jn 5:4; 1 Co 15:57; Is 61:1; Ps 147:3-6)

A couple of Hebrew words that relate to this:

A) Rapha – heal, physician, recover, refresh, see fully healed
Grant relief, repair, doctors, purified, healer, make healthy.
To cure of individual distresses or personal distresses (Ps 30:2-3,5; 103:3;
107:20-22; 147:3; 6:2; 41:4; Is 53:5; 2 Ch 7:14)

B) Chabash – bandaged, binds up, bandage our wounds, doctor, encourage,
govern, bind up (Ps 147:3)

22) God promises rewards for those who diligently seek Him
Diligently – doing something with conscientious and persistent effort or
attention.
Eagerly, earnestly, energetically, enthusiastically, purposefully, zealous,
cravingly, great desire, yearning to do so, intently
(Heb 11:6; Mt 6:33; 1 Ch 16:10-12; 2 Ch 7:14; Ps 9:10; Ps 27:4; Ps 34:10;
Lk 11:9-10; Lam 3:25; Zep 2:3; Jer 29:13-14; Pr 8:17; Deut 4:29; Amos 5:4-6;
Ps 22:26; Ps 69:32; 2 Ch 16:9; Ps 40:16; Ps 70:4; 34:4-5; 145:18-20; 107:13-14;
34:10; 119:2; 24:5-6; 63:1; Ps 27:4-5; Pr 28:25; Pr 2:3-6; Pr 3:6; Lam 3:21-25;
Is 49:23)

23) God promises to give me peace as I seek Him – even peace in the
storm (Is 26:3; Jn 14:27; Php 4:6-7; Jn 16:33; 20:21; Mk 4:35-41; Ps 29:11;
Gal 5:22-23; Is 9:6; 54:10; 26:3-4: Ro 14:17; 15:13; 5:1)

24) God promises to deliver me from fear as I seek Him and trust in Him
(Ps 34:4-5; 56:3-4: 27:13; 46:1-3; 91:4-5; 115:11; 23:4; Deut 31:6; Is 41:13;
Jn 14:27; Josh 1:5-9; Deut 3;22; Josh 8:1; Is 35:4; 41:8-10; Josh 43:1; Jer 42:11;
46:27; Lam 3:57; Joel 2:21; Lk 2:10; Mt 10:26,28,31; 2 Ti 1:7; Heb 13:6;
1 Jn 4:18)

25) God promises to Direct me as He upholds me (Ps 37:23-24; 119:105; 31:3;
Pr 3:5-6; Hos 6:1; Ps 32:8; Pr 16:9; Is 30:21; 48:17; 58;11; Pr 16:3; Ja 1:5-6)
A couple of Hebrew words for direct;
A) Nacah – leade, guide, govern, straitened, transport (Ps 73:24; 139:10; 23:3;
27:11; 77:20; 78:14,53; 5:8; 31:3; 43:3; Ps 61:12; Ex 15:13; Pr 6:22; Ge 24:27,48;
Ex 13:17; Neh 9:19)

B) Nahal – lead, got through, travel, put, carried, give rest, cause to rest,
lead with care, bring to a station or place of rest, guide, refresh,
To journey by station or stages, to lead on, protect, sustain,
lead gently on, to bring to a station or goal
(Ps 23:3; Ex 15:13; Ps 31;3; Is 40:11)
This is a simple "exercise" that can have a profound impact in our lives.

5) THE LORD IS MY _____

There are so many verses where for instance David is writing and saying how the Lord is his protector, healer, help and so forth. These truths and promises that were for David are also for us here and now.

Sometimes we can feel like God is like this for other believers but not for us, and that is simply not true and wrong thinking.

A part of our healing process is to instill into our hearts, mind and soul Biblical truths about God and our personal relationship with Him.

To help drill some of these truths into us I have taken several Bible passages that David and others have written and where the word "MY" is used I have inserted right after it an underlined space. In every space that you see an underline write in YOUR name. Go back and read through that verse with YOUR name in it as often as you can. Some of these I have written out the whole verse and with others I have simply put out the main truth with the verse.

These Biblical truths are for YOU too!

Ps 18:1 – I _____ love You, O Lord, My _____
strength.

Ps 18:2 – The Lord is My _____ rock and
My _____ fortress and My _____ deliverer.
My _____ God, My _____ rock, in whom I
_____ take refuge; My _____ shield and the horn
of My _____ salvation, My _____ stronghold.

Ps 18:3 – I _____ call upon the Lord, who is worthy to be praised,
and I _____ am saved from my enemies.

Ps 18:5 – In My _____ distress I _____ called upon
the Lord, and I _____ cried to My _____ God for
help; He heard My _____ voice out of His temple, and
My _____ cry for help before Him came into His ears.

Ps 42:1 – As the deer pants for the ater brooks, so My _____ soul pants for You, O God.

Ps 42:8 – The Lord will command His love in the daytime; And His song will be with me _____ in the night, A prayer to the God of My _____ life.

Ps 43:2 – God of _____ strength.

Ps 54:4 – God _____ helper.

Ps 42:9 – God _____ rock.

Ps 43:4 – God _____ exceeding joy.

Ps 18:46; 51:14 – God of _____ salvation.

Ps 34:7 – God of _____ deliverance.

Ps 91:9 – The Lord _____ refuge.

Jer 16:9 – The Lord _____ fortress.

Ps 27:1 – The Lord _____ light.

Ps 28:7 – The Lord _____strength.

Ps 23:1 – The Lord _____ shepherd.

Ps 3:3 – The Lord _____ shield.

Ps 3:3 – The Lord lifts up _____ head to look at Him.

Ps 3:5 – The Lord sustains _____.

Ps 4:1 – The Lord relieves _____ in my distress.
Ps 4:3 – The Lord hears me _____ when I call out to Him.

Ps 4:8 – I _____ can lie down in peace at night for the Lord makes me _____ to dwell in safety.

Ps 5:8 – The Lord will lead me _____ when I am surrounded by troubles.

6) PRAYER – ACTS MODEL

One of the major ways by which we can fight off PTSD episodes, depression, our anxieties and to be able to walk through our troubling times is through prayer. This helps us to focus more on God above rather than on our present circumstances. Lifting our minds, hearts and soul up to the Lord in prayer can be a significant avenue by which the Holy Spirit can enable us to fight off the enemy.

Jesus was a man of prayer as He walked this earth. To keep Himself strong and focused He would go out alone to spend time with the Father in prayer. When Jesus was facing His most difficult and trying time of going to the cross for our sins and enduring such great physical and emotional stress and pain that He was about to endure He went to the Father in prayer. So fervent was the Lord's prayer that He even sweet drops of blood. Jesus was a man of prayer. We must be people of prayer.

Here I have given just one model that we can follow to help us to focus on our prayer time. This is just a model and not the only way to pray. We can always walk and talk with the Lord. We can always sit and talk with the Lord. Simply – we can always talk and listen to the Lord.

Here again is simply a model of prayer that can help us to focus on the Lord.

ACTS
Adoration
Confession
Thanksgiving
Supplication

ADORATION

Adoration is the process or way that we regard something or someone with the highest esteem, love and respect. Another word that could be used is – worship. It is cherishing God for who He is. It is delighting in God for who He is. It is admiring God for who He is. In some everyday language it is "having God as your treasure." The more we know about God and spend time with Him the more we will adore Him.

Let your prayer time start out by praising and simply adoring God for who

He is. (Mt 6:9) Think through in your mind some of God's attributes that we have looked at in this book. Take a refreshed look at some of His names/epithets that we have looked at. Think about those truths and then praise Him for them.

Let the sense of God's presence sweep over you. Being still before Him (Ps 46:10). Allow the Holy Spirit to speak to you through His Word and presence (Ps 40:1-3; 90:12-17).

This could also be a time of listening to some praise and worship songs. Let the truths of the songs sink into your mind, heart and soul.

CONFESSION

Because we are human, we are constantly falling short in our lives to live up to the callings that Scripture gives to us to live by. These short comings should not derail us but let them be driving us constantly towards the Lord with confession and repentance (Mt 6:9-13).

Ask the Holy Spirit to search your hearts for areas which you have fallen short of and areas where you may have not done well in. Ask the Lord to cleanse your heart and to get back up and to keep on pursuing Him. I John 1:9 is a good verse to see in how we are to raise up our sins to the Lord. He has already forgiven us at the cross but there is something about bringing them to Him for us to correct areas in our lives that can then as we walk stronger in Him be used more fully in His Kingdom.

Read Psalm 51 and see how upset David was with his personal sin with Bathsheba. He knew the truths of God's forgiveness and he called upon God to forgive him of that sin and to help him to move forward.

THANKSGIVING

1 Thessalonians 5:16-18 is a great verse of truth for us in this. We are to rejoice, pray without ceasing and in EVERYTING give thanks to the Lord. In everything? Yes! Ro 8:28 tells us that God works all things together for those who love Him. So even in our shortcomings and sins God can turn those around for us. Giving God His due thanks for that is a way we can also praise Hiim.

Start thanking God for who He is. Thank God for the blessings that He has given to you. Thank God for what He has done in other people's lives as well. Thank Him for what He did on the cross for you. This might be hard to do at times – but – thank Him for the difficulties that you may be in. These difficulties could be God doing something in you so that He can use you for someone else.

Let me give you a personal example from my life. One day when I got home, I opened up my water bill. I have this taken directly out of my checking account so there are even times when I don't look at my bill right away. This time I know I was led by the Holy Spirit to open it up right then and there. The bill said I owed for that month – wait now – $116,000. That was not a typo. That would be about 120 years of water usage in one month's time. Now I must sadly admit that I know my PTSD rocked me quite a bit. I called several close friends and even someone I knew who worked for the city. The water department was already closed and guess what, it was Friday so nothing with them could be done till Monday. I immediately went to my bank and was told I would need to come back in the morning. My bank told me that it would have been flagged and not gone through anyway. Like I had $116,000 sitting there to be used too! All my friends, including the one from the city told me not to worry about it that it had to be a clerical mistake and it would be fixed. Well, although I probably knew that the weekend was not a good one for me.

I planned on getting up about an hour early on Monday so I could go in and see them first thing before I went to work. When I got up that Monday, I went to my two fish tanks that I must feed my fish. These are not small tanks. One is 75 gallons and the other one that is directly on the floor in front of the TV is about 55 gallons. As I saw the 55-gallon tank on the floor I noticed that about half the water was gone. My first reaction was one of what am I going to do. So not in a smart way I poured more water into it and thought I would deal with it later. Then I came to my senses and realized that pouring more water into it was just feeding the problem and making it obviously worse. So "thankfully" I had another tank sitting there and I began the hour-long process of transferring the water and fish to the new tank. Unfortunately, the soiled fish water had already been spread around on the carpet. This was a problem I would have to deal with after I went to the water department to deal with that problem. So off I went to the water department. And yes, they were able to fix the $116,000 problem right away and they said it was a computer glitch.

So where does being thankful in problems come into this. First, I was thankful that I had been sitting around an extra tank where I could rush my fish into. Secondly later I was thankful that if I had not had the water problem, I would have slept another hour and by that time maybe all the soiled fish tank water would be all over my carpet and a much bigger mess to deal with. Plus, I was thankful that because again of the water problem I had to get up early to deal with the fish in that tank did not die. If I had got up at my regular time more than likely the water would have been all gone from that tank and from what I have been told fish need water to survive.

This taught me firsthand how, even in troubles and difficult situations, how we should and can be thankful to the Lord. We don't know why things happen and perhaps the Lord did so to grab our attention to something or He was using our difficulties to advance His Kingdom in some sovereign way. The long and short of this to train ourselves to be thankful to the Lord in our good times and in our rough difficult times. He is our sovereign Lord in all times.

Ps 9:1-2; 57:9-11; 107:1-3; 100:4-6

Php 4:6-7

SUPPLICATION (Seeking God for answers)

Supplication is a big word for simply going to the Lord with our requests in a humble way. It is a time of requesting God to help us and to help others. Praying for others is a big part of this time of prayer (Mt 6:9-13; Lk 18:1; Col 4:2; 1 Ti 2:1-4).

This is a time when we can and should get very specific with God our needs and request, the needs of others, our leaders, missionaries and the list is endless. We can see through the Psalms how David was constantly bringing up his needs to the Lord.

Hebrews 4:14-16 tells us that we can approach the throne of God with Boldness! He is our loving and caring God who is there for us in all our daily "little" things to our big and difficult situations. There are multitude of times when I am even grocery shopping that I will be praying to the Lord for direction of what to get for food. When I lose something, the Holy Spirit has trained my mind and heart over the years to bring even those seemingly small things to Him. Instead of panicking, which I can do easily, I start literally asking the Holy Spirit to direct me to where the item is. Through these small events it helps to bring me into conversations and experiencing the Holy Spirit.

For some it helps to make a list of things. This could also be helpful as we see how the Lord answers our prayers. Scripture is full of how God hears, listens, and answers our prayers. We must keep in mind that God is sovereign in all areas and to keep ourselves in His sovereign plans through His answers.

It is also vital that in our prayer time we allow ourselves sometime to simply listen as well. Give the Holy Spirit time to quiet our hearts down so that we can hear Him speak to us. The still small voice of the Lord is how He usually speaks to us. Give yourself and the Lord this time to listen.

Keep in mind that Prayer can be done anytime and anywhere!

Blessings

www.ingramcontent.com/pod-product-compliance
Lightning Source LLC
Chambersburg PA
CBHW071718120626
46550CB00001B/285